QUEERING
YOUR CRAFT

QUEERING YOUR CRAFT

witchcraft from the margins

CASSANDRA SNOW

FOREWORD BY MAT AURYN

WEISER BOOKS

This edition first published in 2020 by Weiser Books, an imprint of
Red Wheel/Weiser, LLC
With offices at:
65 Parker Street, Suite 7
Newburyport, MA 01950
www.redwheelweiser.com

ISBN: 978-1-57863-721-8
Library of Congress Cataloging-in-Publication Data available upon request.

Cover and interior design by Kathryn Sky-Peck
Typeset in Soin Sans Neue

Printed in the United States of America
IBI
10 9 8 7 6 5 4 3 2 1

This book is dedicated with so much love to my godchild.
I hope you never have to question or wonder
or worry about whether you are loved,
supported, or capable of great magick.

CONTENTS

FOREWORD

Witchcraft, like queerness, is an orientation of otherness. Witches seek their own connection to the spirit world, divinity, and do not require an outside authority to intercede on behalf of the divine for them. Andrew Chumbley referred to witchcraft as "the lonely road" in the context of a spiritual path. This means it's highly individual and looks different for each witch. It implies that this path isn't the well-trodden path of major religious institutions that most seekers of the great spiritual questions travel. It suggests that our solitary path is going to look completely different from witch to witch, regardless of whether that witch is practicing the same tradition of witchcraft as another or working within the context of a coven or group. In this sense, the witch is the other, an outsider to orthodox and mainstream religious ideology. Both queerness and witchery lay on the outskirts of patriarchal religious norms.

Both the witch and the queer have a long history of persecution and discrimination. Using the word *witch* for oneself is a potent act of reclamation and empowerment, very much in a similar manner to which we reclaim the word *queer*. Historically, if we wanted to find a "witch," we would find one at the end of a pointed finger. In other words, witchcraft was originally an accusation based on bigotry and, in most cases, a false one. Those who were accused of witchcraft were victims—of all genders—of the clenching fist of a patriarchal system where the boundaries between Church and State were blurry at best; if they were even there at all.

Most often they were cis-women who were victims of misogyny. As such, witchcraft today is inherently feminist. Often the woman was accused of having too much power, wealth, or land that was deemed only appropriate for a man to posess within society. For this reason, the logic of the time dictated that such power was unnatural in the hierarchy of "the divine plan" and must have come about by unholy means. Perhaps the woman was too attractive and incited lust within the men. Perhaps the woman was too unattractive and evoked repulsion within the men. Either way, the common denominator of most of the women tortured and killed was misogyny fueled by religious fervor. Likewise, there's an intersection between words and expressions related to witchcraft and queerness that most people don't realize. One of the theories behind the origin of the terms *faggot* and *flaming faggot* as a derogatory slur, which is argued back and forth by academics, is that during the Inquisitions, the inquisitors would tie homosexuals and nongender-conforming individuals to the wood at the feet of the witches and heretics that they burned to death. This explains why a word for a bundle of sticks has been used as a slur against queer men today. There are also theories that the use of the word *fairy* as a slur for queer men is because the fae folk were known for their lack of sexual inhibitions as well as their disregard for gender in their intercourse.

Ancient Pagan faiths were full of gay, lesbian, pansexual, intersex, transgender, gender-fluid, and gender-nonconforming deities. These ancient religions also included these queer individuals within their priesthood, sometimes exclusively—something we also see in indigenous faiths and cultures around the world, particularly before colonization. The idea that the divine is a singular old white cis-het dude in the clouds is a fairly modern idea in the scope of the history of religion upon our planet. The witch remembers this, realizing divinity has expressions and archetypes that are as diverse as nature itself—or at least the witch should be mindful of this, if they have forgotten.

Despite this, modern witchcraft with a focus on reviving ancient pagan practices has not always been welcoming to the noncis-het seeker. The imagery of much of early modern witchcraft is extremely fixated on gender binary with an emphasis on fertility and reproduction. Some of the older traditions straight up refused to initiate homosexuals or allow them in their covens or traditions. It didn't even occur to me that you could have a queer witchcraft until I was working in a metaphysical shop part-time during high school, where I happened across the book *Gay Witchcraft: Empowering the Tribe* by Christopher Penczak. The book changed my whole perspective on what it meant to be a witch who was also queer. The book showed me that the two are not incompatible and that Paganism and Occultism have a rich history of queerness that is often erased or ignored. Years later, I learned that some of the best-selling authors of witchcraft books were also secretly queer and quietly died before having the chance to come out of the closet publicly. I also learned about the hidden queer lifestyles some of the founders of the largest traditions of witchcraft had on the side, the same traditions that rejected queer seekers. I was asked on a radio program why I think there's such a rise of queer witchcraft authors today. My answer is that we have always been here, we're just more visible now, and this visibility is more important now than ever.

I feel that Cassandra Snow's *Queering Your Craft: Witchcraft from the Margins* will do for many others what Penczak's book did for me at that time. Through the pages of this book, Snow urges us to embrace that we are holy and powerful just the way we are, to see all consensual sexuality and gender expression as sacred, as opposed to an act of original sin that we need to cleanse ourselves of or atone for. Queer people have been told by religious institutions that they should be ashamed of who they are and who they love and, in the worst cases, that the divine hates them. They are scolded for being sinful and unholy and often condemned, shunned, or, in extreme situations, abused, Snow encourages you to see the core of who you are as sacred and that your connection to the art of witchery can reflect that. Snow reminds us that witchcraft practitioners and seekers can see themselves in divinity regardless of queerness, gender, or ethnicity. Snow encourages pride over shame and emphasizes embracing our most authentic self in all its unique facets, if we are ever truly going to be empowered in every sense of the word. The empowered witch is sovereign in their self-ownership and autonomy of their bodies, sexuality, and expressions thereof as a sacred right of free will and holds the same to be true for every other individual.

One of the mythopoetic stories about how witchcraft came to the people is found within the Italian legend of Aradia, as relayed by folklorist Charles Leland. In the myth, the lunar goddess Diana sends down her daughter Aradia to instruct the marginalized people in the art of witchery to overthrow their oppressors who are abusing their power—priests, kings, and the rich elite. In this legend, Aradia is the archetype of the very first witch, and therefore she can be seen as all witches: from the most marginalized to the most privileged among us that take upon ourselves the mantle of "witch."

The central theme of the Aradia myth is that of magickal and spiritual powers being placed in the hands of the marginalized to bring about justice in a world where those in positions of corrupt power and prejudice oppress others. Witchcraft in this sense was given to the people by Aradia as the spiritual equivalent of the first brick thrown at Stonewall, the historic riot that sparked the queer rights movement. Witchcraft today remains a practice of the marginalized, which includes a large percentage of queer folks. It's a way of magickally balancing the playing field in a society of injustice. It is the power to fight back. That isn't to say that the path of witchcraft is solely about magickally fighting others to alleviate the suffering of those who are victims at their political hands. It is also a path of healing others and self. It is about understanding where we fit into both the physical and spiritual ecosystem, even as queer individuals. It is about realizing that all of us are connected and that we have an important role to play in the larger balance of the world. Those same metaphorical brick projectiles can be used for more than dismantling, they can also be used to build something greater and fairer for all in its place. For many of us, what we want is true equity, balance, and peace in our world, and that begins with ourselves and the influence we have in our bubble of reality, our actions and interactions in our corner of the world, as much as it does the larger injustices of our world.

Snow encourages us to decolonize our witchcraft as queer witches to ensure the inclusivity of others that may not have the privilege we do. It's important to realize that privilege is a series of scales in different aspects of life, not a one-size-fits-all universal measurement. Recognizing one's privilege is the first important step to creating inclusive spaces. For example, I do not necessarily have heterosexual privilege or the religious privilege that the majority of the population does, but I do have privilege in my whiteness, being cisgender, being male, and other areas of my life. We should empathize with what it's like to be within a marginalized group outside of ourselves and advocate for them when it is necessary, just as much (if not more) as we advocate for ourselves as queer people and as witches.

Snow asks us to look outside our privileges yet to use the experience of our own marginalization and struggles to help us empathize with others to create much-needed intersectionality within witchcraft. We must be able to learn to listen and recognize that we can never truly understand what it's like to experience how others are held back in manners we may not be, but that we can still stand with them in solidarity. Sort of like how a nonqueer person can never truly understand what it's like to feel like you need to be in the closet, that you don't have the luxury of being who you are to the world without the threat of repercussion in one manner or another. Within witchcraft specifically, it is important that queer witches remain visible to the larger witchcraft and occult community, to remind them that we exist and are a part of their community, to help ensure that we have more inclusive and safer groups for those who may not be white cis-het. If these groups do not exist locally, we need to keep creating these spaces for ourselves.

As evident through the pages of this book, Snow holds the vision in their deepest of hearts for the queer aspirant who hears the call towards witchery to find healing, empowerment, strength, and pride through their craft—but more than that, to use that power properly for empowering, strengthening, and healing others just as Aradia did. To use that power properly to elevate others, instead of misusing the tools of the oppressor upon those among us with less privilege and perpetuating that cycle of abuse, is the true heart of witchcraft as a spirit. Snow holds a vision for all people to see the divinity within themselves as well as all others—to honor that divinity by standing up, standing with, and fighting for those whom individuals and institutions are systematically oppressing, until we can all be equal without needing to be the same; to recognize, celebrate and honor the immense diversity that makes us the uniquely beautiful creatures we call human. Yet, the work begins with us. Like lighting an inner flame, it starts inside of us and spreads to our interpersonal level, within our various communities, and eventually to the world. Through creative and unique journal prompts, introspection, rituals, and spells, Snow achieves this beautifully, and herein lies the perfect guide for the queer witch to stand in their power and stand beside others—truly queering our craft with compassion and pride.

—Mat Auryn
author of *Psychic Witch: A Metaphysical Guide to
Meditation, Magick, and Manifestation*

INTRODUCTION

This book is an introduction to witchcraft. It has been written to specifically address the needs of those who are queer, marginalized, living in the shadows, or on the edge of acceptance. It is well known that Paganism and witchcraft have been pushed to the sidelines and marginalized since Christianity began its stronghold. So has queerness.

For most of my adult life, I have practiced and studied magick. I have also studied queer theory, history, and culture. Magickal craft and queerness have gone hand in hand for me personally for so long (and I live in such a queer city) that I forget that my queer craft isn't the norm. Over the course of my practice, I have come up against problematic elements in witchcraft and Paganism that I reconciled and worked out for myself long ago. In spite of those problematic elements, witchcraft gave me the confidence to break from an extremely codependent familial relationship, come out of the closet, and move halfway across the country. Those are probably three of the most groundbreaking, earth shattering decisions I've ever made and magick was there for all of them. I want everyone to have the same access I did to a spellcraft that can change your life

Witchcraft has always belonged to the outsiders and outcasts in society, yet so much of the practice enforces and adheres to the same hierarchy we are faced with in the world at large that isolate and hurt those living beyond society's binaries and boundaries. *Queering Your Craft* takes witchcraft back and helps put it into the hands of those who need it most: queer and marginalized people and their fiercest allies. *Queering Your Craft* will introduce you (or reintroduce you) to magick and spellcraft, and throughout this discussion, I will address the craft from a queer perspective.

This book wraps up everything that is important to a queer practitioner: the personal, the collective, the political, and how deeply intertwined all three are into one useful witchcraft practice that is accessible in both price and grasp (meaning the work is easy to do) while still offering new and inspiring information to those who have been practicing their craft for a long time.

When we look at queering witchcraft and accessibility and the intersection therein, there's an easy in to start understanding how and why it can all fit together: the huge influence of "do-it-yourself" culture and aesthetic that permeates much of the queer community (especially the poor and marginalized queer community that informs this as well). This DIY idea makes its way into every facet of learning witchcraft and many facets of queering things, so if nothing else, *Queering Your Craft* can help push your craft from by-the-book to something that's all your own.

For those who are newer on their path or who struggle to put their practice into words, let's start at the beginning with what magick even is. Magick can be as deep, ethereal, and complicated as you want it to be, but ultimately it is simply using the energy, elements, resources, and tools at your disposal to create outcomes you desire. Everything we know and have and are was created by magick. Everything we know and have and are is maintained by magick. Magick is a skill. Magick is a love song to yourself and the world around you. Magick is internal, external, and beyond even that. Most of all though, magick is your right, and responsibility—as a human living on this Earth.

Put another way, magick is your determination and force of will combined with your desire for something to happen. Your force of will and desire are what bring that outcome into being. This often happens through sheer hard work or by diving into networking. The living of your life is a magickal act. I've written in my personal journal many times some variant of "I haven't done a lot of spell work lately, but I have been reveling in opportunities and adventure and I think maybe that's the same thing." I repeat: *the living of your life (your way) is a magickal act.*

Sometimes we need help, though. In a perfect world our will would be enough to bring the things we want into being, but we live in a world that is far from perfect. Magick is not like it is on TV and movies. We can't blink our way into success or snap our fingers and end up sitting on a pile of money. We're not helpless though, and that's where spells and ritual come in, which is what most people consider the magick. The natural elements that fill our world and make it rich and nuanced also make it easier for us to reclaim our energy, our bodies, and our lives. The stones, herbs, water, other humans, animals, and so on and so forth that we love so dearly can be core components of working magick and helping turn the tides in our favor. Spells and rituals are taking those natural elements and using them to turn those tides.

Your *craft* then, is how you perform the rituals and acts of magick that we think of as spells. Craft is writing and performing spells, but it's also the learning process that goes into *any* spiritual practice. This book focuses largely on the craft of witchcraft or Paganism itself (and therefore the spells and how to get to the spells), but from the perspective of a sick, disabled, fat, often impoverished queer. That means it's a perspective that gets that you don't always have a million dollars for new tools or access to meetups that will teach you what you know. *The most successful witches out there aren't better, more skilled, more magickal than you—they just had access.* This book seeks to break down that discrepancy and grant you access to learn a craft that will become *your* craft.

The majority of this book is devoted to learning spellcraft so you can make spells of your own. This means learning the pieces, tools, and elements involved in craft first. Specifically, when we talk about magickal spiritual paths we are interested in using:

The energies of:

- Animal allies

- Any familiars or pets coming in and out of the room while we work

- Gods and Goddesses

- Others who may be in spiritual communion with us

- Ourselves, including the mood or emotion we're experiencing in that moment

- Spiritual entities like fae or spirits

- The city we're in

- The room we're in

- The vague concept of energy that seeps into most magickal cultures

The four earthly elements:

- Air
- Earth
- Fire
- Water
- And the fifth element—Spirit

Resources and tools, such as:

- Divinatory tools such as a pendulum or a deck of tarot cards
- Friends who have been practicing for longer than you
- Local occult stores who can answer all of your questions and sell you the right stuff at a variety of price points
- Oils, herbs, candles, sigils, artwork, and the like
- The things you need and have at your disposal to make your own dreams come true
- Websites and books chock full of magical knowledge

The last portion of this book is a grimoire of spells to help you invoke or inspire a specific outcome. This section is comprised of explicitly queer spells I wrote that will be easy for readers at the beginning of their journey to cast. Some of the most common forms of magick include love spells, money spells, and protection spells. Other New Age forms of magick include self-love mantras or carrying crystals for grounding and clarity. Old school folk magick or very modern DIY magick can be anything from having a lucky pair of pants that you wore when you aced your midterms to carrying around a lucky penny.

The Necessity of Queering Magick

What we think of as the "norm" now hasn't always been the case. Sexual and gender identity that fall outside of straight and cisgender have had rich periods of acceptance throughout time. We saw it in pre-Nazi Germany with Hirschfield's Institution of Sexology and their successes. We see it in Native and Indigenous cultures even today. There are even texts and other evidence to show that we saw it in pre-Christian times when Paganism was the default spiritual belief throughout most of Europe.

As Christianity gained ground and power, we have seen the reflection of the religion's exclusion get passed down even through other subcultures, like Paganism. When Wicca became really popular through Gardnerian Wicca in the 1950s, male/female polarity was stressed in a way that not only excluded transgender (especially non-binary) people, but also was not very inclusive of gay or bisexual people either. Then there's the Aleister Crowley problem. In the early 20th century, Crowley began his journey to popularize the religion of his creation: Thelema. Thelema is a mystical spirituality (called both a religion and a philosophy depending on who you're talking to) that takes a lot from Ancient Egyptian pantheons and symbolism, general esoterica, and Qabalah. Like the later Wiccan resurgence, Thelema really struggled due to its era: one of generally accepted misogyny and homophobia.

Thelema and Gardenerian Wicca both have foundationally beautiful, magickal, and important principles. They are also both deeply problematic, binary, and full of constraints for people who don't fit into that norm. Because so many marginalized people were looking for something other than Chistianity to rest and relax in, queer people in this period did what queer people always do—they found a way to subvert and reclaim that witchcraft as their own. Nonetheless, neo-Paganism, which largely owes its roots to the creation and popularization of Wicca and Thelema, also suffers from the shortsightedness of its creators and the limits of the language in the early to mid-20th century.

There are also other ways modern witchcraft has been harmful to marginalized people over the years. I have very complicated feelings about the doctrine of "and it harm none," which I'll touch on a little bit later in this book. The phrase itself though is a tenant of most mainstream witchcraft that is well intentioned but falls very short. It's meant to inspire us to do any witchcraft we want so long as it doesn't directly harm someone else. However, what it calls to mind for me is all of the times a marginalized person who has been abused or oppressed, is tone-policed or silenced because they were "too angry." Black activists in particular are constantly being told to silence themselves in order to protect white people's comfort and often language is abused to hold them to that silence.

They are told they are being mean or hurtful but that's not true. That tone policing is a tool of white supremacy to silence dissenting viewpoints and serve the status quo instead of social justice. If we are to be witches, with a duty to humankind and the Earth itself, and to serve social justice, we cannot always be polite and harm free. This is just one way "and it harm none" is nonsense.

In a politically difficult and tense world, witchcraft is a secret weapon. It is catharsis, first—something that helps us purge our emotions and heal. Then it's about autonomy and taking control of our lives. From there, it's about power. It's about the power to create outcomes and wield change. It's about the power to love this world enough to want to make it better. And, it's about the power it takes to make that happen. Because of that, witchcraft has always been something marginalized groups can and should wield. No one is more powerless than those living on the fringes of society, and that is where most queer people can be found. Something quiet, almost secret, happens in those fringes though. Society casts us out into them, but in these darkened shadows we learn to share, to love, and to thrive even in the worst of times.

Those shadows that we thrive in can remain powerful allies in our spellcraft and are a form of shadow work. Shadow work is loosely defined as coming to terms with, and either healing or incorporating the hurt, hidden, or *darker* sides of ourselves. Learning to use the fringes and shadows that we thrive in is much more about incorporating those shadow sides of ourselves into our lives and is therefore the brand of shadow work I prefer. I put darker in italics because, as queer and anti-racist witches I want us to get out of the binary of thinking that *light* magick is good and *dark* magick is bad. This thinking came from very racist roots—a lot of what we think of as dark or *black* magick comes from traditionally Black cultures like *VooDoo*. A lot of what we think of as light magick is often appropriated from other religions largely practiced by white people, such as Christian mysticism. Furthermore, a lot of dark magick is also survival magick. We're told it's selfish or harmful magick because these people are doing work just for themselves. So what? We all have needs and desires. Please don't fall in to the trap of thinking that gaining something for yourself is dark. That is such unnecessary self-punishment, and on top of that, gives in to those aforementioned roots of racism.

The idea of dark magick even existing also comes from conservative Christianity lambasting *all* magick as dark magick. The term light magick was created likely as a way to try to compromise with Christians in our lives, but I don't feel like it successfully does that. We're just giving in to corporate Christian views on dark magick, which is something as queer witches we should refuse to do. I say all of that to show that I think, as humans, we are meant to overcome pain, adversity, and trauma. I don't think we're meant to overcome parts of ourselves (with the exception of any truly toxic or abusive behavior manifestations). When we talk about *queering* magick, we don't just talk about our own shadow work. We talk about group shadow work and honoring the shadows and fringes we've thrived in. Working with your environment is such a crucial and generally accessible part of magickal practice, and for queer people that environment hasn't always been ideal. Yet it's been there, all along, protecting us and allowing us to come into our full selves. Bring that, all of that, into your practice as you continue on your magickal journey.

Queering, to me, means deconstructing something for the purposes of rebuilding it in our own queer image, subverting it in that process, and claiming it as our own. That claiming, or reclaiming, is then an act of power and magick all its own. It makes us come alive and it roots us to the very real, very queer magick running through our veins. Queering magick is necessary because as queer people we have a right to the same power everyone has the potential for and a responsibility to make change in this world. Queering magick is vital because you, beautiful, precious, darling *you*, deserve all of the joy and healing available, which is so much! Queering magick is critical because as we've seen over and over again, the system will not protect or nurture us—so we need to have as many tools as possible in our toolbox to protect and nurture ourselves.

What Do We Mean When We Say Queering Magick?

So often when people hear me speak of queering anything, they think only of sexual and gender identity. If they're pretty well versed they might think of relationship identity or sex-positive connotations. Those are all really wonderful starts to a much deeper philosophy that is anti-racist, anti-capitalist, anti-rape culture (and pro-consent culture), fat positive, disability inclusive, and doesn't leave out those who don't have the financial or social capital to hoard or even access resources. Queering magick must mean making space for those who don't have it elsewhere in the world. Often this means developing or researching accessible resources for new witches, since not everyone has that ability to do it for themselves. You'll notice one thing I seem to be driving at is that even if we are solitary practicioners, queer witchcraft is moving towards a collective *we*. While our own queer wishes and hopes are valid and deserve space, queering witchcraft really is about moving it from the elitist and selfish *I* that even group ritual can enforce to a place where we are fighting for collective liberation as well.

I use a lot of principles of queer theory, history, and culture in my work, which you've already seen if you're familiar with those principles. A few key ones that you'll notice is that I do take the stance that while gender and sexuality may be *partially* socially constructed, they are still vital parts of who we are. That *either/or* binary is a key debate in queer theory, but modern understanding has taken more of a *both/and* approach. One thing that is agreed upon in queer theory, that I also use in my work, is the idea of history as recognition. Queer history is as old as history is, and in recognizing that we recognize that, regardless of the ever-changing social constructs, there have always been queer people. Furthermore, recognizing our history is a gateway to honoring it, and in honoring it we welcome a whole new group of ancestors and a whole new way to venerate them. Sex positivity has also made its way into queer theory, which is another huge foundation of my work as a witch and a writer. We have to honor queer sex if we're honoring queer people, and this book leaves plenty of space for that. If you are queer, you'll see several other overtly queer concepts show up in this book too: community building, resilience, fighting for radical change and activism, chosen family (and how it fails us sometimes), the necessity and vibrance of queer art, and safer spaces, to name a few.

While I've mostly written about the beautiful parts of being queer so far, this community is not any more perfect than any other community. I also seek to dismantle the white supremacy that shows up in our spaces and therefore leaves little to no space (depending on the size of your community) for queer people of color. Because of the DIY nature of a lot of queer space making, these spaces are often inaccessible and overstimulating to people with disabilities. On top of these very large issues, there's also the infighting that happens in a community of mostly traumatized people. There's the way chosen family will give up on you just as quickly as given family sometimes. There's the unique pain that comes from that. In these ways the queer community itself needs to change, and this book strives to open these doors, too.

To make it even easier to understand and break it into bite sized chunks, I've written a manifesto for queer witches below. *I strongly suggest making your own* and using mine as a loose guide instead of prescribing strictly to my or anyone else's version. I can't possibly have covered everything, and if there are hordes of witches each with their own manifesto driving towards social progress, collective liberation, and personal empowerment, then the magick and power in those manifestos' words will automatically begin picking up steam, getting into the universe, and manifesting from there.

A QUEER WITCH MANIFESTO

There are infinite genders and sexual identities. Each one deserves the same space and respect as the next. Each one brings something unique and necessary to a circle should they choose to do magick with us.

White supremacy upholds ideals and expectations that harm everyone, and must fall. Even though white supremacy harms everyone, white people must not center themselves in discussion of it or in plans or spellwork for making it fall.

Because we are fighting white supremacy, *queer magicians must work hard not to appropriate* sacred religious artifacts, aesthetics, and even dieties that do not belong to us.

Sex magick is powerful and beautiful, and like anything sexual, most hold up the idea that informed and enthusiastic consent is mandatory. Our queered-up version of sex magick also fights rape culture, patriarchy, heteronormativity, and cisnormativity.

Though we are anti-capitalist we recognize the constraints of the society we live in and know that money magick is often critical and empowering for those living in the margins.

We recognize that Goddess does not equal womb worship and that anyone can invoke Goddess energy.

We recognize that some witches may have physical, emotional, or mental limits that cannot be overcome with spirituality. We welcome these witches to bring their whole, real selves into a magickal space and cast spells in the way that works best for them.

We recognize that individual traumas may need to be healed before we move on to collective work.

Queer witchcraft can and does include manifesting personal desires so long as they don't impede someone else's autonomy and consent. People who have suffered and been marginalized deserve pleasure, and magick is a great tool for bringing that into being. Manifesting those personal desires is often necessary in a healing journey that needs to happen before we can become empowered.

Magick is a tool for personal healing that leads to empowerment. This empowerment enables us to focus on social progress, empowering others, and collective liberation.

Global climate change is killing us all and *we must protect and attempt to heal the Earth.* This must be a magickal priority for queer witchcraft.

Hierarchies do not work in a queer magickal context. We are equals, even if our jobs in a group working are different.

All bodies are capable of and deserving of magick. All bodies are capable of and deserving of the joy and manifestation magick can bring.

1

WITCHCRAFT 101

Any good spellbook, grimoire, or magickal reference book provides some basics of witchcraft first. This book doesn't stray too far from that tradition as it would be irresponsible not to include foundational information. This is a queer book though, which means as I lay down these foundations for you, everything from here on out is presented through a strictly queer lens with the above manifesto in mind.

Types of Magick

I know that I have probably left out some people's favorite forms of magick in this list. There are infinite ways to express a Pagan or witchy spirituality, and I could not possibly include them all—especially not in a book that isn't devoted solely to different kinds of magick. I did seek to include the most commonly used forms of magick and the types of magick that are accessible at various price points, including zero dollars. I want even the most broke witch, the one struggling with housing and food access, to be able to able to use all of the elements and create beautiful magickal works in their life. Some of these will cost money, but none are more effective than the others. What does make any kind of magick or spells more effective is layering. Layering is the act of adding different tools and skills to a basic spell to boost or underscore it. If you write a list as a spell, layering would mean drawing a sigil on it, waving it over a candle's smoke, or kissing it when you're done as a mild form of personal sex magick.

WRITING POEMS, LETTERS, LISTS

The earliest recorded days of witchcraft and Paganism included deep, beautiful chants and songs and very little else. It doesn't matter if it was Earth-worshipping Druids, followers of Norse Gods, or devotees of Egyptian Gods—it all came down to how deeply our voices were heard by speaking or writing them. This is still a powerful form of magick, and one I'm quick to employ. There's a very modern tendency to rely on the old chants, songs, and spells that we can find in old-fashioned grimoires and spellbooks. I understand that compulsion. It feels witchier and that feeling can be an important boost to our spell. In the end, though, it's just a feeling. Just because something is from ancient times (however you're defining that) does not mean it's more magickal or powerful. The people creating those poems and singing those songs weren't trying to write something timeless that would be used for centuries to come. They were simply calling out to their gods in the vernacular of their time.

If you want a powerful money spell, you don't need to rely on a prosperity spell that was used in harvest times of yore before currency was even invented. It's just as effective to write a letter to a god or to the Earth pleading your case and explaining what you need the money for. It's just as effective to list your goals and stick them on your altar. If you are more artistic or writery than that, then you can absolutely write your own songs and poems that speak to your spiritual connections and desires, and trust me—those will be as well met as any formal group ritual or ancient chant.

As queer people, remembering the potency of our voices is especially important. We live in a world that is constantly trying to silence us, and if we're survivors of personal trauma on top of that, we have likely spent a lot of time learning to make ourselves small and invisible. If we're lucky, we've gotten the help, love, and resources we need to unlearn that. We're still unlearning it though, and it can take a literal lifetime to proudly come into our voice and state our desires, whether they're personal or collective. Starting at a place in your craft where you are directly highlighting your voice, how you're feeling, and what you want is not only an important way to come into your own as a witch, but also is a powerful act of reclamation that frankly, you deserve.

This section is titled "Writing Poems, Letters, Lists." There is no wrong thing to write to cast a spell or even just feel out your voice. I am a terrible poet and sometimes I don't care because it's for the Earth and not for me, but sometimes it makes me too self-conscious for my magick to be effective. My money magick usually consists of several parts but it usually starts with a list of my financial goals and immediate needs and then I add a list of long-term goals. I write a lot of letters—to my family, to my friends, and yes, to my gods. Letters are actually one of my favorite things in the world, and so my witchcraft letters are soaked in love and passion. The reason I listed so many options for magickal writing and left an open-ended "more" is because *what* you're writing isn't important. I've written skits for my gods. I have friends who write chants and songs. Wherever *you* feel strongest is where you should aim your witchcraft writing, and if in regular practice of that you get newly inspired, that's okay, too.

VISUAL ART

Some of you are reading the above section and saying to yourself "that sounds great, but I'm really not so good at the words doing." I would first like to say that A) it doesn't matter, the intention is the point, but also, B) that's okay! We want you to be confident to start, and another really evocative form of magick is creating visual art. This can be a photo you took and had printed off of your family if you're working ancestral magick. It can be a painting of endless Celtic knots or spirals to remind yourself that life is about cycles and you'll come out of this one okay. It can be a sculpture you created of a god that you're interested in invoking or working with. Just like with writing, the only rules are that you should be confident in what you're doing and that it should have a specific intent (even if the intent is "to be happier" or "to be more magickal").

In terms of queer identity and visual art, so many of us are artistically inclined that it almost goes without saying that this is a potent form of magick for queer witches to try. Even if you yourself are not visually creative or skilled enough to give this a go at this time, buying art from local queers that speaks to your altar (or an upcoming spell) and displaying it proudly is a solid way to keep that energy vibing throughout your space for the foreseeable future. Not everyone is verbally or literarily inclined, but visual art is another way for queer people to start reclaiming their voice and space in this world. Sometimes we don't operate in words and clear thought, we operate in colors and feelings. That's an energy you're encouraged to bring into your life as a witch too, and it's one that visual art (your own or someone else's) can really allow you to thrive in.

INCANTATIONS AND MANTRAS

Sometimes our practice includes writing, visual art, or both and over time we notice that there are distinct words and themes that come to the surface of our practice no matter which form of magick we've been using. These often drive at deeper needs that developed and weren't met for a sustained period of our life. This can be scars from trauma or oppression, or it could be a need or desire we never learned to voice. In either case, a deeper healing is needed. In these times, words can still be our deepest allies even if we feel like we aren't good at them.

Incantations and mantras are all of that pain, those needs, those desires condensed into short, quick verbal spells like:

"With the power inside of my heart and gut, I will attract a new lover thus.

But I am content until they come and I am joyful on my own."

Or . . .

"As I work throughout the day, I attract so much money to me."

Or . . .

"I am connected to my gods and the Earth in all things."

Or even just . . .

"I deserve to be happy."

Incantations and mantras can be said at the start of your day, in your head while you're brushing your teeth, out loud in between taking your meds, or hummed to yourself while you're feeding your pets. They can be spoken any time you get anxious about your intention not being met throughout the day. Write them in a journal, put them on sticky notes on your mirror or the fridge, set an alarm on your phone that sends them through to you.

Words have power, and, while I am a believer in manifestation, I do not think that oppressed people create oppressed circumstances because of lack of self-esteem or anything else. I do not think that people deserve their trauma or illness because they didn't think positively enough. Sometimes things happen simply because other humans, and the institutions they've built and run, are terrible. That's it! That's the reason! Still, our words *do* have power and the most important words need to be repeated back to ourselves over and over again. That's where incantations come in. So often as marginalized people, our healing and our abundance is up to us. That isn't because it should be or because it's fair, but because often we don't have other options. Yet thinking about taking charge of your circumstances and trying to outsmart *The Man* is incredibly daunting. We can start by writing out a few incantantions, putting them everywhere, repeating them often, and trusting our inner power to allow those shifts in language to cause shifts in our behavior that cause shifts in our life. It's not a perfect art, because we still love in a society full of hate. It can, however, dramatically alter the power and autonomy we feel in our lives, and that can open an infinite number of doors for ourselves.

MEDITATIONS, WISHES, AND PRAYERS

When we grow up queer, especially if we grow up in the closet or in an unsafe area, we learn to be very careful about when and where to speak our attractions or desires. Often our parents or the communities we grow up in reinforce the idea that we need to be quiet about what and how we feel. Over time this disconnects us from our inner voice and our own intuition. I want to say that, first and foremost, this is not our fault. A lot of us who grew up in traditional and queerphobic faiths have also learned to internalize guilt and wield even our own sheepishness against ourselves. That's a lie though—it's not our fault, at all, that we do any of this, or that we've become disconnected from our own divinity.

The first steps to getting your divinity back can often be linked to intentional time spent trying to connect with it again. Prayer itself is one way to do this. It doesn't matter to whom. It doesn't have to be *to* anybody. Prayer is so easy, free, and accessible that anyone can do it. It's also such a beautiful connector to divine energy that everybody *should* do it. I also recognize from experiencing it firsthand, that those who grew up in a prayer-heavy faith might have trouble connecting to this too-familiar path that might even make you feel kind of icky at the start. I'm not trying to override your religious trauma. If you try a prayer to the Earth, a god, your ancestors, the Universe, love, and it doesn't work, if your inner critic comes out or your trauma screams "wrong," that's okay. Step away for a few minutes. You'll get there. Try easing into it slowly. A quick prayer that is literally just "thank you" when you get unexpected luck or a despairing "please help" when you're feeling your absolute worst is enough. The intention is clear. The Divine is listening. You'll grow slowly from there.

Prayer has, over time, become a way I fill time on bus rides, waiting for clients who are late, and trying to fall asleep at night. It also keeps me rooted in Divine energy all day long and therefore helps me bring that same consistent energy into my practice. I have learned that the gods didn't hurt me. People did. Society did. Institutions developed by the power holders in our society did. My gods only ever stepped in to help. It's okay if you're not there yet, but by slowly easing into prayer, eventually you will be. From there it's only a matter of time until you feel comfortable using prayer as a form of spell. For those of us who are already there, think of prayer as a way to cast small spells of gratitude, closeness, and your daily goals throughout the day. Sometimes I write down my prayers, mostly I don't. Divine energy isn't necessary for witchcraft unless you want it to be, but for those of us who do rely on it, prayer is the way in.

Wishes are a form of magick too, though you often don't realize it at the time. I often tell witchcraft students or tarot clients to be diligent with their wishes because if we really want something in the moment and really send it out there as something forceful, they are likely to come back to us in some form or fashion (within reason). That person might not fall in love with you, but you might find that person's best traits with someone else. Or, if you weren't careful with the wish, it could be their worst. Wishes can happen on shooting stars and eclipses, they can be said during ritual or in our beds when we're crying late at night. There are wishing spells and rituals, some of which are included later. Some of those you already know. Throw a penny in a well. Wish upon a shooting star. This is a form of magick, and for queer people who are feeling disconnected from their ability to pray, it functions in a relatively similar way.

Another thing I lump in with wishing and praying is meditation. Meditation is also flexible, but the basics are to find a seated position where you're relatively comfortable. I know for those in chronic pain or in a wheelchair that might be difficult, and I know you won't get to total relaxation—that's okay. Get as comfortable as you feasibly can. I tend to recommend closing your eyes, because life is distracting. If you're physically able to, fade into deep, even breathing. If you can't do that or even temporarily can't, still focus on what your breath is doing naturally, as it's able to. Try to clear your mind—really try. A lot of people are really resistant to meditation because they can't clear their mind for that long. Some of them have perfectly valid reasons for feeling that way—anxiety disorders, ADHD, a legitimately overpacked to-do list that they haven't really chipped away at yet. These are exactly the people who should be meditating, though. The dirty little secret of meditation is that it's actually startlingly rare for people to clear their minds for any length of time. Most of the work is in trying to clear your mind. This practice alone, believe it or not, does deepen your connection to your own intuition over time. Your intuition is often what connects you to spiritual energy, and developing this takes time but is completely doable.

Once you're pretty skilled at getting into a clearer headspace (knowing that it's rarely a perfect art), you can start doing either guided or self-guided meditations for specific purposes. Your incantations can come in here. Get into that clear headspace and then just think your incantations. If you are in a panic prior to meditation, you can just repeat them over and over. If you're having a good mental health day you can say them once, allow the words to sink into your body and your brain, and then repeat them. Take it slow again.

For queer magick users who have been disconnected from their own voice, meditation is a game-changer. You sit there connecting to your body and what it's trying to tell you and you find pretty quickly that the practice works. Meditation alone can continue to serve as a form of witchcraft, regardless of whether we're trying to clear our minds or attract certain energies to us. I try to meditate every morning, before I jump into any physical therapy I need to do that day. I don't always get there, but I do manage to clear my head for long enough to focus on a goal for the day. From there I can connect back to that energy more easily throughout the day, again, keeping the witchy vibes flowing no matter what I'm doing.

SIGIL MAKING

Witch confession: I only starting working with *sigils* in the past year or so. Sigils are technically defined as any magickally infused picture, letter, or symbol. What most witches mean when they use them are a specific group of or aesthetic of symbols, similar to the one shown here.

Sigils like this are used most often in chaos magick, a form of ceremonial magick that doesn't pull from a specific line of witchcraft other than it's own. You don't have to be a chaos magician to use them though. The thing to know is that they're often thought of as signatures of angels or other spiritual entities. I often use them as messages from my loved ones who have passed on, or honestly just a magick symbol with energy from other planes or realms. Like most of the types of magick we've talked about in this section, sigils can be used for anything and everything. You *can* find sigils for any purpose under the sun by using Google Search, and most of those images are safe and bewitched for you to use.

Sigils can be drawn (or doodled!), carved into candles, or just scrawled into your journal or grimoire (more on that later). You can keep any that are done on small pieces of paper on your altar, in your wallet, in your pocket, or bra, wherever. I tend to not think of these as spells themselves. They're more like spell booster or amplifiers. That's not true for everyone of course, and there is one glaring exception to that rule—when you create your own.

We've talked ad nauseum about why creating something in your voice, from your point of view is important for queer witches so I won't reiterate it here. I *will* say that all of the reasons you would write or draw as a spell likewise apply to your sigil creation. I will also say that a lot of times the reasons we're seeking magickal intervention in our lives as queer people is because there aren't ready made ones for a lot of our very real needs and goals. This is one of my favorite things about sigils. I don't need to find one that speaks to me, I just need to find pieces or ideas of how I want one to look that speak to me.

There are several ways to go about creating your own sigils. One common folkway of doing it is to write out a word or short phrase that sums up your goals. Then cross out the vowels. From there, play with combining the consonants into one symbol or letter until you're satisfied with what you're looking at. Remake that final one into the *official* sigil you're using, and incorporate it however you need to.

Another practice I really like is to find several different sigils that *sort of* hit on what I'm looking for and play with turning them into one until I'm satisfied with what I'm looking at. This can be done by laying them on top of each other in Adobe PhotoShop, and futzing with them until you're content. It can be done by drawing one then incorporating pieces of the others. It can be done by looking at several, praying or meditating on it, and allowing a totally new vision to come into your mind of what it should look like.

If you're feeling pretty good and pretty in touch with your intuition, you can also do a meditation meant to bring a specific sigil to the forefront of your mind that you can use as, or in, a spell. I actually struggle with this since I'm not a super visually oriented person, but I know of a lot of wildly successful witches who come up with their own sigils by praying or meditating on it until an image rises to the surface.

POPPETS

I cannot contain myself when I start talking about poppet magick. I just love poppets so much. Some of it is that I'm a Pisces with a Pisces moon, and as a people, we really love cute or pretty things. A lot of that excitement is because there's a misunderstanding of creating and using poppet magick where people think it's too deep and mystical to understand and yet it is absolutely one of the most accessible forms of magick that there is. You just need some stray fabric, cornhusks, or anything else fibrous that holds together and won't rot, and something to fill it with like cotton, dry rice, more fabric, cornhusks, or whatever is handy.

That accessibility alone is one of the reasons I think queer magicians should absolutely be making and using poppets. Poppets are a type of sympathetic magick, which basically just means that the doll represents you or whoever you're doing the spell on. Poppets are most common in hex spells, and that is how I came to them. Poppets are such a clear stand-in for another human being, that it makes sense to use this as your hexing default. This practice comes from HooDoo, VooDoo, and folk magick practices. Poppets allow you to tie the energy of a person or group of people you're hexing to the poppet by using some hair, a photo, or other similar implement of theirs. You simply stuff those items into the body of the poppet. But we'll get to that in a moment.

There is also so much beautiful sympathetic magick that can be done for ourselves (especially as queer people who need some extra boosts of empowerment), each other, and community with poppet work, too. I've done spells where I make a couple of poppets to represent my neighbors or my queer community members and enchant them with protection. On particularly arthritic days, I'll make a poppet that represents me and do a healing or an anti-pain spell on myself. If a close friend is struggling to keep their business afloat, I'll make them a poppet stuffed with cash that I've doused in prosperity oil. With any kind of sympathetic magick, you don't want to rule out that you might need to do a hex in protection of self, loved ones, or community. You also don't want to think of it only in these terms when it can be yet another type of really wonderful magick for empowerment, strength, and knocking out those goals.

To make a poppet, first clearly define what you want the poppet to be for. So far I've primarily discussed types of magick that can be used for general healing, prosperity, confidence, and so forth. Sympathetic magick is not that. You need a specific person with a specific goal in mind. Please note that for the rest of the steps in your poppet making adventure, you'll want to keep your energy and intentions right at the front of your mind and heart. You want that energy to be pouring off of you and into your poppet. Say the intentions out loud. Talk to the poppet as you make it. Tell them about all the great things you're going to do together.

You may want to draw out a pattern first. All you need to do is draw a rough image of approximately what you want your poppet to look like on a piece of paper, cut it out, lay your poppet material, on top of that, and cut accordingly. I do recommend making the poppet pattern bigger than you want the poppet to be, because if you're not experienced with sewing, you'll likely be tying off your poppet and that can create too small of a poppet and too tedious of a process if you don't. Even if you are good at sewing, remember that this is a process that includes stuffing, so the shape will be different than you anticipate.

From there, lay the poppet fabric down and put your filler in. I do recommend using filler that corresponds with your intention. If this is a poppet meant to make you rich, try symbols of wealth like uncooked corn (which represents a harvest) or shredded money. If it's a poppet that rep-resents the ideal lover you are trying to bring to yourself, fill it with dried flower petals. This isn't wholly necessary, because this is an accessible process, but you can enchant even cotton or dried rice to the intention that you're looking for. Simply hold it in your hands, close your eyes, and think about intention. Picture a ball of energy moving past your skin and into the filler. Once you feel ready, put the filler in the poppet. I would also include with the filler any small things you want that represent the goal or energy you want the doll to be imbued with. An incantation or sigil written down on a small piece of paper and folded up, a coin, a trinket or charm, or a handful of herbs are a few examples that will do the trick.

There are a couple of different ways you can pull the poppet together into a poppet or doll instead of just random pieces of things. If you're skilled with sewing, you can obviously sew it all together in a way that makes sense for you. I usually grab smaller, thinner but long strips of the same material of the poppet and tie the poppet together. That means in my pattern portion, I don't cut the fabric into halves, I let it stay attached because then it's easier to tie together. I do one strip to create a head and neck division. I do one around the waist area. I usually also tie off shoulders, and arms and legs where the hands and feet would normally be. Poppets are not supposed to be pretty or cute (but I think they are!) so if yours bulge weird or don't look perfectly even at first, don't worry. It's still a poppet and it'll still work. You can also tie it off with twine, yarn, or chunky thread, especially if you're working with a less pliable material like cornhusks.

A couple of final touches you can add once you're all sewn up or tied together include: oils, sprays, or perfumes. Feel free to douse the poppet, especially a fabric poppet, so long as you can stand to be in the room with the strong smell. Obviously these should correlate to the poppet's overall purpose, too. You can also decorate the poppet. Use some thread or buttons to make eyes or a smile. Sew on patches or buttons wherever you want them to represent any final touches you want your spell to have.

Once your poppet is complete, hold it in your hands and do any last incantations or energy push. Place it wherever you'd like—your bed, your altar, a random bookcase, and go about your day. Every few days you should check in with the poppet, either chatting with it (I like to let mine know about the progress we're making towards the goals) or recharging it. Eventually you might feel like you don't need this poppet anymore. If it is a hex poppet, destroy it and throw it away. If it was a good-to-you poppet, you can unstitch it and use the pieces and ingredients for later spells, or just hang on to it. You can dispose of it if it feels respectful to do so, but I know a lot of witches get attached to theirs. I have a small box where I keep several former poppets, and I just try really hard not to outgrow that box. Eventually though, I do toss a few out. I made them so long ago that I no longer remember what their purpose was, or their goals were hit so long ago that it feels like I'm holding on to a former, and sometimes lesser, version of myself. Feel it out and trust your gut—just like in all things magickal.

KITCHEN WITCHERY

A *kitchen witch* is someone who focuses their craft in their home, particularly where cooking, baking, and using nontraditional magickal tools is concerned. All that this path requires is a base knowledge of cooking, baking, and which herbs are used for what in magickal practice. (Actually, using Google Search in place of knowledge is pretty useful too, so don't get stressed or hung up on that piece.) An advanced kitchen witch might also grow their own herbs and flowers, or even have a full-fledged garden of edibles that they tend. I'm including kitchen witchery in this section because it is a deeply accessible and flexible form of magick, and one that I think takes on a whole new life of its own once we start queering it.

Kitchen witchery has been one of my favorite forms of magick to reclaim over the years. As an ardent queer feminist who grew up in an unstable home, I used to turn my back on anything that felt homemakery. When I started learning witchcraft I had no concept of hearth and home. I wasn't concerned with creating warm and safe spaces for others because I didn't have that for myself. As time passed and now that I'm well into my mid-thirties, I feel very differently. The shift into kitchen witchcraft came naturally. First I had to fall in love with having a stable home and partnership. Then I had to want to create that space for others. Then I had to fall in love with cooking. Then I had to find my way on this new branch of my path. As a bona fide queer, I never found kitchen witchery necessary for the reasons I described above. I have subverted homemaking and kitchen magick now; these can be a powerful way to remake what home and family is. Which is something I really needed to find.

In a nutshell, kitchen witches spend a lot of their time making food and drink that is infused with witchcraft and magick. They might take wheat as a symbol of harvest and bake bread that they've enchanted with a spell for ongoing harvest and abundance. They might make cookies with fresh flower petals loved by the fae baked into them in an attempt to woo the fae to their favor. They might make teas that are meant to help you with everything from menstrual cramps to sex magick and back again. They usually have an altar in the kitchen, though certainly that isn't a requirement.

We are living through a time where things like cooking, baking, and even keeping house are having a kitschy resurgence as hipster hobbies, and for that reason information about kitchen witchery abounds. To follow this path, it's easy enough to research online some simple starter recipes that are also spells, and some herb and ingredient correspondence lists. Any time you want to do something really tangible and creative with a spell, kitchen witchery is a beautiful place to start, especially if you really have no idea what your creative skills are. Kitchen witchery is also generally accessible. It's tempting once you're on this path to acquire all of the fanciest kitchen gadgets and highest quality herbs, but it's also completely unnecessary. Some salt thrown into your dish can help with protection magick. Some pasta sauce out of a jar can honor a god that is associated with nightshade plants. It doesn't have to be complicated. You can even just research "magical use of X" where X is a random ingredient you have to work with.

There is something truly invigorating about actually ingesting your magickal spell. You are putting something special and divine that you created with your own hands into your body. Even if you're not at a point where you're interested in reclaiming the idea of home, kitchen witchery can pay off big for you. It's incredibly rooted to the body, which is often the first thing I see queer clients needing to reclaim. When you ingest your own magick and let it run its course throughout your body, you are staking your claim to and owning your desires for your life.

Most queer people are concerned with helping the collective, and not just themselves. Kitchen witchery can allow you to take your few sparse ingredients and turn them into a magickal meal for your chosen family and loved ones. It helps you bring something inspiring or community building to the potluck beyond just food itself. If someone in my community is struggling with food insecurity, I'll likely make them some food and then enchant it with a spell to help them overcome this hurdle and enter a more prosperous time. If someone in my community is struggling with new physical pain, I'll try to pull together a tea known to help in their situation and further bewitch it to help them see new paths towards healing that pain. I think a lot of the reason kitchen witchery wasn't hip for a while was because on the surface it seems like it would be for traditional homes, individuals, or families only. Once we think about what our community actually needs though, it cracks this idea wide open. Queer communities love getting together to feed each other and share our hearts. There is no better magick to incorporate into this practice than kitchen magick.

FASHION AND STYLE WITCHCRAFT

Don't skip to the next section just because you don't fancy yourself a fashionista! I don't either! I have three different palates—mermaid, black and silver, and autumn—and they do not go together logically. I was thirty-one when I finally gave up on learning how to style my hair and just started dumping wild colors in it so no one would question it. I can't even wear heels because of rheumatoid arthritis, but I *do* wear a lot of orthopedic shoes at the tender old age of thirty-five. Trust me, I am not making anyone's list of style icons anytime soon.

The good news is that none of that matters for using clothes, makeup, hair, and beauty routines as a form of magick. It really, really doesn't. Fashion and style witchcraft are about coordinating your look, however lackadaisical that may be, with whatever your spiritual goals or magickal intentions for that time period are. The easiest way to do this is by pulling out your outfits in advance and using color correspondences. I usually wear silver on days I'm doing moon magick, since it coordinates with the Moon. Alternatively, I'll wear gold or bronze details on days I'm trying to connect with Sun energy. If I'm looking for love, I might wear a deep burgundy shirt to color-coordinate, but another way to use fashion magick is to pull whatever you think says love, money, or other intention out of your closet and wear that. So I might color coordinate with correspondences for love, but I also might pull out the outfit that I want an ideal partner to fall in love with me in, instead. If I want to get a lot of writing done, I might pull out a purple outfit for creativity. I also might pull out a long pencil skirt and a button-down to give myself that "professional writer" feeling.

I listed some pretty femme examples up there, and it bears mentioning that I'm genderfluid but tend to present femme publicly. Anyone can use this style of magick though. A cis gay man can rock a pink shirt with yellow details to work on making friends in the queer community, for example. In fact, one thing I've really been playing a lot with with fashion magick is the idea of gender magick. I'm loosely defining gender magick as magick that either reinforces how I want people to see my gender or intentionally shakes up societal views of gender. If I want people to see me as more masculine, I might put on a muscle tank top (one of my favorite kinds of shirts). If I want to mix up people's perceptions of gender as a construct though, I might pick a pink or purple one. I might put on a suit that accentuates my curves or a dress with a binder under it. Just like there's no one way to be whatever gender you are, there's no one way to do gender magick.

Queer aesthetic is obviously a *big thing*, and that includes a lot of gender fuckery. Infusing that with magick gives you even more entitlement over your own image. I think fashion and style (like songs, poems, and bread) are magick innately. We usually dress with intention and accessorize to boot. We want people to think we're tough so we throw on a vest or combat boots. We want people to think we're soft so we wear fuzzy sweaters. Or we want people to not know what to think so we wear both. This is already a form of magick. Adding a specific protection intention to your combat boots is only going to help you on your path as a witch and your path back to yourself.

I've mostly talked about clothes here because everyone wears clothes. Underwear, accessories, makeup, face washes, and the like can all be used in this type of magick, too. Just pick out some beauty, style, and fashion pieces that scream your current intentions, and rock them. You'll probably even notice over time that doing this boosts your confidence even if you never specifically cast a spell with your eyeshadow for confidence. That's because you're walking around all day in something that aligns you to your deeper needs and higher callings. Staying connected to those things is bound to boost your self-image, especially for those of us whose queerness meant we were consistently put down for our style and presentation for much of our lives.

Finally, there are other things you can add to your fashion magick! You can lay your clothes out overnight and charge them with crystals that correspond. You can light incense or candles for your spellwork, and (carefully) wave your pieces over that smoke. You can dab them with oils, douse them in perfumes (so long as you're not going somewhere scent-free that day), or do any number of things to further enchant them. I usually incorporate mantras or incantations as I get dressed, saying something as simple as "May this necklace help me fill my pockets today" for prosperity or "May this vest keep me safe from catcallers on this bus ride."

Obviously anyone can do this kind of magick and it takes almost nothing but the clothes already in your closet. Even if you don't think any of your clothes or beauty products quite fit your current intentions, you can use the stones, incense, oils, mantras, and so forth described above to get your intended result. Style and presentation are a huge cornerstone of not all, but a lot, of queer culture. Amplifying something you're already doing with spells is the easiest transition into a magickal lifestyle. The reason style and presentation are so important to queer people, though, is specifically because our voices and forms of expression have already been stifled for so long. One of the first things we figure out on our own is how we want this out-and-proud version of ourselves to look to the rest of the world. Witchcraft is also about reclaiming your body and space in this world. This means fashion plus magick is a ready-made pair up, eager for you to jump in and start using it.

SEX MAGICK

We go into sex magick multiple times in this book, especially as we edge ever closer to the grimoire at the end. Sex magick has a couple of different facets, but one very important thing to know is that this is not *just* about attracting sex into your life. *Sex magick* is a catchall term for any spell that incorporates sex or masturbation (especially that is meant to bring you to orgasm) into your spellcraft. This is a great form of spellcraft because it's free, it's pleasurable, and if you're queer, then boom! It's automatically queer. No further thinking or nuance needed.

Sex magick is also wildly powerful. The general theory behind it is that we are at our most vulnerable and most receptive post-orgasm. As the aftershocks pulsate through us, we are able to use visualization or other free magickal tools to begin manifesting specific desires. Any intention you have, sex magick can help with. I know some people may not be ready for it because of sexual trauma, but I still encourage you to explore your body as a form of healing. Learn what makes *you* feel good, remind yourself that as a human capable of that pleasure you deserve that pleasure, and know that there is healing in that. It just takes time.

The easiest way to learn the art of sex magick is, I think, via masturbation. Involving other people is beautiful and boosts our magick, but it can also complicate things for us, stress us out, cause us to perform instead of enjoy, or mix with energies that may not boost us magickally. To start then, we do need to break down our relationship to masturbation and our own bodies. I know a lot of people who are otherwise sexually empowered still feel certain ways about masturbation. I would practice masturbating a few times with *no* magickal intention. Use toys if you have access to them, and don't use toys. Use your hand, use pillows, use whatever you want. Try porn, erotica, and your own imagination. You don't know what gets you off in this way until you know. Take the time to explore your body. I'm sure you won't be surprised to hear me say that regardless of your intentions for actual sex magick, learning your body and how to make it come is a form of magick that roots you in your body and allows you to fall into pleasure, thus making you more open and receptive to pleasure in the first place.

Once you have a handle on your body and what gets it off, pick a night when you feel really sexy and go to town in the way you get off most often. Before you jump in, spend some time thinking about your intentions for the sex spell. Often I tell myself to picture a *very* wealthy bank statement as I come as a form of money magick. If I'm seeking a sexual partner, I'll set the intention to visualize other hands (or other body parts entirely) getting me off as I come.

If you have a sexual partner or potential sexual partner that you feel spiritually drawn to, sex with that person can also be a spiritual act. Instead of masturbating, have sex with them and use the same visualization techniques above. If you fully trust this sexual partner, then have them visualize the same thing or a complementing vision with you. Hold each other afterwards if you're both comfortable with that, and congratulate each other on a magickal job well done as your bodies cool down. If you love threesomes or group sex, and if you have other witches that you sleep with, these are tactics that can be used in those group scenarios, too. Trust each other and trust yourselves—but know that team visualization, especially during and post-orgasm, can take your magick to totally new heights.

Journal Exercise

New and seasoned witches, it's time to check in with which of the above methods resonate with you and which don't. Using a journal or some paper, take some notes on anything that struck a positive or negative chord with you. Which magicks do you currently practice? How is that going? What do you want to try next? Is there anything that you feel called to do but are afraid of right now? Journal about all of this, and then leave it be for a few days as you rest your psychic self.

THE PERKS AND PITFALLS OF GROUP WORK

One of the questions I get asked most often by new witches is whether I'm in a coven or not. Full disclosure: I'm not, and while I used to really rail against anything that felt organized or hierarchical, I am currently open to the right coven under the right circumstances. It just hasn't happened yet. A coven is a group of witches, usually formalized, who practice magick together. That's it! Some denominations of witchcraft will tell you that it should be three, or four, or thirteen, or some other arbitrary number but at the end of the day if you're a formal group with similar goals who practice working toward those goals together magickally and you call yourself a coven, you're a coven.

For the record, there *are* incredibly formalized, hierarchical covens. Some of them I've practiced with during public ritual, a time when those covens may design a ritual and then open it up to the public. Some of these formal covens I've studied with and under and ultimately decided not to join for one reason or another. Most covens tend to be very rooted in a specific path such as Wiccan, Thelemic, Satanic, or the like, and I honestly take from all of those paths, many other paths, and create my own way a lot of the time. That eclectic method is becoming more and more common, and that means that not as many people are joining the super formalized covens. Those covens are shrinking, and smaller ones are disappearing altogether. They do serve an important purpose though, namely they make witchcraft and Paganism look like a viable religion in a society that normally thinks we're absurd, goth teenagers who saw *The Craft* a few too many times. Covens are an important part of a lot of my favorite witches' practice and some of the public rituals I've attended have changed my life even if I decided that ultimately those covens were not for me, so I'm not here to put them down. They aren't as visible or prevalent as they once were though, and even when they are, they're not for everyone. There's nothing wrong with *not* joining a coven, but I do want to explore our options a little bit further.

If you're someone who is on a specific path or is willing to work within a specific path while you're otherwise learning the ropes, covens are a good place to learn, network, and grow as a witch. If you do better in a group setting than not and are more of a follower than a leader, then covens are likely a good fit, too. Another reason a coven may work well for you is because a lot of spells, specifically those aimed at changing culture and public policy, are more powerful when you get more voices behind them. Personal spellwork works just fine on your own, but the power of having multiple people helping you heal and grow cannot be overstated. If you feel like your spellwork would benefit from organized coven work, then doing research in the area you live is your best bet. Attend some meetups for witches or metaphysical/New Age types and see if you connect with anyone there. If there aren't formal covens in your area, you might meet some people who are interested in starting one with you.

There are downsides to formal coven work, especially for queer people. I grew up in the Bible Belt in a church with a clear hierarchy that was both formal (imbedded into the laws of the church) and informal (rooted in class or things like who had the most time to volunteer) and those at the top of those hierarchies set the tone and rules for everyone else. This was stifling as someone who was assigned female at birth and hurtful as someone who was in the closet. I am not the only person with this reaction to church, and an incredibly disproportionate number of queer people suffer from the newly named and relatively newly understood, Religious Trauma Syndrome (RTS). That means a lot of people in our community have an aversion to having one person in charge or even a group of people in charge. To make a coven work effectively, that's often the breakdown that's needed, which does mean that being a part of a coven is not right for those who struggle with those facets of formalized group worship.

Additionally, covens often cost money and time that are too scarce in queer community. It's hard to rally your energy for a coven event when you have work during the day, a show you're in at night, and community members crashing with you until they get on their feet. It's hard to justify the budget line expense for coven fees (which are totally fair because witches should be paid, especially those organizing big things for everyone else) when you're asking your friends to send you money on Venmo so you can eat until your next paycheck. This might sound dramatic, but that is the reality many, many queer community members face. Additionally, covens are traditionally very white and the queer community would be nothing without the Queer and Trans Black and Indigenous People of Color (QTBIPOC) who have paved the way for us. Covens are also often very straight or emphasize all male or all female breakdowns that are traumatic and isolating for trans and non-binary people.

As I mentioned earlier, covens are also disappearing, which means that even if you think you want to join one, you may not be able to find one, depending on where you live and how many spots the covens around you have open throughout the year—if there even are covens around you! Throughout witch history there have been solutions to the social problems I listed above, but as Black and Indigenous, People of Color (BIPOC)-run organizations and queer-run organizations are disturbingly underfunded, they're often the first to fold when something, like coven work starts going out of vogue, meaning the odds of finding a queer friendly and racially inclusive coven are almost nil right now.

While I do think working as a solitary witch is the right path for me and so many others, I also know firsthand the unique gifts and power that group spellwork can give us. There are a couple of other options that modern queer witches are turning to instead. The most obvious and common of those is informal covens. This is, essentially, witches who know and trust each other turning to each other frequently for spiritual backup and group spellwork. There's usually no hierarchy, though often if one witch is more advanced they might take the lead without thinking about it. If someone in the group doesn't like that, it's an easy discussion to have so everybody gets time as a spiritual leader and to just take part in the spell. Unofficial covens often happen if a group of friends or chosen family all happen to be struggling in the same way at the same time, such as financially or in dealing with societally imposed trauma. I do think it's important to work together when you're *not* in crisis, too. It's in those times when things are fine that your strongest relationships with magickal entities and each other grow the most. Not having an immediate problem to solve means the spell serves to pull you closer and allows you to explore your spiritualities separately and together. This is foundational work that will serve your craft for years to come, and foundations can only benefit from the love and support of other witches.

Many witches turn to the Internet now to find community and tips, which is another reason covens have become arguably less necessary. It used to be that there were a limited number of ways to find out how to do magick and you almost needed a coven in your area to figure it out. Things in general aren't so regionalized now, and most of us have the entire Web at our fingertips. Some of my best witch friends are people I met online. Some of those friendships have stayed online, and we have coordinated spellwork and done spells for each other. Some of them have become strong, potent IRL (In Real Life) relationships that I would be totally lost without. None of that even touches on the scores of resources, spells, and information out there. Facebook groups, shared Pinterest boards, and community websites abound and it's a wonderful way to meet people and learn the craft, especially if you're explicitly looking for queer community.

Of course, it's easy to get lost online. Someone close to me is trying to slowly learn witchcraft as we speak and has panicked over inflammatory and false articles like "Are you a natural born witch?" That's why finding witches you connect with online should be a first step, not a secondary one, and using social media platforms to find unofficial covens should be a priority. There are usually people more experienced than you willing to guide your hand, many with your same identities. Those people can point you in the direction of useful resources and help you build your magickal skillset.

There are, of course, pitfalls to working with groups for magick. It can seem clamorous to bring in a Heathen, a Druid, and an eclectic witch all into one circle. It'll take time to learn how to work together. That time is completely worth it, and those differences can make powerful shifts as multiple gods from multiple covens join in to work together. There can also be squabbles, differences in culture, and differences in core values and beliefs that can make working together seem insurmountably difficult, and you should consider how you and the people you're considering working with handle conflict and differences before jumping into spiritual work with them. If everyone is open to new ideas and communicative, proceed. If not, take a few steps back and figure out if there's a common ground to be had or not. If not, that's okay. You'll find your witches. This just ain't them.

Whether you want to make witch friends or join a formalized coven, whether you want to use the Internet or not, witchcraft itself is growing even as covens shrink and disappear. Do research into your area and look for classes, meetups, or even just spaces where the witchy types hang out, and be friendly. Witchcraft is also really, really common among queer people, and even if no one you know practices witchcraft per se, there are likely people interested in New Age, occult, or metaphysical things, which can be a first step towards practicing craft. Don't roll your eyes at your queer friends who are going on and on about astrology, manifesting, or ghosts. Engage them, and allow both of your senses of spirituality to deepen from those conversations.

Magick isn't always formalized. There's wishing magick, which is exactly what it sounds like. There's prayer. There's the magick of living your life in the way that suits you best that can open the floodgates to dream opportunities and paths for you. When we think about group witchcraft, it doesn't have to be about covens and meetups. Surrounding yourself with people that affirm your identity and support your dreams is a type of magick, too. Queer community calls such people chosen family. RuPaul famously comforts queens with unsupportive families on *RuPaul's Drag Race* by reminding them that as LGBTQQIA2SP+ (Lesbian, Gay, Bisexual, Transgender, Queer, Questioning, Intersex, Asexual, Two-Spirit, Plus) people, we get to choose our own families. This is an honor and a gift. Yes, it is often absolutely steeped in the tragedy and pain of being forced out of your given family. No one can override that pain. You need time and distance to heal from that. You *can* surround yourself with people who will support this process, though. That's chosen family, and honoring this group of people as family, loving them as family, trusting them as family is its own form of magick.

That's not to say that chosen family always gets it right. Humans are imperfect and they will hurt you. You will have to forgive each other a thousand times over, but as long as they're working on themselves and you're working on yourselves and you're both working on the friendship together, it can and will be salvaged every time. So love the people who love you and have shown you acceptance. Honor chosen family and let them into your heart. Support others the way they've supported you. If magick is often about living our lives as we want to live them, and it is, then creating a team of strong, generous, loving people around you is the strongest kind of magick there is. No coven needed, just open hearts.

A PRIMER ON SHADOW WORK

Throughout this book so far, I have alluded to and talked about shadow work, which is a very specific type of spiritual work where we face and come to terms with our shadow selves. The shadow self is that side of you where all your fears and anxieties are kept. It's the side that you often don't like. It's the part of you that doesn't want to heal and move forward because it's still feeling the pain of everything so deeply. Our shadow self doesn't always look like you'd expect, given how I just described it. You'd think mine would be a sniveling, insecure child but instead my shadow self comes out and makes me mean and gossipy sometimes. It makes me overreach so that when I'm let down it reinforces my low self-esteem. It's rooted in that same fear and insecurity, but how it manifests is personal and different for everyone, because of the hows and whys of your shadow self. Why is it there? Who lied to you by diminishing your worth? What traumatized you? How did that play into building the shadow self that you're still dealing with?

Shadow work is about healing, but just like our shadow selves, that doesn't always look like we expect it to. If your shadow self can be manipulative or have a lot of badly aspected trickster energy, your healing is often coming to peace with this side of yourself by learning to find healthier ways to work with it. If you get jealous and anxious easily, healing might be learning to look for the root of why and bringing new goals to the forefront. Sometimes it does just look like plan old healing where you don't see your shadow self as often, or you'll heal the first layer and realize there's more.

I don't want to set up that expectation though, and in some cases, for queer people, the idea of squashing our shadow self is a bad idea. Your bossiness could be dominance, but because you were shamed for it your whole life, you banished it to the shadow when you could've really come into yourself sexually. For some of us, promiscuity is listed as a shadow self quality but I would argue that it's not, as long as we're not doing it to hurt ourselves or someone else. It's a lot to untangle though, and I don't want people who have been shamed or abused for their gender and sexuality to come into this section hoping to *cure* things that were never wrong with them in the first place. In the tarot, the Devil often represents the shadow self. This card shows up dripping with sexual energy and an indulgent attitude. Tarot lore says that's bad, but a good reader will probe you to go deeper and figure out where you've been restricting and why. A good shadow work teacher will do the same thing.

In making peace with our shadow selves we say that there is no part of us that is bad. There are parts of us that we hide. There are parts that can be harmful if we don't learn how to dance with them. There are parts that we have been told are bad that we can reclaim now. There are parts that are hurting, parts that just need attention, parts that need to play. There are not parts of you that are wrong. Queer people face backlash about how we are always *wrong* no matter what we are doing. Over a lifetime we internalize that and we believe it, but it isn't true.

Practice Time!

Now that all of that is settled, let's look at some practical ways to work through some shadow work. Start by sitting in a safe, comfortable space and clearing your head. Set the intention "I want to see my shadow self" first, if you're brand new to witchcraft. Meditate on that idea and sit for several minutes. Pay attention to your breathing. It will get uncomfortable. It is supposed to get uncomfortable. I cried for a nice, long time the first time I sat and really looked at the ways I'd hurt other people and the ways I'd hurt myself. You don't know what you're working with until you really sit with it, though.

After that, do some self-care. Journal about the experience, or talk to a metaphysically inclined friend. Think it over from an emotionally safer space for a couple of days. From there you can develop a plan to learn to make peace with those energies and pains, and what using that side of yourself in a healthy way looks like. Write that plan down—sometimes our shadow self needs reminders, and we don't want to let this important work get away from us.

And It Harm None?

As you're reading this book and researching witchcraft, you'll frequently come across the phrase, "and it harm none." It's how we're supposed to conclude our spells and rituals, and it's the basic tenet that a lot of witchcraft is built around. The idea is a good one, in theory. It is supposed to be our reminder that, while we can be selfish, we shouldn't actively work to hurt others. It's a reminder to keep our magick light and airy and not dig into the nitty gritty, because that's painful.

I do not subscribe to this. For starters, this phrase doesn't make logical sense in our society. If you do a love spell to meet the right monogamous person, there are exes and people who have crushes on both of you that are going to be hurt. You will never have no baggage or spark the interest of others who have no baggage. Saying "and it harm none," means you honestly may never meet that person. Love also hurts. When my anxiety is working overtime or I am doubled over in Polycystic Ovary

Syndrome (PCOS) pain, those who love me feel emotional pain, too. This is technically doing harm and setting your spells to not cause any harm also blocks out a lot of really beautiful things in life, like love itself.

Another example of how "and it harm none" doesn't work is if you're doing a money spell. Sorry not sorry, but capitalism, and therefore money, is inherently harmful. We need it! It's a necessary evil, but people did get hurt for that dollar to hit your hand. I know these are bold statements and I might make a lot of witches wildly unhappy with this statement, but for most of our goals and intentions to be met, that means someone else's won't be. We can't say "and it harm none" and have our spells work. If they do work, we're kidding ourselves to think that no one got hurt somewhere along the way.

Furthermore as marginalized people, in order to have anything worth having, we have to unpack a lot of deep, heavy stuff. It isn't all fun. If "and it harm none" is meant to include ourselves, and why wouldn't it, we'll never get anywhere. We have to hurt to heal. We are literally uncovering wounds so they can feel the air and get better. It is an innately painful process. When we love, it hurts—even if everything in the relationship is healthy. My queerplatonic partner struggles with severe depression and my heart breaks a thousand times a year wanting to help and knowing I can't. Our love hurts and I wouldn't change it for all the "and it harm none" in the world.

If we're looking at collective movements, we cannot afford to tack "and it harm none" on to our spellwork. What do we think is going to happen if we overhaul the government? What do we think is going to happen if we decriminalize nonviolent behavior? The state will suffer. People with jobs at the state will suffer. Children of people with jobs at the state will suffer. I don't take this lightly, but we have to work towards creating a more fair and equitable society if we're going to call ourselves witches, but there will be people who suffer in the transition. That's just how it is. Furthermore, marginalized people, especially women of color, are constantly being told not to even speak up or make waves for the sake of being "nice" and not offending anyone. This is not actually coming from fear of people being hurt. It's coming from people who think marginalized people should know their place and not strive for a better society. If we're going to do activism, we will have to challenge the status quo and make a whole lot of well-meaning people uncomfortable. We can't afford "and it harm none." The stakes are too high.

That said, I do think we should wield our spiritual gifts responsibly. We shouldn't hex people for the hell of it or because we're jealous of them. We should aim to do as little harm as possible. We should act out of love of community and a better world and not out of fear or hate. Yet as queer witches we have a responsibility to make waves and make change, and I don't think we can do that without hurting people. I think we deserve money, love, and all of the joy that this world has to offer, but we have to be realistic about it or our spellwork and our spiritual growth will be stunted. It makes you a better, more aware person to know that sometimes, through no fault of yours, people get hurt. You are not responsible for that as long as you're behaving responsibly.

So forget what you read about "and it harm none" and just try not be a jerk, okay? Oh, and recycle. Please. The planet needs you, too.

2

MAGICKAL
BEST PRACTICES

Once we know the basics of working with the elements and what a ritual is, we're ready to build a manageable daily practice that will keep us in our power as witches all day long. However, the truth is, no matter how devout you become you won't feel like a witch 24/7, and that's not an expectation you should put on yourself. Our society really tries to drive home being productive at all times, and even when we're defecting to take on something like witchcraft that internalized idea of always feeling *on* follows us. That doesn't mean you won't *be* a witch 24/7 though, and that's an important thing to remember. It's just as witchy to rest, even if it doesn't feel like it. It's just as magickal to laugh with friends about sitcoms for a few hours as it is to keep a grimoire, even though you may not feel like you're creating magick.

As we're building a regular practice for our craft, the first step should be to add some cornerstones into our practice that will help us learn our witchcraft style and grow as witches. Regular practice is not the same as big rituals where we call the corners and call in gods. Instead it's tending to our magickal spaces and taking care of our magickal selves. This is an absolutely crucial part of our work because this is often where the big breakthroughs happen. A lot of what I hear from those newly taking a witchier path is that they don't even know where to start because working with the elements and tools at hand can feel so overwhelming. To those people, I encourage the use of grimoires, journals, and meditation to help take care of their spiritual selves, and slowly building altars to take care of the external pieces of their magick. Proper self-care is also important for your craft and is especially important for queer people, disabled people, trauma survivors, and people of color trying to survive the systems that drove us to the margins in the first place. Pleasure is resistance. Self-care is resistance. Period. It feels like it's not important, but what you're doing when you're taking care of yourself is telling those that do not love or support you that you are fine without them. You are telling our society that you are worth taking care of even if they don't see it. This is rebellion. On top of that, it's straight up necessary no matter how busy you might think you are. You cannot give from an empty cup. Superheroes aren't real, and if they are, it's dubious that you are one. Learn to relax, and learn to allow yourself joy. Call it magick. Call it a political act. Call it whatever you need to. Just please, do it.

Magickal best practices are the specifics of how we can keep up a spiritual practice in the worst, best, and busiest times. These are all tangible steps you can take and practical things you can do in your own time, to take care of and grow into your witchy self. As your craft gets more ambitious and bigger, these grounding principles will help you keep track of what's working and what's not. The best practices I recommend are building and maintaining our altars, using a combination of journals and either a grimoire or Book of Shadows, meditation, and proper self-care.

Building and Maintaining Altars

As witches, focal points of our practice should be sacred spaces carved out in our home that we dedicate to magickal purpose. I am talking about altars, of course. Altars can be to specific gods or deities. They can be for specific purposes, like community building or making a smooth gender transition. They can be for our ancestors, or for those we love that have passed on. It's also common to have a general altar to witchcraft itself. Each altar will look different depending on how you want to focus it. Altars are an important way to send ourselves, as queer people, strong reminders of what our goals are whether that goal is hexing the patriarchy or casting glamours until your self-esteem builds back up. It's easy to get distracted or carried away by the whirlwind of just trying to get by in the systems we have to work within. Having a sacred, beautiful space in your home reminds you that skating by is not all you are doing.

Altars can be tables, windowsills, tops of dressers or bookshelves, or shelves hanging up on the wall. It just needs to be dedicated space that is big enough to support the things you want to decorate it with. Common altar accoutrement includes candles, charms, incense holders and incense, flowers, bowls of herbs, Moon water, and artwork—but this list is not comprehensive. These are just the first altar decorations I could think of. Anything that aligns with your goal, your god, or whatever else your altar is for, can go on your altar. Most people recommend having separate altars for separate purposes, but I suggest starting with one basic witchcraft altar until you have a handle on maintaining it. This altar should contain tools of all five elements, and any symbols of your goals as a witch. It can include starter altar items for gods, ancestors, or specific workings you're ramping up to.

Queering our altars can start with aesthetics alone. What screams, "I'm here, I'm queer, and I'm doing freaking magick!" to you? Add all of that to your altar. Add subtle rainbows or go all in on the glitter. Make it the punkest, most DIY looking altar that ever existed, full of patches and ornaments made out of bike tires. Use poppers in place of rum to serve your deities. Put an Indigo Girls poster up. Get creative, and get queer—but do make sure it circles back to the reasons for your altar in the first place.

To further queer your altar, think beyond your basic magickal goals and the focus of your spirituality. What unique barriers do you face to those goals as a queer person? If I set up a money altar, I put something that represents the fact that I am competing with straight white men for clients, who are often taken more seriously than me with my nasal voice and blue hair. While I don't love living in a state of hyper competitiveness, the reality is that's what my tarot practice faces. So, if I'm including a querent caller in my money work, I need to face that reality. If I'm looking to work with a politician to change legislation to be more queer-friendly, I'm facing even bigger obstacles. I would almost have to have a patch that says Hex the Patriarchy sitting front and center. I might also print out and roll up what my legislation's ideal wording is and stick it in a bowl with some herbs for luck and dab it with oil that helps us within the justice system. If we're looking to honor a god associated with queerness, we're probably in the minority of people that look at that aspect of that god. They'll greatly appreciate any identity-affirming tokens you can toss on to the altar.

I include altars in this section on regular practice because it provides a visual that will reinforce your intentions. Altars should be cleaned and tended to with regularity, and those are often the first steps to regular practice. Candles that have fizzled out should get thrown away. Stones that have cracked should be removed. Any incense dust should be swept away. Your altar doesn't have to look clean and Instagram friendly (I would be the worst witch ever if that was the case), but it should show respect to your intentions, which shows respect for yourself. The practice of maintaining your altar also physically connects you to the altar, creating an opportunity for you to work one on one with your gods and goals.

For queer people dealing with housing instability, or, alternatively who are so successful that they're traveling to present their queer art to new places or fighting with Washington bureaucrats even though they live in Montana (there are queer people in Montana, I promise) you need a travel altar. This can go in a cigarette case, an Altoids tin or a bigger box, if you're able to acquire one. It would be mostly tokens, charms, very small candles like tealights or miniature tapers, and mini-vials of oils or herbs. The same principles we've been talking about apply. Once you're in your temporary spot for the night, pull it out and set it up. If you aren't in a place where that's safe or practical, keeping it on you until you need it works just as well. That physical closeness with your magickal implements does the same good that having an altar in a home does, keeping you connected to your magick and your intentions (as well as your ability to do that magick).

Grimoires, Books of Shadows, and Journals

I know not everyone fancies themselves a writer or a journaler, but I cannot stress enough the importance of writing down and tracking your spellwork some way or another. The clearest example of that is using a grimoire, a Book of Shadows, a journaling practice, or any combination thereof. We've already talked about the power of our words, written or verbalized, and a way to make them gain power is to write them down so we can keep track of them. The terms grimoire and Book of Shadows are often used interchangeably, so I'll break down the difference between them.

A grimoire is a book of general knowledge about your craft and practice. Using one means taking notes on the witchcraft books you're using and noting your knowledge of plants, stones, and more as you learn it. It can include spells or spell formulas, too. Many witches also use their grimoires to take notes on magickal tips and tricks they pick up along the way, for example, herbs that can be used in a variety of spells or what certain dream symbols have come to mean to them.

A Book of Shadows is a personal record of your journey as a witch. It's similar to a grimoire; both are where you design and write down spellwork. They are sometimes considered slightly different because a Book of Shadows focuses more on the spells than the basic knowledge and ingredients that a grimoire often focuses on and includes personal notes tracking which spells work and which ones don't.

What I do is slightly different. I use my personal journal for all of that as well as general journaling. I do think that the magickal (read: healing and empowered) living of our lives is a deeply magickal act and don't like to separate the two. Some witches don't like having the petulance and darker thoughts that can show up in their journals in their grimoires and Books of Shadows and that's okay, too. Journaling is not a witch-specific practice, but it is one a lot of witches use to keep detailed records of how their life is going and, therefore, how their magick is working. Journaling as a way to process your emotions so you don't go into a ritual overloaded or overwhelmed is a good part of a witch's process, too.

Writing itself is an important part of spellwork, so you have to do what works best for you. Take your accessibility needs into account here, too. You might have much more luck going digital or even using voice-to-text apps for your digital record.

• • •

It's fine to combine these things into one book, or have separate accounts—one solely for magick and one solely for feelings. I like keeping mine together because the bleedover of spirituality and my emotional self is so intense for me, but I'm also a triple water sign who is as sentimental as I am spiritually gifted, and I recognize that separate accounts work much better for a lot of witches. Separate accounts also make it easier to find your spells and the work you've done on them.

Grimoires, Books of Shadows, and journals are so deeply personal that the concept of them queers themselves. Queer community has always been drawn to personal accounts and the written word, and these can be a fantastically witchy way to own and tell your own story as you move through it. Sure, you can decorate it to look more queer or personal and include explicity queer stories and spells, and I recommend all of those things. It's also worth noting that recording your own triumphs and pitfalls and chronicling your own journey towards liberation (not to mention that of any movements you're a part of) is a badass move all its own.

Regular Meditation and Grounding

Grounding is an important part of your craft overall. It is the act of centering yourself, steadying your breathing (if that's something you're physically able to do), and becoming more calm and rooted into where you are and what you're doing. It looks like a lot of different things for a lot of different people. I tend to sit in a comfortable-ish position (with my arthritis it's never fully comfortable) and do some deep breathing or a body scan. I work into feeling my body and how it connects to the floor and wall, or whatever else I'm sitting on and against. For some people it's standing and stretching. For others it's focusing on a candle's flame as it flickers and steadying their breathing. It's whatever helps you calm your breathing as much as possible and gets you focused for either your day, or whatever task is in front of you. Grounding is an important piece of ritual work, and I strongly recommend you do it before putting up a circle in a big spell or meeting up with a group for group work. Grounding is something I do before I start writing or seeing clients for the day. It's the practice of putting yourself back into the present and into your body—and it's an important part of building a meditation practice.

Meditation is the act of clearing your mind and either keeping it clear or focusing on specific thoughts and ideas for a certain amount of time. There are relaxing components to it, too. This should be a comfortable, peaceful exercise that brings you a sense of calm. Meditation can be virtually spirituality-less—used only to clear your mind and to relax, or it can be focused on an intention or spell you've been working. There are also, countless YouTube guided meditations that will walk you through deity-focused meditations that bring you closer to understanding and connecting with a god, so depending on your beliefs and needs, deity-focus can be a good way to use your meditative time and energy, too.

Anyone can meditate, and here's the dirty little secret: no one is good at it all the time. While you'll have significantly more luck meditating if you throw some grounding work into it at the beginning of your meditation, the reality is that our minds are often scattered with dozens of other things we should be doing—among other distractions. The feedback I get when I push tarot clients to meditate is that they could only clear their minds for a second or two at a time. Please know that, especially in the beginning, this is not a failure. It is part of the process. The good news is, you *did* clear your mind for a second or two. You know what that feels like now, and you can build from there. This is an exercise, especially in the beginning of your journey as a witch, to get you to sit still and find clarity. Give it space and over time you'll be able to clear your mind for longer and longer stretches. Please know, though, that even those who lead guided meditations, who teach meditation classes, who put their dedication to meditating on their Tinder bios absolutely do not clear their minds for an hour at a time or more every single day. They have days they can't do it, or moments in the meditation that they can't calm down, or entire weeks that are basically wasted, meditation-wise.

Meditation is an important part of a witch's journey because you need time, even just five minutes a day, where you sit with your body, mind, and soul and focus on that. You need space where you can be comfortable and connect your gut to your higher intuition, your intuition to your body, your body to the world. For queer people whose heads are constantly being filled with doubt about if they're queer enough for this friend group or too queer for the rest of the world or somehow both, it's especially important. This is time alone with yourself to develop your craft, and it gives you more of a blank canvas to start from than going in without meditation.

If you have not yet incorporated meditation into your spiritual practice or self-care routine, you should start with basic meditative rituals to clear your mind. Once you feel like you kind of know what you're doing, you can include intentions or follow guided meditations. Meditation classes might be good for that if you feel like you need an instructor. Breath work is another common group working or class that you might be able to find if you live somewhere with any kind of New Age scene. Breath work isn't meditation specifically, but it follows a lot of the same principles and will give you a similar outcome.

You don't have to write about your daily or thrice weekly meditations in your journal or grimoire if you don't want to, but you can. I would take note of any emotional or spiritual breakthroughs that you have, and if you have a day where you're unusually able to focus or unusually unable to focus, I would note that, too. Over time, this practice should bring you increased peace even in trying and borderline traumatic circumstances. It should help you access new levels of spirituality, and that means your spells will be even more powerful. Most importantly, your meditation should, in time, connect and root you deeply into yourself, where you are. This is a form of reclaiming your body. You'll notice as we go that so, so much of queering your craft is making it yours. To get there, you have to make *yourself* yours first, and for that, you have to connect with yourself and that's what meditation gives you.

Self-Care

Marginalized people are ridiculously resistant to basic self-care principles. Between internalizing a hypercapitalist society that forces go-go-go all the time, the ensuing cult of busy that follows after living like that for too long and the queer ideal of focusing on community first, we insist that we either don't need or don't have time for self-care. Sometimes we insist on both. Yet not giving space for self-care inhibits your witchcraft. Even beyond the spiritual sense, I want to reiterate that you cannot give from an empty cup, and you will burn yourself out if you don't engage in self-care. Burnout will leave you no time or energy for making enough money to survive or taking care of your loved ones, let alone creating change or community.

So what is self-care? In this Instagram age we think of this as taking entire nights off on a whim to live in the bubble bath. For some of us, this is a form of self-care because pleasure is a human need. Why do we have pleasure receptors, points on our body that feel good, taste buds, and so much more if we aren't supposed to use them? Many of them serve no other evolutionary purpose beyond enjoying them, which means that need needs to be fulfilled. I think what makes this form of self-care so easily scornable is that the same things do not bring us all pleasure. For me, bubble baths are a very real physical health need to help my body physically relax in the face of pelvic floor disorder and rheumatoid arthritis. Automatically condemning this form of public photo-worthy self-care is short sighted at best and ableist at worst. What's worse though, is you could be shutting out your own ability to feel pleasure in some way.

Again though, not everything that is pleasurable to some is pleasurable to all. For some people really good food tingles our senses, and for others it causes eating disorder related anxiety. For some of us sex and masturbation are incredibly pleasurable but for others it can remind us of trauma that we've been through. For me, laughter is key. I need anything hilarious, several times a day whether that's goofing off with friends or putting on a stand-up special to watch as I decompress from the day. Figure out what brings *you* pleasure and incorporate it into your life. Pleasure is absolutely a self-care need, and one you need to suss out and prioritize for yourself.

Of course, self-care is not our only need. We need to be well fed, well rested, and feel like we know where we're going and what we're doing on any given day. That means incredibly boring things like keeping your freezer stocked with frozen burritos on weeks you're really busy. Brushing your teeth, taking your meds, and showering are forms of self-care. Exercising, if you're physically able to, is self-care because it focuses on what your body can do and celebrates that. You're also putting endorphins straight into your brain. Rest, though critical for self-care, is a hard one because most of us really do try, but sleep eludes us. Improving your sleep hygiene, then, is a foundational form of self-care. That means setting an actual rough bedtime for yourself, fluffing your pillows, and settling into a nighttime routine that is restful. You may need to do some body scans or deep breathing to get into a sleepy headspace. There are witchy ways to meet this need, too. There are stones like scolecite that help with sleep, or lepidolite that helps with rest. There are relaxing teas and lavender scented sprays.

You'll notice that some of these things overlap with things that bring us pleasure. Our needs are not meant to be isolated, or sectioned off. They feed each other, and when we feed each of them we operate better as humans and as witches. I really wish I could tell you that sheer will and determination can bring the most powerful of spells into being, but you have to take care of your body as well as you are able to. Our bodies and our spirits are the most powerful energetic tools we have, but they both need to be running as well as possible for the other to function. A better rested witch is a more successful witch.

As queers, let alone as queer witches, there is a lot to be said for self-care as resistance magick all on its own. One of my heroes, adrienne maree brown, has a whole book called *Pleasure Activism,* that you should read if you struggle to see why self-care and pleasure, especially, are important. We owe it to ourselves to claim these tired, sick, hated bodies back from the gatekeepers that made them this way. And, we absolutely need to develop a standard self-care practice to get there.

3

WORKING WITH
THE ELEMENTS

The *elements* as referenced in witchcraft explicitly mean the collective use of these four things: Fire, Air, Water, Earth. They each have their own magickal purpose, and they have purposes that can be specific to queer practitioners. The elements are foundational in learning tarot cards, group magick, and solo work, just to name a few. You can (and I often do) work with each element as an individual tool, but the work that is created when all four elements come together is absolutely Divine in every meaning of the word.

When we talk about divine energy we also welcome in a fifth element that many witches, myself included, believe in fervently and use as the centerpiece for all of our workings. That element is Spirit. In witchcraft I largely use Spirit to mean the idea of spirituality in general, the energy that comes from working with a goddess or specific spiritual energy, or the feeling that we get sometimes of being *in the spell*. Spirit is also the human spirit, especially the human spirit of someone who has been through the ringer. Spirit is the element of survival and strength, and to that end, when it comes to witchcraft, Spirit is our own ability to manifest our needs and desires. Historically, Spirit is also listed as *idea*. For innovation, creating change, and art we rely on Spirit to bring us new and fresh ideas.

The four elements that are not Spirit have tools and correspondences that are more tangible and straightforward. While some of these tools can be costly, I've tried to highlight affordable and free options for each one, too.

A fun fact about witchcraft is that the pentagram often associated with witches and Pagans is meant to encompass all five elements.

This goes back to Marcus Vipsanius Agrippa who, in the 15th and 16th centuries, attributed this symbol to magic, and used the points of the star to represent the elements. In a pentagram, the top point represents Spirit, and the other four correlate to the other elements. In ceremonial magick there are entire Greater and Lesser Rituals involving different types of pentagrams, so if this is something that interests you, don't stop at this book. Anything about Golden Dawn, chaos magick, or other forms of esoteric, ritual-based magick will include this work. A lot of these books have their problems with gender, binaries, and hierarchies that are a hindrance to queer people, so tread carefully and take care of yourself if you find exclusive and hurtful ideas and language.

The Elements are frequently used together in witchcraft when you begin a spell by casting a circle and calling the elements. Casting a circle just means pulling all of your necessary witchcraft materials into the area where you'll be doing your spellwork, and casting a protective circle around where you're working. Casting the actual circle usually means envisioning a protective white light coming from the floor and enveloping your room or area in a circle. This is meant to protect the work you're doing from outside eyes and ears, and to protect those practicing the magick from any ill-intentioned spirits that might try to sneak in. The circle, in my experience, also serves as a pressure cooker for all of the intention and magick that you deal with during the spell. By that, I mean it amplifies this energy by keeping it central and focused in this one area, allowing it to build to something really powerful instead of having it scatter all over the space you're working in.

Calling the corners as part of this means calling in each of the elements at the beginning of your process. This is largely a Wiccan practice, but one I often still do, as it is a way to connect to each element individually before I begin my work with those elements. I don't always call in every element either—if my spell is specifically mixing a potion for Water magick or unlocking the magick in a plant I'm growing, I'll just call in Water or Earth, respectively. I know witches who don't call the corners for any magick that isn't sitting in their sacred space or in a group working. I know witches who call all four corners every time they do anything. Like most things, I fall somewhere in the middle and like anything I talk about in *Queering Your Craft*, your voice and decision-making are the most holy things you have. Do what works for *you*—because otherwise it *won't* work for you.

If you want to call the elements into your work at any point, know that each element is thought to have a home and guardians of that element in the North, South, East or West. I'll include what directional corner they're coming from and a short mantra I use to call them in, in the individual element chapters. My mantras are largely influenced by my tarot practice and understanding, so a fun exercise is to pull some cards or do some divining about each element to see how each one wants you to address it.

Many witches, regardless of whether they call the quarters or not, use elementals, myself included. Elementals are a short one-word way to say that we work with energies or spirits related or connected to the elements. You'll see examples of those in the following sections as well.

Fire

Fire is often featured at the bottom right point of the pentagram. This is the element of passion, excitement, lust, and pleasure. Fire is that thing that wakes us up in the morning, puts that bounce in our step, and gets us amped up. It is that feeling of blood boiling, for better or worse. Fire is largely what inspires us to action in our own lives. Fire *is* the action and fight of the spellwork. Anytime we are doing magick, we should aspire to perform those actions on our own, which means most spells have an element of fire in them. The idea of action and fight gets tricky when we're queering our craft though. We have to take into account the myriad mental and chronic illnesses that disproportionately affect the queer community when we talk about and quantify action. Chronic and mental illness, especially with someone who is otherwise marginalized and running low on energy, means we don't always have the clarity, the wherewithal, or the physical prowess to perform the actions we need to better our lives within the ideal timeline. In addition to getting external action going, Fire energy can be used in these cases to inspire or motivate ourselves to start working or fighting again or to figure out the creative workarounds that so many of us use in our daily lives. Fire is creativity too, and for a lot of queer folks that is what we need to rely on as we think about which actions we can take, while also caring for ourselves.

Fire represents transformation. Because Fire burns away the old to make way for and create fertile ground for the new, there is also a history of linguistic tradition that aids this thought—like saying something tough and resilient is "forged in the fire." When we're doing activist work or work that is meant to pull ourselves out of traumatic or oppressive situations, we want fire on our side. This element's ability to turn something or someone into a better, tougher, wiser version of themselves is exactly what we, as queer or otherwise marginalized people, want to do when we think about a troubling present versus a potentially beautiful future. Fire is one of our strongest allies for doing so. For trans people going through gender transition, Fire's relationship with transformation is the perfect thing to work with. Doing a fire-heavy spell while starting hormones, buying new gender-affirming clothes, and considering surgery options (if you choose to and have the resources to do so) will help you feel truly reborn as you navigate away from your assigned gender and into the best gender for you.

For a lot of queer people, our greatest passion *is* our gender and sexual identity, or it's the activism and advocacy for the rights of those identities that society basically forces on us. That means most queer people I know have endless fire spells going to aid them with any aspect of their life that needs it and even loosely correlates: relationships, standing up for ourselves, and the work itself (however we are defining that). Fire, as you'd expect, is *big* energy, but it can also be a peaceful and important spiritual ally for those of us struggling to name ourselves and come into our own.

Fire is useful for spells that intend to kick queerphobic people out of our life. We can then use that same fiery energy to rid ourselves of those hurtful peoples' influence. We can use Fire when we are working through dysphoria or gender transition. We can call on Fire to help us in our activist or social justice work. I've already mentioned that Fire is amazing for sex magick, and for queer people it can be an especially powerful ally. I've definitely used Fire magick during Pride month to help me celebrate my sapphic self by getting laid. As a fat, mentally ill, physically ill, genderfluid lesbian what I really need sometimes is the strength to get through the day and continue the part of my activist work where I resist just by being myself. Fire is wonderful for that. I'm in a really strong, wonderful queer-platonic partnership. Even though we choose to keep our partnership free of sexuality or sexual tension, we are so passionate about each other and our lives together that I use Fire in the ongoing spiritual work of keeping our relationship strong.

Fire energies are most often symbolized by salamanders, but when we get to the DIY portion of this book you might realize there is a completely different animal, spirit, or elemental (like a type of fae or an anthropomorphized flame) that you attribute to Fire. Always trust your inclinations over someone else's. Witchcraft, like any faith at its best, is supposed to focus on a personal relationship with whatever gods, spirits, or energies you believe in. Other common elementals used to bring fire into ritual include dragons, lions, scorpions, or a Phoenix.

Sometimes Fire is South and sometimes it's East. I usually work with it as South because that's the way I learned it a decade and a half ago. I should also point out that these are the the assignations in North America—if you're reading from somewhere else, your Fire might come in from somewhere different. Basically, wherever you feel the Sun is placed is where your Fire element should hail from.

The mantra I use most often to call in Fire is:

Welcome, guardians of the watchtowers of the South,
Keepers of fire—and therefore lust, passion, action, and excitement,
I welcome this element and its keepers to this circle tonight.

TYPES OF FIRE MAGICK

- Bonfires, campfires, fireplace fires

- Burning paper, herbs, and the like

- Candle magick

- Connecting with a deity that is heavily associated with fire

- Doing spells during the day, under sunlight, as opposed to the more common Moon magick

- Exercise that stretches and builds strength in the gut and groin area

- Intuitive work that focuses on raw gut instinct

- Tending to the mantle above the fireplace in your home

WHEN TO USE FIRE MAGICK

- For any spellwork associated with the things you're most passionate about

- For gender magick, especially related to transition

- For sex and love magick

- When you need inspiration, ideas, or motivation

- When you need to get rid of negative energy that's been hanging around you

- When you need to transform something in your life (or yourself)

- When you want to amplify your will or determination in a manifestation work

FIRE CORRESPONDENCES

*Please note that these are just some examples to get you started. There are *tons* of correspondences for each element.

Magickal Tools

- A lamp, or anything that offers light

- A lighter, matches, or anything else that can create fire

- A wand (or anything you would use as a wand like a sanded down branch that is meaningful to you)

- An athame or dagger, though this is most often associated with Air

- Fire itself, such as candles or a controlled fire

Stones

- Carnelian—especially in work where you're trying to amplify your own will

- Red jasper—especially as a source of inspiration and motivation or to cleanse negative energy

- Ruby—for a whole plethora of reasons

- Volcanic stone like obsidian—especially in transformative work

Herbs

- Allspice—to increase energy and determination

- Garlic—especially for sex magick (it has aphrodisiac qualities) or for general courage and fight

- Nettles—especially to break a spell or to drive out unwanted energy

- Onion—especially for banishment

Water

Water is my favorite element, but then again I am a Pisces with a Pisces moon and a Cancer rising so that energy is, and has always been, a driving force in my life. Water is all about emotions, expressions, and the manifestations of those things (like art or relationships). Water also oversees our journey towards emotional healing. Healing work is a critical part of witchcraft, whether we're talking about the emotional or the spiritual. Because water itself is a life source and is healing, I tend to use it in both kinds of magick. Even in the super practical we see this application—if you have a physical burn, the liquid part of the aloe plant is our best salve for that. If you're ill, they tell you to drink a lot of fluids. Water's healing energy is prevalent in science and medicine, so it's certainly applicable in witchcraft. If you're reading this book, you're likely concerned with collective healing too, and so much of that is done using Water as the primary force.

Water represents the "heart's desire" element that is so critical to witchcraft. This element forces us to get real about what we want so that we'll have the audacity to ask for it. As queer people especially, so many of us are divorced from our heart's desire because we spent a lot of time convincing ourselves we are wrong or mistaken about what we wanted back in our closeted days. Even if you've largely healed from that time as you've started coming out and coming into your own, denying yourself attraction and pleasure eventually dampens your ability to understand what you want. That makes formulating spells, even for the collective, difficult. For this reason, Water magick is often a first step in witchcraft. It can help us to see what we want more clearly and move forward from there.

Of course, because Water rules emotions and therefore love, Water is a great ally for love magick of all types. I cast spells for new friends (or to find time with old friends), and I know friendships and chosen family are generally a priority for queer people in a very specific way. Certainly Water can help us find new romantic relationships or strengthen standing ones. That clarity around your heart's desire is important here, but so is Water's natural capacity to aid us in other ways where love is concerned. Queer people are more likely than nonqueer people to deal with unsupportive or toxic members in our given family. While Water can be used in magick that is meant to bury the hatchet or smooth things over, when you get clear on your own desires you might find that what you really want is to not hurt from those scars anymore and to move forward in your own life. This is a combination of love and healing magick, and Water is excited to work with you in those instances.

Water is the element of artists and philosophers, and while Air also has a stake in literature and literary careers, Water is focused so much on expression that of course our written words are highlighted in this element as well. Along this line, Water is also super powerful for those using psychic prowess or intuition in their career. Water work is a key part of any of my career or money workings. Water wants what we want, which for me is to be a successful writer, tarot reader, and theatre maker. Because it works in those forms of expression too, it's wildly powerful in career work when our careers are, essentially, creative, psychic, or both.

However, Water is not concerned with overt success the way Earth or even Fire is. Water is about the expression and art or psychic work itself. That means most intuitives and creatives would do best using Water spells when they're stuck in a rut and can't access those parts of themselves, when they want to turn their ideas into something real and tangible, or when they are working through a project or process. Water as an aid for expression just wants it to be expressive, and can absolutely guide you on that process.

Water is associated with the West, and the mantra I use most often to call in Water is:

Welcome, guardians of the watchtowers of the West,
Keepers of water—and therefore emotion, love, beauty, and art.
I welcome this element and it's keepers to this circle tonight.

TYPES OF WATER MAGICK

- Cleansing your home with Florida Water or other known magickal cleansing liquid

- Creating drawings or other visual art for deities or spell purposes

- Creating Moon water, which is a simple practice of leaving a container of water to charge and cleanse in the Full or Dark Moon and using that for magickal purposes later

- Dressing candles in oil

- Drinking magickal tea

- Magickal baths

- Really any use of magickal or essential oils, including making your own mixes or sprays

- Using magickal sprays or perfume

- Using salt water as a cleansing and protecting agent

- Writing songs or poems for dieties

WHEN TO USE WATER MAGICK

- For Moon magick in general

- For queer love magick, be it romantic or otherwise

- For spiritual or emotional healing in energy work or spells

- For workings that are about balancing your emotions

- In the process of making art or other creative work

- To draw new friends or artistic collaborators to you

- To inspire your creative muse

OTHER WATER CORRESPONDENCES

Magickal Tools

- Any cup or vessel used to hold water

- Chalices

- Large bodies of water

- The Moon

- Water itself—especially purified or with salt

Stones

- Amethyst—especially for any spell using or enhancing your intuition

- Dried coral

- Lepidolite—especially for stabilizing, balancing, or sleep work

- Moonstone—especially for Moon or healing magick

- Rose quartz—especially for love magick

- Seashells, starfish, sand dollars, water snail shells

Herbs

- Catnip—especially for love magick

- Echinacea—especially for any work where you're calling on river or lake dieties

- Poppies—especially in magick for love, for magick to happen in your sleep, or for general watery good luck

- Rose—especially for love work

- Valerian or valerian root—especially for healing and soothing work

- Vervain—especially to open psychic channels or for creative purposes

Air

 Air is the element I have the most trouble connecting with and, not surprisingly, it's the one that comes up the most as energy I need to fuse with or take on. Air correlates to the intellect, which I love, and is often the energy that writers or those whose jobs deal with a lot of communication need to call on to get through their work life. Because Air does connect so much to the mind, it's also the energy that anyone in a Science, Technology, Engineering, and Mathematics (STEM) field would call on for success in their career. This piece of Air I love. It wants to get our brain going and nurture us on our journey. Air is all about helping us look for the right words to back up our actions.

Air is also (like Fire) all about those actions. Where Fire is about taking action, creating change, and inspiring new action, Air is sometimes the type of action we don't like to take. Air is using our mind to outsmart or outclever someone. Air is about getting rid of the excess things you don't need in your life, and working to cut out old habits and vices that don't serve you. Air is also sometimes (though not always) about being the bad guy.

As queer practitioners though, working with Air is a critical skill to learn as witches as much as we may struggle with it. In the personal, so much of what we need is to cut out and move on from toxic relationships with queerphobic people or systems in our life. In the collective, sometimes what we need are direct actions that will bring those systems to their knees. Air is perfect for this type of work and is therefore an energy that we must learn to wield successfully.

Another important piece of queer witchcraft that uses Air energy is something I talked about in the intro to this book—*shadow work*. Air brings clarity and sharpens our mind, which is a perfect first step towards facing your shadow head on. Air can bring up those difficult or traumatic times in our life (of which queer people have many), and while this isn't always pleasant, if we're trying to navigate through shadow work it's an absolutely necessary step. Often times shadow work is about cutting away the things that aren't serving our highest self, or coming to peace with and integrating them fully into our lives, which are actions we know Air is an agent of.

Air usually comes from the East if we're calling corners or guardians of the watchtowers. The mantra I use most often to call in Air is:

Welcome, guardians of the watchtowers of the East,
Keepers of Air—and therefore logic, judgement, and decision.
I welcome this element and it's keepers to this circle tonight.

TYPES OF AIR MAGICK

- Creating or using sigils, or both

- Doing work outside on a breezy or windy day

- Mantras and incantations

- Meditation

- Using incense

- Writing poems, letters, or lists of goals

WHEN TO USE AIR MAGICK

- As a first step towards shadow work

- For any spell where you need to think logically to follow through when the spell work succeeds

- For clearing out old, harmful, and stale energy from our home, work space, or own energy field

- If you're a writer, working in STEM, or have a communications heavy job and you're looking for inspiration or a career boost

- To inspire logic and clarity within yourself or another

- When you have big decisions to make and big actions to take

- When you need a cool, clear head to make decisions

- When you need to cut people, situations, or energies out of your life

- When you need to cut your own bad habits and vices out of your life

OTHER AIR CORRESPONDENCES

Magickal Tools

- A knife or athame

- Incense

- Pen and paper

- Sigils

- Writing and words

Stones

- Citrine

- Peridot

- Sapphire

- Topaz

- Tourmaline

Herbs

- Basil

- Calendula

- Comfrey

- Eyebright

- Lavender

- Poppies

- Valerian

Earth

If Air is the element I have grappled with the most, Earth is the one (alongside Water) that I have innately understood time after time. Air is all around us all the time, but we can't see it. Earth is right under our feet. Most of the things we pick up and hold on a daily basis have Earth imbued right into them. Earth is dirt, grass, herbs, wood, stones, and so much more. In the magickal, Earth is what grounds us and roots us. One of Earth's goals as an element is to keep our feet firmly planted on it, so that we don't get too overtaken by the other elements. Earth is also about planting seeds, watching things grow, and pulling in a harvest when it's time for that.

Traditionally, a whole lot of magickal practitioners use Earth when they're looking for growth in their career, finances, home, or family. These are things traditionally thought to root us. For queer practitioners, it's important to hold space for the fact that some of the images and values that those words conjure can cause tension or even distress. When your childhood home was fraught with tension, the idea or dream of "home" might be very vague, or potentially harmful. The same goes for family. It's important, though, for queer people to remember that we deserve those things, and even if they aren't present in our lives now (and even if we don't want them to be), we can use Earth energy to help us reconcile those images or feelings that come up with those words.

From there we can even reconsider or reconfigure what those words mean or look like to us as individuals, and stop chasing the societally approved versions of those things. The next step would be actually casting your spells, setting your intentions, and doing the work to acquire those newfound visions of home and family. I know not every queer person had a difficult upbringing and I'm not trying to isolate those who love their parents and have no issues with them. As a subculture though, queer people are usually not driving towards the same life and visions that our parents were, or that they wanted for us. Regardless of where you are on your own journey, Earth magick can help with all of the steps outlined above.

Career and finances are tricky for me as a queer person. I am really critical of the systems that push us to produce-produce-produce. I'm very aware of the fact that my community, especially LGBTQQIA2SP+ people of color, live in disproportionate amounts of poverty and struggle to get and maintain jobs at all, let alone anything that can be called or considered a career. It has made a number of us, myself included, disinclined to fall in line and hop on the 9–5 train for the sake of doing so. Yet we do live in a capitalist system, and we do need money to survive. That's the reality of it. Earth energy can be called on to keep ourselves and our community members financially safe, and from there we can focus our energy on success as we define it.

All of that being said, large numbers of queer people, myself included, do have very real hopes and dreams for our careers. While many of us have to start our magickal practice looking for a baseline of financial safety, from there we can cast spells and wishes (which are just short, fast spells) for those careers. It's also worth pointing out that a lot of our careers are tied up in our identities. A lot of us are working that nonprofit life trying to do good in the world, going into politics to try to protect the rest of us, creating resources for our community, or making art that highlights the plethora of untold stories from queer history and culture. Earth energy is absolutely what we want to call on in all of those cases.

Another use for Earth energy or magick that shouldn't be queer specific, except that queer people and people of color are usually the people I know who are most concerned with this, is setting up and establishing resources for community. So many in our beautiful community are not explicitly focused on the self and are much more interested in creating safer and better resources for their communities at large. Earth energy *loves* this type of magick and would be elated to be called on for this. I think this is the most pure and beautiful use for Earth magick, truth be told. As humans, we should be pushing towards community and interdependence, especially in a time of climate crisis and worldwide financial instability. Earth wants us to be stable and secure, and for that we need each other. Most of us have privileges, resources, and ideas that will benefit the community, and Earth energy wants you to give as much or more than you take.

Earth can be called on from the North almost always, regardless of where you are in the world. The mantra I use most often to call in Earth is:

Welcome, guardians of the watchtowers of the North,
Keepers of Earth—and therefore planning, growth, and stability,
I welcome this element and it's keepers to this circle tonight.

TYPES OF EARTH MAGICK

- Doing magick outside, especially in wooded or, alternatively, desert areas

- Kitchen magick

- Protecting yourself with sea salt or black salt

- Working with herbs—dressing your candles in them, making teas out of them, and more

- Working with stones

WHEN TO USE EARTH MAGICK

- For queer money and career magick

- To do work aimed at providing essential resources for your community

- To ground or center yourself

- To help come to terms with and reconfigure your ideas of home and family—and then achieve them

- To protect and heal the Earth itself

OTHER EARTH CORRESPONDENCES

Magickal Tools

- Anything respectfully taken from or being used in nature

- Chunks of wood

- Dirt

- Herbs

- Pentacles/pentagrams

- Salt

- Stones

Stones

- Agate

- Aventurine

- Jasper

- Onyx

- Tourmalated Quartz

- Tourmaline

- Turquoise

Herbs

- Cinquefoil

- Horehound

- Pennyroyal

- Slippery elm

Spirit

The four elements listed above are the ones found here on Earth and the ones that we can harness in very real and tangible ways. There is also a fifth element that is here on Earth with us, but it exists in such an ethereal way that some new or young witches really struggle to understand where it's coming from or how to use it. I'm talking, of course, about Spirit. Yet Spirit as an element doesn't need to be this big, mysterious thing.

Before you dive into the rest of this section, I first want you to sit back, close your eyes, and think about what even just the word Spirit brings into your mind. Let those feelings, words or images linger for a few minutes and then move on to the rest of this piece. Maybe take some notes about it, because you should incorporate that into your understanding of working with Spirit as an elemental.

Spirit can be thought of in a number of different ways, as I'm sure you realized when you were thinking through it. In terms of witchcraft, you can absolutely think about Spirit as the synthesis of the other four elements. Spirit is what happens when Fire, Water, Air, and Earth come together to move in and through your life. Individually these elements can make incredible things happen in your life, but when pulled together there's almost nothing you can't do. That, in essence, is Spirit.

When I think of Spirit I also think of the spiritual energies and entities that often come into our sacred spaces to work with us. This can be literal spirits or ancestor energy. It can be faeries, or animal allies, or even the spirits within your plant allies. It can be the actual deities you work with should you choose to work with them. This is a very literal interpretation, admittedly, but if we're queering witchcraft, then we need to make it accessible to people who may not have a lot of resources. That often means the literal is the most necessary, and certainly when we're talking about magick I would argue that the use of spiritual entities and energies is among the most important pieces of our work.

Spirit is also the human spirit, especially when we're queering the tarot and looking at marginalized identities. So often the missing piece in our spells is *us*. It's the magick that comes from ourselves, our hearts, our souls, our bodies. I say that this is especially true for queer and marginalized people because the human spirit is resilient, and that is never more true than when we're looking at people who have been oppressed and forced to the sidelines by society. Resilience is a key magickal ingredient regardless of what we're doing magick for. That comes from Spirit, which comes from us as much as it comes from outside of us. Spirit is the element that brings our work together and takes it to magickal realms while also keeping us full of the energy, confidence, and determination it takes to make our spells come true.

Spirit isn't hard to define, harness, or work with once you know what you're doing, but it is a mutable force. If in thinking about Spirit, none of the words or ideas I wrote work for you, that's okay. Spirit is what you want and need it to be, and that can't come from a single teacher. It needs to come from your ideas and your understanding. Whatever it takes to get you from thinking in vague ideas of what Spirit could be to thinking in incredibly straightforward terms about what Spirit is to you, is the right way to access Spirit and incorporate it into your work.

Because Spirit is so mutable, there aren't necessarily specific correspondences I want to list at this point. Often a spell will call on you to bring something you own, carry with you, or both into a spell and set it with your other tools. That is usually the correspondence I use for Spirit. Occasionally belongings of my loved ones who have passed on, images or idols of the gods I work with, and random string, trinkets, or stones I find, make it into a ritual or onto an altar as a correspondence to Spirit. It's always deeply personal and it changes every time—just as Spirit shifts, changes, and moves within you, around you, and way above you.

How to Set Up a Ritual or Circle

Working with the elements is a necessary (and hopefully fun) building block for your magickal practice, and it's where a lot of books start for a reason. One thing I really faltered with in a lot of my early witchcraft study was understanding what to do with my elemental knowledge. This book later gets into specific spells and rituals, group work, and the like, but I don't want you to feel totally lost in the meantime. As you're beginning your witchcraft practice, I strongly recommend building an altar to your craft itself. First find a flat surface that you can clear off, set up, and devote to the tools and symbols of your intended goal for as long as you need it, whether that goal is worship, connection, or something more specific that we'll get to later. To begin working with the elements, including Spirit, before you know much more, start decorating a simple altar with symbols and tools of all five elements. Visit it every day, touch or use your tools, and learn slowly over time through meditation, study, and this practice where you should be going from there.

Another thing to know about using and working with the elements is that for most spells you do, you'll pull either the element you're working with or all five elements off of your altar, set them on a separate spell space, and work with them more actively. I do advise casting a circle even if you choose not to call in the elements every time. This costs no money and only a few moments of your time before you begin a ritual. Once you have your elemental tools around you, imagine a spot on the floor, wall, or wherever you want, of glowing light, black smoke, or anything else that makes you feel calm and safe. Then envision that spot growing into a protective circle around your spell space. At the end of the ritual, you'll imagine that space coming down. The point of this pre-spell practice is to keep your space concentrated so the magick is really strong. It's a protective circle, too. No energy should be allowed in or out of the circle without your permission from then on. You might notice it feels really warm and cozy or cool and calm in the circle. It functions to make your spellwork as comfortable as possible. When we're more comfortable we're able to let our spiritual guards down. I especially recommend this practice for LGBTQQIA2SP+ people, people of color, disabled people, and those who are otherwise marginalized, because to me it so often represents that I'm blocking out a world that has been hurtful and painful and focusing exclusively on my goals, pleasure, and community for the time I'm in this spell. That visualization alone is a powerful spell because it prioritizes those things in your mind and allows you to take the first steps towards liberation.

A final thing I recommend doing with your new knowledge of elements while you're learning your path is spending time outside, on the Earth. Even if you live in a big city without a lot of green space, your feet hitting the cement or your face feeling the breeze is an organic connection to the magick of our world. Magick comes from inside of us. It comes from gods or the Universe if we believe in those things. It also comes from the Earth. Our job as witches is to respect and fall in love with the world we live in once again, and as we're learning to get a handle on the elements, getting outside and really rooting in and experiencing all of those elements at once is a beautiful way to awaken your own witchery.

4

MAGICKAL TIMING, MOON MAGICK & SABBATS

Given how much DIY witchcraft I do, it might surprise you to learn that I actually follow Moon magick and Sabbats rather closely. I am someone who likes having a basic framework, and following existing witches' calendars gives my craft a backbone and a discipline. While I ultimately think that the best timing to work your spells is when you most need and want to, I also think there's something to learning the best times to do your work and using the world's natural cycles to support your goals and intentions. That's basically all magickal timing is. This chapter is geared towards helping you get a handle on working with the natural cycles of this world we live in and the Universe above that so that your magick is rich with layers and filled with allies guiding you along the way.

Moon magick is the basic principle of intentionally casting spells when the Moon is at a certain point in its monthly cycle. Full Moons are when a lot of people do big spells with big intentions or group work, especially geared towards breaking bad habits or oppressive holds on us. Sabbats are Pagan holy days and each has a specific purpose, but they're almost all a really good time to give thanks. Like any magickal practice, magickal timing can also be deeply personalized, and the end of this chapter lists and describes several other days you might want to set aside for magick.

In very devout witch circles, it's not uncommon for there to be a little bit of a pressure cooker to mark every important Moon cycle phase, every Sabbat, and every personal meaningful day with *big magick*. This can be exhausting and unnecessary, especially for queer people who are already running on a deficit of time and energy since they're likely engaged in activism, trying to unlearn harmful cycles and "isms" that they've internalized, and are often working more than one job while trying to make art and also, somehow, find time to be a witch. It would be ridiculous to expect you to do all of that and honor every single important magick day. It's also possible that after seeing how certain days' magick and energy is worked, some of it might not feel relevant or important to your life. I have a very close, very witchy friend who doesn't practice Sabbats. I am close with a pair of romantic partners that don't do big astrological markings. I generally practice in all of the days I'll refer to in this chapter, but not every time or every year.

Instead of jumping in, head first, to every single magickal date you come across, I suggest sitting with these energies and ideas for a while and figuring out which ones really resonate with you and which ones don't. You might find that the public religious ecstasy of Beltane is right up your alley but talking to the dead on Samhain still scares you. You might find that you feel nothing on the Full Moon but exhaustion but light up on the Dark or New Moon. For now, especially, work with the things that light you up and make you really excited to get down to witch business. Do leave some space for flexibility and change over time though, because as your relationship to witchcraft and whatever spiritual entities you're working with change, so might the days and times that are important to you.

Moon Magick

We're starting with Moon magick, a surprising commonality between most witches regardless of path, tradition, or how DIY their magick is. I touched on this briefly earlier, but Moon magick refers to a type of spellcraft that follows the cycles of the moon and casts spells according to what the moon is doing. The idea is that the Moon itself is magickal. There's also some really interesting pseudoscience to back up this idea that I do subscribe to. The Moon absolutely has an effect on what happens here on Earth, as does the Sun. Growing up, my mom was as Christian as could be, but whenever other drivers on the road would start swerving and cutting us off unpredictably and dangerously, she'd mutter that it must be a Full Moon. This shows that during this time emotions are high and behavior is wild, but as witches we have a very real opportunity to use that energy to benefit us. While the Full Moon is the most noticeably different energy, at least by mainstream standards, every phase of the moon cycle can be useful in our metaphysical practice.

The Moon is often referred to and revered as the Divine Feminine, with the Sun as the Divine Masculine. As queer people, it's up to the individual whether you subscribe to this or not. I will often work with this and then decide that if this is true, the Earth must be non-binary. Sometimes I throw it out all together. Sometimes eclipses are about integrating into something genderqueer or beyond the gender spectrum for me. If you want to work with this idea, the Moon is great for trying to heal from patriarchal trauma, transition to a more feminine gender than the one you were assigned at birth, or to welcome in goddess energy.

A lot of queer witches turn to Moon magick first because it's easy to follow. The sky usually tells us what we need to know so there's not a lot of need for extensive calendars or tracking. Additionally, many of the religions a lot of us grew up with focused on or exclusively showcased the Divine Masculine and Moon work is thought to be decidedly feminine. That makes it different enough that in our young, forming queer brains we consider it the opposite and therefore the best way to go. While I, and most other witches, grow to respect and worship Sun and Sun gods as well, we often start our journey looking to the feminine. From there, we find the Moon rather quickly.

There are exceptions to literally everything in magick, so your experience might not match the common one outlined above. For Norse practitioners, Sol is the female Sun god and Mani is the god of the Moon. In Shinto, Ameratsu is a Sun goddess and her brother Tsukuyomi is god of the Moon. It's notable that regardless of the pantheon we're pulling from, the Sun and Moon gods or the Sun and Moon themselves are very often related, siblings, or brother and sister. As a genderqueer person, I tend to think of those things as a metaphor for being a part of a greater whole. I am not more feminine or masculine when I am working with the Sun or Moon, and the Sun or Moon isn't always either. Rather there is a related or sibling face that makes the greater whole of the celestial beings we can utilize for magickal purpose. As a genderfluid person, I sometimes find gendering the Sun and Moon to be a little baffling as a practice. While I understand why certain gods and goddesses have genders ascribed to them, and while many of those ascriptions really do bend gender expectations in ways I find delightful, I don't think it adds to our practice to think of the Sun or Moon either way, with one exception.

When I think of or refer to the Moon as a gendered entity, it's because I'm thinking of it as a more feminine face of the Divine. I keep coming back to this idea in large part because of my own upbringing in the Bible Belt where everywhere you look, it's a specific Divine Masculine that kept me in the closet for years. Then when I came out as a lesbian, that Divine Masculine even kept my ideas of dating and sex very gendered. When I was looking for alternative spirituality, I wanted to embrace nothing but the feminine. This is true for so many queer magick users and magick seekers. Even cisgender queer men are likely to turn away from the Divine Masculine because of the stress dominant organized religions put on them, which makes working with the Moon as a feminine energy a rebellious and righteous way to reclaim our physical selves.

Regardless of how you look at the moon, its magickal pull in our lives is undeniable and fantastic. We'll talk about the Sun and Sun magick in this book too, but Moon magick persists as a common form of witchcraft for a whole slew of reasons. One of them is simply that the Moon's phases do shift and change, which is not an experience we have with the Sun. That means its energy and pull in our lives is also shifting and changing. We can ask the Sun for a favor any time, but it feels special and important to work with a specific phase of the Moon. A lot of witchcraft isn't quantifiable. We work with the Moon because when we do, our magick works. The Moon is one part magickal ally, one part late night confidante, and two parts badass spiritual gift that can boost our confidence and helps us through the complicated swirl of emotions that it can also bring.

As we move forward, spend some time over the next few weeks checking out the Moon's cycle and seeing how it affects your moon and spiritual energy. I strongly recommend tracking that somewhere too. You might be surprised to learn that certain issues regularly pop up over the same Moon phases, or that you get really excited really easily at certain times. As you track it, start setting intentions when it makes sense and feels natural. From there you'll be able to develop a relationship with the Moon that can alter the course of your magick forever.

FULL MOON

O There are basically two lines of thinking with a Full Moon, and either is totally valid for magick. One is that because the Full Moon is when the Moon is at its fullest and brightest, we should be using that time for *big spells* or major group work. These are spells that aren't just meant to bring in a couple of new clients or a new flirtation, but to bring life-altering love into your life or break you out of poverty for good. In those cases, you'll need to do the same working over several Full Moons. Group work refers to the work done by a group of witches working together on the same spell at the same time, be that in person or otherwise. Like big spells, group work will likely take place every Full Moon until the intended purpose is met.

Another way to think of this kind of Moon work is as *emergency* spellwork. These are spells that you might have to do only once, but that you really must do to have a basic need met, like housing or mental clarity. These are emergency situations that require immediate action, and although I would argue that that spellwork can be really potent at any time, the Moon certainly helps aid that process. In the beginning of a queer witch's journey, it's likely to be all emergency spellwork all the time. While I urge and encourage Pagan students of mine to set one intention at a time until it comes true when they're starting their path, I understand firsthand the urge to wildly light emergency spell after emergency spell. When you've been hurt and traumatized by religion, by our society, by your own friends, family, loved ones or partners, it's hard to know how to prioritize. You're likely short on resources and shorter on knowledge. In those cases where there really are endless urgent situations, you'll want to use the power of the Full Moon for the most urgent of those emergencies and learn how to use the other Moon Cycles to keep this powerful energy going.

After the Moon is full, it wanes. Waning means the moon shrinks, basically, making each part of itself slightly less visible with each passing day until the Dark or New Moon. Waning Moon energy is good for getting rid of things, which we'll expound on in a bit. Once you have a more sophisticated relationship with the Moon and its magick, you'll learn the second line of thinking about the Full Moon: it's good for setting big intentions to get rid of certain things (habits, energies, situations, ideas), then using the following Waning Moon to continue to clear that energy out. Examples of things you might want to get rid of include your attraction to a type of person you know is toxic for you, poverty, the effect that daily microaggressions have on your heart, a caffeine addiction, or a tough relationship that you're finally ready to let go of. Beyond being good for big spells and getting rid of things, the Full Moon is not very picky about what we come to it with.

A sometimes-forgotten purpose of the Full Moon, (since this is when the Moon is at its most rounded and visible) is specifically for those like myself who connect deeply to the moon, its magick, and the myriad of purposes we would work with it for. This purpose is to do the deep, personal inner work it takes to heal from those sources of pain and trauma that sit within all of us. The Moon is a diviner's ally, but it's also a healer's ally. This Full Moon magick can work deeply through us in a healing spell and help us make huge changes to our harmful mindsets and deep-seated trauma that we've been trying to work through. Any healing work is well aspected now, especially as we dive into two weeks of *waning* after this where we can see the magnitude of our pain shrink daily if we set our intention so. The phrase "deep inner work" means something different to everyone, but a Full Moon is there to help us through the plethora of personal complications that can come up when we're trying to do magick.

For anyone starting a Moon practice, starting with Full Moons, inner work, and the overlap therein is a perfect primer and a great way to cut through any harm that previous religions or circumstances have caused you. Witchcraft is not a perfect art. Nothing in this book is going to give you everything you want and topple capitalism overnight. We can wield these tools for dramatic shifts and changes in our lives, and when it's that inner-self soul piece that needs healing first, the Full Moon has our back.

The Full Moon does like ritual, so using the Full Moon for any of the above kinds of magick does mean committing to a formalized spell or ritual. It doesn't matter what kind—but there are other kinds of magick where you just have to passively light a candle and go about your day or say a quick prayer in the shower. Full Moon magick is not that. Clear off some space in your calendar when the Moon is shining full, and pull together the tools and objects you want to use. How you set your intention and perform the spell is up to you. The Full Moon just really wants some more extended time and energy from you to see your desires through.

DARK AND NEW MOON

I have learned only recently that not everyone refers to or uses the Dark or New Moon interchangeably the way that I do. I have always referred to both as the time where you can't see the Moon at all (hence the phrase "Dark Moon"). This is when the Moon phases start over again, and over the following two weeks the Moon will become slightly more visible. This is referred to as *waxing*, but before we can get there we have to experience the moonless nights known primarily as the Dark Moon. Some people use New Moon to refer to the next day, when we do see a tiny sliver of the Moon, and set this apart as a different Moon phase. Spend some time looking at the Moon on the few days surrounding this time to figure out what works for you. Magickally, they work similarly, but there are a couple of subtle differentiations you can use if you choose to.

If the Full Moon is for *big (emergency) spells*, group work, or getting rid of things, the next sentence probably won't surprise you much. The Dark and New Moon are best for magickal maintenance and resetting day-to-day magickal intentions *or* bringing something major to you. If you're someone who works with both Dark and New Moon energy as separate energies, I would use Dark to set the intention and do the big spell part at the New to reinforce that and reset your attraction magick for the weeks to come.

Attraction magick refers to any kind of spell that's meant to bring something to you. Money magick is attraction magick. Magick meant to bring you new flirtations is attraction magick. Spells to bring a safe space or new resource into your community are types of attraction magick. Because attraction magick is one of the primary types of magick that we hear about, a lot of witches actually favor the Dark or New Moon over the Full Moon. That's okay too. If you don't feel like you have much to get rid of but definitely need to build your toolkit and lists of resources, it's totally fine to take the Dark Moon as seriously as a lot of witches and witchy writers take the Full Moon.

I will also say that any kind of magick that you want to do can most likely be rephrased or reworded to to apply to the Moon phase that we're in. If you want to gain money, but the Moon is waning, you can ask the Moon to help you repel poverty and debt. If you want to get rid of someone in your community who's dangerous but it's a New Moon, you can ask to attract safety to your community.

Another thing that the Dark and New Moon are exceptional for is taking stock (especially prior to setting any of the aforementioned intentions or attraction goals). Whereas the Full Moon can (and often does) probe you to go deep into your own subconscious and work through big healing goals, this phase of the Moon happily aides in helping you sort through the external manifestations at play in your life. A Full Moon might ask you who you are and how to sort through your pain, but a Dark or New Moon focuses on how many resources are available to you, how close you are to your goals, and what you can do about any gaps therein.

WAXING MOON

The Waxing and Waning Moons we've touched on already but they absolutely have a very special magickal purpose and intention, too. While the Dark Moon or New Moon is seen as spooky and mysterious and the Full Moon is bright and flashy, a Waxing Moon is hella powerful attraction magick as outlined above. Waxing takes place over a period of two weeks (literally fourteen days) and that can be an incredible time for daily rituals like meditations or lighting candles that have already been enchanted each night to bring you your desired outcome.

If you've already set your intentions and are in a waiting or holding pattern for them, this is an ideal time to prepare yourself mentally, emotionally, and spiritually for the changes coming. This is a type of attraction magick, but it requires different work on our end. Instead of just setting the goal to gain or attract the thing we're trying to bring in, preparing ourselves means doing any processing around things holding us back from our goals. It means working through any blocks that are still remaining. It means making space and time in our schedules and energy and love in our hearts for the new things that will come into being. This is work and magick (which we know by now are basically the same thing).

I sometimes think of using the Waxing Moon as a time to slowly build up to new ideas or energies as we inch slowly towards the Full Moon. For those of us who are LGBTQQIA2SP+ and because of that are divorced from our desires and needs at an early age, it can take a lot of guts to ask the Moon to help you with something big. It's not unusual then to make your New Moon and Full Moon spells related. From there you'd use the Waxing Moon to work up to the big ask of the Full Moon. The New or Dark Moon would be setting a basic, easy-to-ask-for intention. Then you'd do the work to process and prepare for what you need to process and prepare for over the two weeks of the Waxing Moon. When the Full Moon comes, you'll be ready to release your big blocks and ask for that big request that you've been sneakily setting intentions for by doing this other work the whole time.

The Waxing Moon inspires and encourages us to set daily habits and practices that serve our long-term spiritual and emotional goals too. Not everything in our lives is about big magick. Sometimes we've worked through our big blocks and now we just need to get in the habit of lighting our candles at night, cleaning off our altars each day, and praying while we're on the bus. The gentle energy of a Waxing Moon can ease us into these new habits in ways that feel natural and easy, and from there our practice can thrive in new and radical ways. Even if the habits you're trying to build aren't spiritual, this is the time to start doing the easy, daily work of starting them. After the 2016 United States election that shook a lot of us up, I used a Waxing Moon cycle to get in the habit of reading news and texting Resistbot daily, accordingly. I used another one to start saving just a few cents a day to eventually save up enough to send to nonprofits that are doing the important resistance and activist work that I'm not able to. This energy was affirming and inspiring and helped build the foundation I needed to take on bigger projects and bigger work later.

WANING MOON

Just as the New and Full Moon can work inversely, so can the Waxing and Waning Moon. *Waning* is that time when it looks like the Moon is shrinking, and it's the perfect time do the work of letting go of the things that are no longer serving you. If your Full Moon spell is a full-on repulsion spell, the following two weeks should take you on a journey of learning to slowly release and let go of the thing you've gotten attached to, but now need to let go of. It's also a time to slowly get rid of the mundane things that aren't serving us either. If you're trying to let go of an ex-partner but have a bunch of their stuff sitting around, the Waning Moon encourages you to destroy, abandon, or (if you're kind) return their belongings a little at a time so you don't have this pile of physical reminders. If you're trying to release the effects of poverty trauma, the Waning Moon might have you slowly developing better financial habits. Maybe you set up a savings account one day, start tracking your finances, and cut a few unnecessary expenditures. (Those are just examples, and I recognize that you need to be in a place of relative privilege for a lot of them.)

One bad habit that most of us need to cut is letting life pass us by and in that way, taking for granted that we will have more days coming. Queer people are no stranger to grief and loss. We lost an entire generation to the AIDS epidemic, and that's not the first time we've suffered a collective loss that lives in our subconscious memories. Yet in the struggle to get through the day, and then the next day, and the next one, we often lose track of our own goals, desires, fears, griefs, and so on. The Waning Moon is sometimes thought of as a good couple of weeks to develop a gratitude practice. This is part of the process of learning to release pain and ego according to a lot of New Age thought. I think some of that thought is harmful and can quickly give way to spiritual bypassing, but it's true that a gratitude practice for the (sometimes admittedly sparse) blessings that do come your way can shift your thinking in ways that allow for huge breakthroughs and healings that will benefit your overall spiritual goals exponentially. It's not the easiest thing to do, and I try not to push it on people too hard because I don't want to overlook the very real pain a lot of us have been through. Still, if you're looking to start a gratitude practice just to see how that shifts your thinking, the Waning Moon is a strong ally and gives you roughly fourteen days to do so.

Daily mantras to live as your best, most generous self or alternatively, to build safe and solid boundaries around yourself can really take hold in fierce, important ways during a Waning Moon. Just like the Waxing Moon wants us to slowly build good daily habits for attraction, the Waning Moon wants us to build good, daily habits for cleansing and release. That might mean smoke cleansing after the end of each long workday during this cycle. It might mean setting those mantras and incantations to shred your own worst habits. It might simply mean reminding yourself daily what you're letting go of. This phase tempers down to a Dark or New Moon, and if we're doing any big magick then, we want to be at a phase where it's all new skin and shiny hope. That means using the Waning Moon wisely to shed the skin that was constricting you.

MOONS AND ASTROLOGY

If you're super new to witchery and therefore divination, you might not realize that in addition to Sun astrology, there's Moon astrology, too. Your Sun sign is most likely the sign you know and use. It's the culmination of the rest of our astrological charts and how it all gets synthesized. We *are* our Sun signs, and I'm not denying that. We are also the rest of our astrology. The Sun spends about thirty days in each sign. The Moon spends only three (approximately). Our Moon sign is who we are in the shadows or at home when no one is watching. The Moon sitting in a sign gives it the positive and negative benefits of working with that sign, and allows our understanding of the Moon and ourselves to deepen.

Personal astrology aside, this is still building block information for a Moon magick practice. If after reading through the rest of this chapter you're still not sure which Moon phases you're attached to or not, it might be that the missing key is the astrology of the moon at any given time. There's no instant way to tell where the Moon is, but it's not hard to find by using Google Search or downloading moon tracking or astrology apps. Knowing where the Moon is before starting your spell can help you personalize your working or navigate it differently. It bolsters the energy of the spell, and can reveal a shadow side of your intentions that might be difficult to come face to face with but is nonetheless important for us to know.

Examples of using the Moon's astrology would include:

- You're doing a money spell, and the moon is in Aries. Aries is a passionate and impulsive sign, so you could ask for quick money or a totally surprising opportunity that will change the course of your financial life but is not at all what you had planned.

- You're doing a spell to help soothe your friend's heart through their gender transition. Ideally the Moon would be in a caretaking sign like Cancer or Pisces to guide your magick, but you have a Sagittarius moon to work with. Sagittarians are known to be full of life and laughter instead, but never fear! Laughter can still soothe the soul. Your spell is most effective by gearing it towards fun that will help your friend cut loose for a while, thus lightening their load and their heart.

- You haven't been feeling super cute lately, so you're thinking about a glamour (a spell performed with the intention for other people to see you a certain way) to hold you over while you work towards building confidence. The Moon is in Pisces. Pisces is a sensitive, compassionate, and relatively New Agey sign. Your glamour benefits from this energy by allowing you to reflect your inner beauty outwards, and it wraps you in a little bit of intriguing mystery.

It is absolutely not necessary to incorporate the Moon's current astrology into your Moon magick, but doing so can amplify your message and spellwork. The most exciting part is what the Moon's astrology can do for deepening and nuancing your Moon work. Those astrological signs can implore us to see our own desires and their possibility through a specific lens that both cracks our thinking wide open and narrows the scope of our spell. Both of those changes are great for magick of any type. Furthermore, the whole point of magickal timing is that working with the Earth and the Moon's natural cycles calmly helps your work and allows it to thrive in unique and profoundly life-changing ways. Adding the Moon's astrology to the mix gives you another layer of magickal intention and protection and boosts your message loudly into the Universe, ultimately bringing that intention and the purpose of that message back to you.

Traditional Pagan Holy Days, A.K.A. Sabbats

Sabbats, put simply, are Pagan holy days. They can be thought of as witch calendar markers, times that anyone regardless of deity worship or not, can sit back and take in the lessons of the season as they continue on their journey through this life. For those of us who started a Pagan or witchcraft journey as a response to a stifling brand of organized religion that we grew up in, Sabbats can either reflect the restriction and organization that we're uncomfortable with or welcome alternatives to the steeped-with-Christianity mainstream holidays. If you are uncomfortable feeling like there are too many days you have to, or should, celebrate, then take this section as primarily informational so you can keep up when your witch friends who do celebrate talk about them. It's also not uncommon to have an initial discomfort or disinterest in Sabbats and then grow into a practice of taking them later in your journey.

For those of us who are looking for ways to mark our journey and want an alternative to Moon magick for working magickal timing, Sabbats offer that and so much more. I am a deeply Sabbatical witch, meaning that these days are really important and holy to me. Because of my schedule and how my journey may be going, I don't celebrate every Sabbat every year, but I do note them on my calendar and at least specify a prayer or journal entry for that day.

Another reason I love Sabbats is that even if I don't do a big ritual with that holiday's intention, thousands of other Pagans across the world are. This means even my minor intentions can ride the backs of other spells and take a foothold that can prop up my work until the next Sabbat. Not only is that a joyful thought that brings ease to the day, but it also makes me well up with joy to think about so many other witches celebrating the day with all of the woo and witchiness and weirdness they can muster. Even if I don't set my own intentions, I give thanks for witches the world over, and trust that collectively we are all doing what we should be.

The Sabbats as a collection of days are often called the Wheel of the Year, which I love. I think that title makes the rest of the information about each Sabbat more accessible and clear. The Wheel of the Year emphasizes that, for the most part, these days are just about noting where we are and taking the time to do spiritual work or celebrate (which *is* spiritual work, and the Sabbats remind us of that).

Of these eight holy days, four of them are equinoxes and solstices, and the others are cross-quarter days, which essentially just means they are between the equinoxes and solstices. It's thought that the equinoxes and solstices are Sun Sabbats and the cross-quarter days are Earth Festivals. We talked about the traditional thought of the Moon as feminine, and here we see the integration with the masculine Sun via those equinoxes and solstices. I have been working with the cross-quarter Earth days as nonbinary, fluid, genderqueer energy for years. Queering our craft does not mean just honoring the inherent queerness in what's already there, and it doesn't *always* mean shunning or chucking every binary assignation out the window, though it can mean that. Queer people have always created our own thoughts, ideas, art, and communities. We get to create these things in our spiritual life too. The Earth holds all of us, of all genders, and it's always changing and evolving. I think it makes perfect sense if you want something non-binary to worship, like I do, that it can fall on

the Earth. (Really it can fall anywhere. Queering something means taking queer and DIY principles to it—but for me the Earth has always felt like it's all of us and none of us at once.)

Different schools of witchcraft will assign more importance to Sun or Earth days, but for the genderqueer reasons outlined above, I don't. The important Sabbats for your year are the ones that speak to you, and the ones you think you can get great work done for yourself and for the collective of queers and witches trying to survive in this world.

A lot of Wheel of the Year myth is steeped in specifically Wiccan myth and culture, and I am not Wiccan at all. Yet this wheel, in so many ways, transcends space, time, and culture to provide a framework that any of us can use. A lot of that Wiccan myth takes from other mythologies, meaning that my Celtic roots or someone else's Egyptian roots shine right through on these days too. For this book, and for that reason, I've chosen to leave out as much myth about the Sabbats that one could leave out and still have the day make sense. I've chosen to focus on the universal purposes of the Sabbat, allowing for free thinking and exploration as you move through the year.

Before we dive right in, I want to address the idea of a Pagan New Year. There's a lot of heated discussion in Pagan community about when that is. Do we follow the mainstream New Year? Is it Samhain, when autumn is in its full head of glory and we're preparing for things to die off? Is it the Winter Solstice when things are actually dying off for the year ahead? Should it be Ostara when things are being born again? How does that change as we shift hemispheres and therefore both cultural and climate markers? There's not a wrong answer (surprise!), just the one that works for you. As for me, I like to keep things as simple as possible so I follow the mainstream Western New Year since that's the culture I live in. Our witchcraft is so often thought of as a subculture that completely exists by its own rules. For those of us who are queer, marginalized, or both, that can be amplified even further. Even so, because I see the Wheel of the Year largely as a way to keep track of our days and practices, it makes the most sense of me to address both my culture's dominant New Year and note when Pagan energy resets. As such, I'm starting the Sabbats off with Imbolc—the first Sabbat you'll see in a mainstream New Year.

There are definitely specific and specialized ways to celebrate each Sabbat, but there is also work you can plan for for each one. Setting a

single intention for your Wheel of the Year and figuring out how each Sabbat fits into that intention is a beautiful way to get to know your own magickal skills and still have that goal met. Setting an altar for each Sabbat is a sweet, easy way to honor these days in your home. Planning to write something—anything—in your grimoire for the day to denote where you are on a spiritual journey is another good practice. I personally like mixing it up, so each Sabbat does include some specific ways you can celebrate and honor the day.

IMBOLC

Imbolc is a cross-quarter holiday, and the first Sabbat of a numerical New Year. It falls right about halfway between the Winter Solstice (Yule) and the Spring Equinox (Ostara), putting it on February 1st for most witches in most countries. (For those in the Southern hemisphere, August 1st is often Imbolc.) Imbolc basically represents the beginning of Spring, and has a variety of rituals and intentions associated with it correlating to that. While it will still be winter for several more months, Imbolc marks the changing weather and lengthening daylight hours therefore promising that Spring is, in fact, coming. Potential for new ideas and beginnings runs rampant. Hope abounds. If we use our Yule to do deep inner work, then Imbolc allows us to shed the gravity of the winter and spring forth like a laughing, joyful, reborn person.

Imbolc can have a lot of meaning for queer magicians because of all of that hope and promise coursing through the day. For those who are recently out or grappling with their identity still, the sun being up for a few more minutes a day each day is a symbol that your own life can reset to something lighter, too. For those of us who grapple with unfortunate and unfortunately often true queer cliches like codependent relationships or tumultous chosen family drama, Imbolc is a sign that relief is coming (so long as we are doing our own inner work). For the all-too-high number of us who live with mental illness (myself included), Imbolc can be a day to celebrate the recovery we're working towards. I don't know a single queer person, regardless of their religion or spiritual path, that doesn't know the metaphor and the reality of coming out of a dark time and into a better one intimately. Imbolc gives us a specific day to revel in promise of that lighter time.

Healing magick works really well during Imbolc, especially if it's an emotional or spiritual healing that we're looking for. Those source spots of

our trauma that sit in our guts or our hearts can see significant progress after an Imbolc ritual. We can feel lighter ourselves, not just joyful about the days getting lighter, if we aim our craft that way on this day. For herbalists and kitchen witches this is prime time to plan and begin implementing their growing season. For energy healers this is honestly a great day to make some extra cash by pulling in extra clients who are trying to shrug their own emotional weight as we head into Spring.

Attraction magick works well during Imbolc too, and for queer witches who don't feel like their calling is in healing this is a good time to set your intentions for Spring and Summer. Imbolc in a lot of parts of the world does mark a slow descent into Spring, so these are attraction intentions that start small but grow over time. If you're trying to start your own business or nonprofit but aren't quite there yet, Imbolc ritual should help you attract what you need to get ready. For queer artists, writers, and activists who spent the winter hibernating, this Sabbat can be used to bring new ideas and inspiration by doing something as simple as lighting a candle.

While some of our Sabbats see very specific intentions and therefore rituals (looking at you, Samhain), many of them can be used or tweaked to fit the holy day nicely. Imbolc is great for any spell that requires hope, making healing and attraction magick the big attractions for the day. Getting rid of the yuck from winter and therefore doing some early spring cleaning is also a form of ritual that can set you up for the season to come. This day in Wiccan and Celtic lore belongs to Brighid, a goddess of poetry and home. That means regardless of your pantheon, spells for those things are well aspected. Traditionally those who work with Brighid will use her energy to cast protection spells on Imbolc too, so it really is a day with a lot of options. It just depends on what spiritual entities you work with and what your needs are at the time.

While I'm choosing to omit most myths from this section, a fun trivia about Imbolc that gets lost is that it used to be a holiday where we marked off part of the day to practice weather divination. Weather divination is an almost lost form of divination where we (as people) use a natural divination method like observing animal behavior to figure out what the weather is going to do over the next several weeks. If this sounds familiar to you, it's because as time has gone on, American culture specifically has rewritten this cultural milestone and rebranded it as Groundhog Day. Groundhog Day is when we see if Puxatawney Phil, a groundhog, will see

his shadow or not. If he does, that supposedly foretells six more weeks of winter. If not, Spring should be on its way.

I bring up weather divination and how it's been rebranded not only because I think it's interesting, but also because as growing witches and Pagans it's our right to note when our culture pervades the mainstream, instead of the other way around. Weather divination is hardly the point of Imbolc, but it shows that Imbolc energy is alive and well, and therefore accessible to us with something as basic as watching the Groundhog Day ritual on our TV.

OSTARA OR SPRING EQUINOX

While Imbolc might represent the hope and potential of an impending Spring, Ostara, which is also blatantly known as the Spring Equinox, represents the Spring in its wholeness. Night and day are equal in length on this day as we officially move into Spring proper. Because we do so much of our preliminary magick for Spring during Imbolc, this equinox is considered a time of balance and equilibrium. Ostara can take place any time between March 20th and 23rd, as that balance of night and day, light and dark are what we're looking for.

Ostara, also known as Eostre, is an Anglo-Saxon (often German) lunar goddess of fertility. There are actually several goddesses with similar names and similar affiliations throughout the whole world, so if you're a deific witch you don't need to focus exclusively on a German pantheon for this day and it's magick. You might also find as you begin independent research that Ostara is affiliated with hares and sometimes eggs, which might strike you as something Christians have blatantly appropriated from Paganism and watered down for their own spring holiday, Easter. You're right. I'm not a Pagan who gets super upset at how much witchcraft has been pushed to the margins, especially because I know for a lot of queer witches, that's how we were able to find and access it. The incredibly purposeful appropriation of our holy days and symbols does get to me sometimes though, and the symbols of Ostara are an important example of that.

As we get back to a queer Pagan understanding of the Spring Equinox, though, we understand that this time could and should be about our own power to bring almost anything we want from conception to fulfillment. Fertility magick is big during Ostara, which makes sense given as

that's how we're ringing in Spring. Fertility magick can be quite literal and for queer couples who are looking to expand their family through adoption, conception, taking in those who need homes, or any other way you can build a family, this is the time for an intense ritual aimed at that expansion. Fertility magick can also be a metaphor. Fertile ground is what we call land that is perfect for growing crops, and this is a great green witch's holiday, too.

I didn't start off as a green witch, but as our climate continues its descent into madness and as my activism has grown to include that knowledge, I've learned how to give back to this Earth. A lot of that does come down to green witchcraft. It seems so simple, but planting plants, especially trees or bee friendly plants, is critical right now. If we have outdoor space, we should be doing it. If we don't have outdoor space, we should be piggybacking on the efforts of those who do and contributing in any way we know how. Green witchcraft isn't exclusively about plants and climate change, but it's an important step toward it. The Spring Equinox is a great time to learn what that means for you and how you can contribute to the Earth's ongoing fertility and to start doing so if you're ready.

Fertility magick is also a metaphor for any magick for any intention that you mean to take from conception to growth. If Imbolc was about making business plans for a new business or non-profit that benefits your community, Ostara is about filing your paperwork with the state. If Imbolc was about seeking inspiration as an artist, writer, or activist, Ostara is about getting those projects going hot and heavy. If you're moving out of toxic relationships, Ostara can be about meeting new people and planting seeds for future connection.

Most of the Sabbats represent time to step back and take stock of what we've done and how we've grown as witches and as people. Ostara is no exception to this. This is a perfect day to look at where you were during Yule, where you are now, and chart what that growth has looked and felt like. It's a time to recommit to your journey, but before we can recommit we need to take stock of what's working and what isn't. Hopefully your winter was one of learning and stretching, and now you have a better idea of what you want things to look like. Once you have all of that written down or etched into your brain, it's time to do the spellwork meant to keep you on track.

Ostara can be a powerful time for magick or for the paperwork maintenance of our emotional and spiritual lives, which we've seen above. I also sometimes use this day just to give thanks back to my gods, to the Earth, and to those I do magick with. I might buy fresh flowers for my altars at home, or take my best witches out for a nice meal. While I almost always have magick for my own self I could be doing, I often choose to use this day for collective workings and magick. Queer witches should be focused on community and the world, and this day has enough power to help your big queer dreams for a better world on their journey to come true. This might mean breaking ground on a new homeless shelter for queer youth or doing the magick to bring one into being. It might mean starting work on a campaign for a political candidate you actually agree with. It may simply mean using your spiritual gifts and the depth of your heart to dream of new ways to give back, and begin doing so as soon as possible. Ostara is all about Spring, which is all about hope and new life. Don't limit your own imagination and what this equinox could mean for you and those you love.

BELTANE OR MAY DAY

May 1st has always been one of my favorite days on the calendar, and as I learned and grew into myself as a queer witch, it's abundantly clear why. This is another cross-quarter day, this time between the Spring Equinox and the Summer Solstice. This is thought to be the day when, historically, pastoral animals were sent out to pasture to do their grazing and fattening. Protection rituals for those animals abounded, with an obvious undertone of "please bring money to this house." Often these protection rites were done with fire, which leads us to how most of us see Beltane today. It's also worth noting that Spirits and faeries are thought to be particularly lively this day as they help us transition into summer with joy and levity.

Today, we largely celebrate Beltane as a time to honor life itself as our plans and spells move from potential to conception to existing. This is a time to celebrate and mark growth. It's also time to celebrate fire, heat, passion, and sensuality. Even the most sex positive witches don't always take time to denote the Sabbats as particularly sexual days, but Beltane doesn't really let us forget its purpose. There's something in the air on this Sabbat, driving us towards spiritual and physical ecstasy. There is something deeply tantric permeating the whole day, and sex magick is highly electric on Beltane. The

idea is that we're at our most receptive when we're at our most vulnerable, which is thought to often be post-coital. As someone who has had a lot of good and bad sex, and who has seen both result in orgasm, I'm not sure I agree that this is always when we're at our most vulnerably receptive, but so much of magick is putting ideas and intangibles into tangibles. For that, the idea of sex magick absolutely works to attract whatever it is you're trying to attrack to your life, and on Beltane that can absolutely mean a new partner or partners. Beltane is the time when a lot of covens do group sex magick, but that isn't necessary. Masturbating or sex with a partner you trust can drive you towards that same religious ecstasy and point of receptivity if you set the intention for it to do so.

As a queer person who was told for years to keep her sexual identity to herself, as a kinky person who sometimes still, decades after becoming sexually active, feels *domme shame*, and as a deeply romantic person who does see sex as sacred even when it's not for sacred purposes, I cannot express enough the importance of Beltane for those living in the margins. If we are taught to be ashamed of something, making an entire day to celebrate it is rebellion and resistance at its finest. This day has helped so many queer witches I know reclaim their bodies and the idea that they deserve pleasure, and it can do that for you, too. Even if sex isn't your bag or you're struggling with sexual hangups or gender dysphoria that prevent sexual pleasure, sex is so often a metaphor for pleasure as a whole and I absolutely think that that rings true in Beltane. Where in your life do you feel so much joy, so much ecstasy, that it renders you incapable of turning away more pleasure for yourself? That's how you should spend your Beltane, whether you have a specific intention for that moment of peak pleasure or not.

If you are someone who is still unpacking the years of shame that too many queer people know too well, that's okay. You don't have to be one hundred percent at the top of your game to achieve Beltane greatness. There are some standard images and rituals you can partake in. One of my favorites is fire magick, but I'm not talking about candles. Beltane is almost synonymous with big bonfires. This can be a spiritual event where you and your loved ones burn objects that are no longer serving you, dance around the fire in shared love and enjoyment, or anything else that feels spiritual and sacred. It can also be an emotionally significant ritual where you cuddle with your close friends, drink some quality beer or seltzer, and

give thanks to the fire and summer itself. If this Sabbat is meant to help us bring in summer with all of its fun and fieriness, then getting cozy and laughing around a fire is a splendid way to use that energy.

While this might be harder to come by if you don't live in a big city, public *maypoles* tend to signify May Day and Beltane, too. A maypole is a tall, wooden pole usually in a public space with ribbons hanging off of it that you can grab and dance with, or mold into various shapes with other ribbon-holders. You can do a version of this yourself at home. If you have yard space, you could obviously pitch a much more modest version and invite just a couple of people over to play and dance around it. You can also make a replica for your altar or as a table centerpiece to ring in the day. Grab a wand or a smooth stick (you don't want splinters!) and attach some ribbons to it. You'll probably need a holder for the base too. This image recalls something deep in our souls and you'll be inviting in summer and all of its pleasure with your personal maypole.

More modest ways to celebrate include flower crowns, glittery (but Earth safe) makeup, and time spent outdoors. Even though I am deeply introverted, I make a concerted effort every May Day to spend it with other people, ideally people whom I think the world of that I know think the world of me. For queer witches this means time with community who affirm our identities and hold space for our traumas. For everyone, it means spending some time with people who laugh and bring you to ecstasy. A big part of manifestation that is a part of a lot of spellwork is the idea that "like attracts like." While this is deeply problematic thinking because we do not "earn" more trauma by being unable to move on from traumatic circumstances, when we're setting positive intentions we can use that idea to reinforce that we're looking to melt into Pleasure Activism and joy during Beltane.

LITHA, MIDSUMMER, OR SUMMER SOLSTICE

As exciting as Beltane was to dive into, Litha has been just as important in my life and on my journey as a queer witch. This day happens between June 20th and 23rd, whichever the longest day of the year happens to fall on. The longest day means this is the day when we have the most sunlight, and when our night is the shortest. This is the year's energetic peak. It's when the Sun is at its shiniest. It's when all of that summer fun hits a head.

The Sun is a tricky spiritual entity though. On the one hand, the Sun brings us joy and pleasure and fun. On the other hand, the Sun illuminates anything that we were trying to keep hidden or keep under wraps. Spiritually, that makes Litha an incredibly powerful time for releasing any emotions that we've built up since our last major release. It means this is an exceptional Sabbat for doing energy cleansing or energy work as we work towards maintaining our spiritual selves. We know how the Wheel of the Year operates by now, and we're realizing that for every (metaphorically) sunny day there's a rainy one. It's time, not necessarily to prep for snow or rain, but to recognize our aversion to it and honor those emotions too. As a day for release, Midsummer also acknowledges the happier side of this coin. This is a day for a final (for now) release because the harvest days are coming, and we want to spend that time focusing on all of the beautiful times we've grown and built.

I talked above about how crucial Litha has been to me as a queer person. There is so much joy in this day, but sometimes my heart feels so heavy with the pain and trauma that I've endured over the years that I cannot merely celebrate what's come of me even though it's mostly good. Instead, the fact that Litha upholds and honors me but gently encourages me to release that pain has been pivotal. Litha is a day where queer witches can gather together to hex queerphobic systems and release the effects they've had on our psyche. It's a day we can spend alone, contemplating what we've been through and deciding where we want to go from here and where we want this tumultuous journey to take us next. The release available on this Sabbat often goes overlooked, but it's one of the more important parts for anyone whose society oppresses them. It's a whole day where our gods or the Universe or whatever spiritual energy we connect with agrees to take on and shoulder our emotions so that we don't have to—and if that's not a reason to celebrate, I don't know what is.

Litha is a summer holiday, which means it is not all heaviness. It's also a day to focus on the things we're trying to manifest again. With harvest Sabbats coming up before we know it, it's time to get serious about our workings. Flowers should be in full bloom everywhere we look, so finding some for wishing or attraction spells should be easy for us now. For queer people who sometimes have unique desires (by which I just mean "desires you won't find in a mainstream spell book") this is probably our

most powerful day for making those wishes. This is partially because we are as supported by the spiritual powers that be as I described above, and partially because of the abundance of flowering plants, herbs, and other goodies that we can use for our magick.

In recent years, my Litha wish has been for my magick to become more powerful. Magick is a lot of things to a lot of people, but I keep coming back to how valuable a tool witchcraft is for queer people. Because of who we are, how we love, or both, we are so easily and quickly cast to the side even by people we trust (and absolutely by society at large). It is our right to take that power back in whatever ways we deem necessary and possible. Witchcraft can be a huge asset for that, as it's all about coming into one's own magick and power. I'm not sure people who have not been put down by loved ones, who are not at risk of hate crimes, whose own government doesn't hate them, truly understand the complexities and nuances that challenge us and prevent us from stepping easily into our power. It's not easy for queer people, or, I would argue, for people of color or disabled people, to step into our power. It can be done though. We *can* reclaim our own selves. Litha will not make or break our ability to become powerful witches, but it will aid us, uphold us, and support us on our journey to do so.

LUGHNASADH OR LAMMAS

Finally we arrive at the first of our three harvest Sabbats. This is a cross quarter day between Summer Solstice and Autumn Equinox and it's brimming with opportunity for us to claim our dreams, harvests, and desires as our own. This day is usually August 1st, though not for those in the Southern Hemisphere who may celebrate it during Spring. Lughnasadh is named after Lugh, a Celtic Sun god, but even though I'm as Celtic as they come I tend to prefer the more expansive and inclusive term Lammas.

During Midsummer and Litha we were told to set some goals and think about what we were trying to manifest or wish for. During Lammas, the first thing we need to do is check in and see how that's going for us. In some cases, we're starting to see buds of success that just haven't had time to hit full bloom yet. In that case, what I refer to as *magickal maintenance* is needed. This just means smaller spells or rituals designed to recommit us and our magick to the previous intentions, essentially hitting "repeat" on a previous spell. In some cases, we still have a lot of work to

do on ourselves or towards our goals before there's even a reset button to be hit. That's okay. This day can be used for correcting course, however that works in your situation. Some of us though, will see ourselves ready to metaphorically (or literally in some cases) pull out our first harvests.

Whether you are recalibrating, recommitting, or straight up harvesting on Lammas, this is a day for giving thanks for that harvest and for feasting. *I really want to emphasize that even though this is a day for giving thanks, it's also for feasting or whatever way you express that you are full and have enough for now.* Many of the organized and oppressive religions queer people grew up in have convinced us that the holy days are not about us. They are about a capital-G God, and nothing we do can ever be enough to live up to that God's promise. They are about a life and a death we had nothing to do with, and yet we're supposed to give everything over to that and honor it. By contrast, Sabbats are so much about you, your work, and your pleasure. This is a criticial lesson for queer witches and one I didn't learn for way too long.

Yes, we should absolutely use Lammas to thank our Divine. We should do a ritual of thanks. We should plan to use the blessings that have been sent wisely. We should honor that we had Divine intervention in our lives. We should also use Lammas to pat ourselves on the back for our own hard work that we're finally starting to see pay off. In the metaphor of growing crops, you needed Divine intervention for good weather, fertile soil, and to protect your crops from predators. Yet your gods did not plant those seeds. They didn't water them. They didn't pull bugs off of their leaves, talk to the plants, put up a fence around those plants that the rabbits really liked to eat. You did all of that. So give yourself a pat on the back and prepare a literal or metaphorical feast as you settle in to finish up this growing season. Tomorrow the sun will rise and you'll get back into the work. Today, on Lammas, you can melt into the joy that your hard inner and outer work has wrought.

MABON OR AUTUMN EQUINOX

I freaking love fall. I am one of those annoying people with too many sweaters and a hot coffee or, yes, the dreaded pumpkin spice latte in hand as I stroll through as many whirlwinds of red and orange leaves as possible. Growing up, fall meant new possibilities as school started. I tended to hop around friend groups and my course load ended up being wildly different

year to year. I would be trembling with excitement for what could come every Autumn. I never really grew out of that, especially because I love the breezy weather and seasonal treats so much. So obviously, when I started learning witchcraft, the Autumn Equinox was one of the Sabbats I was most excited to learn about.

Mabon takes place between September 20th and 23rd, whichever day recalibrates our days and nights so that daylight and nighttime are equally met again. Mabon is traditionally celebrated as the second harvest Sabbat, though some of the language around it is a little bit weird because it alludes to this being a complete harvest. What that really means is that though you'll continue to reap the benefits of your harvest for a little bit longer, your job on this set of intentions is basically done unless you decide to continue your work on it. Though harvest holidays on the whole are happy, joyous occasions, on this equinox we do begin facing the reality that we should start preparing for an emotionally intense and often isolating winter. In Paganism though, none of the seasons are considered bad. There are just those that require harder inner work, and those that are about joy and giving in to pleasure.

Mabon falls on a harvest day, which signifies thanks, but does bring that autumn chill in the air. It makes sense then that this is a day where we focus on balance. Your spell's intentions are best served to find that work-life balance people are always going on about, to welcome an element that you haven't felt as connected to lately back into your life, or to work through any funky energy in your aura or home as you reset for the rest of the year. As queer witches, my close friends and I spend a lot of Mabon energy trying to cleanse and recharge from our busy lives as activist-artist-witches, often with day jobs or things bringing in the money. In a gig economy, most of us pushed to the fringes of society are working multiple gigs at once and Mabon can bring a natural rest and pleasant reset to help us power through the rest of the year and continue the hard and necessary work we do.

Mabon is a harvest holiday, and I've talked at length about how important it is for queer witches to take these harvest days as days of gratitude, pleasure, and rest. It's so easy to wear ourselves out without realizing the effect of a callous society or unsupportive living community has on us until it's too late. Mabon can be used to take stock of how we're feeling regarding trauma and energy and to do whatever magick we need

to balance those scales for ourselves. Traditional witchcraft can sometimes stress family harvests for Mabon. As queer people we get to decide who that is. We get to decide if that means our family of origin, a chosen family of other queers and outcasts, or a community center where we show up with a basket full of baguettes. We get to decide if that includes our artistic collaborators, our political allies, our fellow regulars at our favorite gay bar. Family can be anything. It's rarely perfect, but it can be fierce and full of love. Those people can share in your Mabon feast—and you can shut the rest of the world out while you enjoy each other's company and hearts.

Mabon is the Autumn Equinox, which means we are preparing for the dark. For LGBTQQIA2SP+ people, we're used to the dark. We're used to the fray. We're used to the side, where hedges are overgrown or cities are eroding into rubble because that's where our dominant culture pushes us to. Mabon is about honoring the dark, but for queer witches this is often easier than for our straight and cisgender counterparts. We have learned to thrive and be happy in the dark. The dark is where we're left alone to explore our bodies, our hearts, and our souls. It's where we can whisper to our lovers without judgment or try on new identities for size with minimal stakes. Queering things is sometimes about subverting them and making them ours, and for that reason queer people gravitate to the dark naturally. It's why so much of our cultural touchstones happen through nightlife. This darkness allows us to thrive and as we return back to it, we can think about this time as *our* season. Mabon can be about thanking the dark for all of this protection and concealment in a thanks-giving ritual or by setting an altar with all of your favorite symbols of darkness.

Mabon is about the harvest and about the feast above all else. Queers love a good party, and this does not have to be a small, intimate affair. If you've gone through this section and realize you want your Mabon to look like decadence and wider community, costumes and drag, fancy food and fancier footwork (dancing), then do it! I've spent Mabon at quiet safer spaces with chosen family and in my own apartment. I've also spent them dancing the night away and eating my weight in tater tots after a burlesque show. Some of us need quiet and space and you shouldn't feel any pressure to break loose on this or any other day. Most of us do need to cut lose once in a while though, and Mabon is a perfect reason to do so.

SAMHAIN

Samhain is the witchiest and spookiest of Sabbats, and because of that, it's so many witches' absolute favorite. I am including myself in that number. Samhain happens on October 31st and arguably over November 1st as well. This is a cross-quarter Sabbat, right between the Autumn Equinox and the Winter Solstice. It marks the end of the harvest festival so it's a good day to bring in the final fruits of your labor from the previous several seasons and store them for the next several months. It is, as all the harvest festivals are, a good day to give thanks and spoil yourself with the gains you've made. It's also, like the other harvest sabbats, a good day to take note of which seeds that you sowed grew and which ones didn't, and to recalibrate for next time.

Samhain is so exciting though because it shares space with Halloween and Day of the Dead in a number of cultures. It also shares purpose, traditions, and ritual potential with those days. Samhain is when the veil between our and other worlds is the thinnest, which makes it ideal for spirit communication and visits. It also makes it ideal for *any* magick and witchery. Any intention set or spell cast today will be heard loud and clear by the spiritual realms. Ancestor veneration and necromancy are *big* on these days, but I've also used the powerful energy for love and money spells that changed my life, too.

When a queer witch studies under me or takes one of my classes, I push them to think more deeply about queer ancestry. Statistically, there are absolutely queer people in your lineage that you may be able to connect with. For some of us that's a lot more difficult. Some of our families have intentionally written out any queerness in our family tree. For Black people, entire histories and lineages are often unknowable due to the egregious crime of slavery where, on top of everything else, those stolen had their histories intentially obscured. For adoptees or children of immigrants, it may be that any paperwork tracking is too much effort or not even possible. There are a couple of different ways you could still try to connect, especially on Samhain. You could do a spirit connection ritual to specifically seek out LGBTQQIA2SP+ ancestors from your history. You could do a similar ritual to find those ancestors in your more recent family history because again, statistically, there have probably even been a couple in the past couple of generations. You could also connect to the idea of chosen ancestry. What queer people from history do you connect

with? Could you do some research to find known queer people from your city or birthplace's history? (You probably can!) Connecting with those spirits is well aspected on Samhain. My favorite way to connect with queer ancestry though is to set a spirit reaching ritual that invites any LGBTQQIA2SP+ spirits and souls that want to connect with me to come in. That means sometimes I do get direct ancestors, and sometimes I get someone else entirely. Either way, I haven't imposed on someone who is resting peacefully and I have connected with sacred queerness.

Connection is only part of how we can reach spirits on Samhain (or anytime). In traditional lore, this is a time to honor our loved ones and ancestors who have passed on. As we feast and give thanks for the things we've grown and are now harvesting on Samhain, make sure you give thanks to any souls or spirits that have passed on who you feel have aided that growth. I built my "dead people" altar one Samhain, and update it annually on the same day. While all of the harvest days can be used as feast days, this one is notable because we're meant to leave meals and spaces at the table for those same loved ones. A prayer of thanks or love is heard easily by those spirits on this day too, so it doesn't have to be a big ordeal.

Samhain is very much a witches' Sabbat, and using this energy to grow your abilities as a witch, psychic, energy worker, or any other type of occult worker is exceedingly well aspected. Underworld or so-called dark gods love to be called on and are more accessible over this two-day period, making it a perfect time for big asks to help step into and grow your own power. While many of the Sabbats offer chances for queer witches to step into their power and grow as a person, Samhain offers this explictly for our witchcraft. While none of our spiritual practice has to be for other people, it can be. If you're developing skills to help heal and empower marginalized seekers, Samhain is a beautiful time to power up.

YULE OR WINTER SOLSTICE

Finally, we arrive at Yule on the Wheel of the Year. Yule is the Winter Solstice, happening festival style over many days. Yule begins roughly between December 20th and 23rd and lasts for approximately twelve days. Yule is when the dark half of the year gives power back to the lighter half of the year, which is now impending. Solstice night is the

longest night of the year, and things do begin getting brighter for longer, slowly but surely after this night.

Yule shares a lot of tradition and symbology with Christmas, its Christian and overpoweringly mainstream counterpart, which makes celebrating Yule an easy yet tricky thing. As a witch who does celebrate secular Christmas, learning and keeping the boundaries between each holiday took some time. Yule is specifically meant to usher in the new and coming lighter portion of the year and therefore the rebirth of the Sun as it begins to hang longer for each day. Yule feasts and bonfires are common, though bonfires in the American Midwest where I live are quite a tricky feat to find or pull off. Cozying up by the fireplace is a welcome, modern interpretation of this that still grants you the time with loved ones that both Christmas and bonfires can represent.

Any ritual that is meant to release you from a darker time or usher in a lighter time is welcome at Yule. Symbols of Yule include mistletoe, yule logs, wreaths, and bells. These are all easy to come by during the holiday season and can be easily rethought to welcome the Sun back literally or metaphorically. A lot of queer people are living in dark times right now whether that's because of given family, society, politics, the faiths they were raised in, or some combination of these factors. Queer people live with higher probabilities of trauma response and mental illness. Some queer people, like trans women of color, live with terrifying statistics and realities about their life expectancies and income caps. While a single Yule celebration can't make all of that pain shrug off and disappear, we can hold rituals that are more like a catharsis where we're letting go of some of our pain and the tight hand we hold close to our chest and agree to allow for the possibilities of lightness. It can be a day that we hold as a day to find lightness where we are and allow more to grow from there. We can do anything that releases that pain we've been holding on to, regardless of what pain may or may not resurface in the future. This is a common time of year to get into therapy or to conceive a new artwork. While those might not seem like witchy manifestations per se, they will honor our Yuletide goals of moving towards the light.

Over time, Yule and Christmas have blended together, which is both good and bad. On the plus side, Christmas is often a time to show our loved ones how much we love them with gifts, parties, and attention. I want to emphasize here that gifts do not have to be bought, expensive,

or more than a quick poppet made out of leftover cornhusks. They can be thoughtful and free, 100 percent. I love the bleedover of this into Yule and the idea of giving witchy Yule gifts that are not cost prohibitive. A kitchen witch friend made me a prosperity ornament one year. Another witchy friend regularly reads my runes around this time, giving me a gift of labor and spiritual insight that I hold very dearly. I bake a lot of enchanted Christmas cookies for people around this time, taking taste and diet into account. A beautiful idea that goes into secular Christmas is that if you give something, you get something back. This is a popular witch principle too with the rule of three, and though I don't believe in "three times three" exactly, I do think getting a rune reading in exchange for something I thoughtfully witchcrafted is an excellent, real-time example of this.

I know Christmas is so hard for so many queer people who come from unsupportive families, but as you grow as a witch you have the power to rewrite your December holiday. You can make it Yule. You can make it about welcoming the metaphor of light and relinquishing the metaphor of dark. You can kiss the genders you prefer under mistletoe knowing that it's really a symbol of metaphorical fertility—affording you many more kisses with that gender or those genders under much more mistletoe. You can use silver bells to wish away negative spirits in your home, even when those are spirits from holidays past. You can burn a Yule log in a friend's fireplace and watch the stress from the season melt away. Yule, for queer witches, is a time to remember that your life is your own and an opportunity to think about rebuilding it in your own queer, witchy image.

Creating Your Own Sabbats

A beautiful thing about queer culture is that not only can we reclaim and subvert Moon magick, Sabbats, and other traditional holy days, but we also get to make up a lot of our own touchstones, too. There is such a rich history of unique people, events, and circumstances in our own queer lives and in queer history. Magickal days abound throughout the year, between Sabbats and Full Moons and everything else if we but name and honor them. Below are examples of personal Sabbats that you can create and celebrate as seriously (or even more so) as the other times outlined in this chapter.

STONEWALL ANNIVERSARY AND PRIDE

On June 28th, 1969, queer people gathering in secret or mob-run bars got tired of police shakeups and brutality and decided to fight back, begetting three nights of riots that we continue to honor today with Pride Festivals where we celebrate and fight for LGBTQQIA2SP+ rights. These protests, known as the Stonewall riots, were led largely by trans women of color like Marsha P. Johnson, Miss Major, and Sylvia Rivera. They were supported by their community, with droves of queer people coming out over the next several days and nights to riot against the police (and by default, the laws that protected the police and outlawed any LGBTQQIA2SP+ behavior). The next year, the first Pride Parade was held in honor and memoriam of this event.

Pride Festivals today have a lot of the markings of some of the Sabbats described earlier in this chapter, such as food and drink aplenty, public affection and sexual activity, and a general feeling of celebration and festivity. This is a huge accomplishment given the pain and heartache that Pride Festivals come from. It's easy, as a queer person in 2019 to be skeptical and critical of Pride Festivals losing their meaning and giving themselves over to debauchery but I don't think that's losing their meaning at all. Pride started as a riot that now centers around peaceful protests, like being who we are, loudly and unapologetically, in the public sphere. There are still protests at a lot of Prides and there is still queer art, like drag, happening at and right outside of these festivals. There are free goodies and celebrations galore, for entire weekends—often even longer.

Still, I understand the complaint that we've fallen so very far from our roots where trans women of color were fighting against police brutality that was meant to shame and literally harm them for being their true selves. While I think Pride has deeply spiritual feelings, roots, and rituals it is okay if you don't feel that way. You can honor Stonewall in your own queer and witchy way. I often do quieter rituals as well as take part in Pride in my city. I build an altar to Marsha P. Johnson and Sylvia Rivera. I light candles for queer people who have been murdered and committed suicide that year (the ones whose names came up in the news, at least.) I have a couple of quiet nights or brunches in with close queer friends and chosen family. While Pride festivals are rich with bacchanalia imagery and spirituality, that isn't for everyone. Even if it is for you but it feels incongruent with how you feel during Stonewall's anniversary, that's okay.

This is a deeply personal day or series of days that will strike each person differently.

Regardless of how you choose to celebrate this time as a witchy time, if you do, if you give back to those who have paved a better way for all of us and set clear intentions for your Pride time, than you've marked it as a sacred Sabbat. You can expand on this—or not—as necessary, as your witchcraft grows. Because this is a time to fight for queerness and against persecution, this is a great time for gender magick, love spells, sexual intentions. Be clear about what you want, and turn it over to the queer spirits who have passed on. Then go celebrate our freedoms and protest against the ones we still don't have in whatever way feels best to you.

DEATH DAYS

Most of us have known and loved someone who has passed away, and in many cases there was a deep abiding spiritual connection that still persists. We don't lose our connections with people just because they pass on. That's why ancestral magick works too, and why you still feel a pull to some ancestors or other people you consider kin that have passed on. While we talked about what makes an ancestor and how you can work with them on Samhain, for some people Samhain doesn't work quite the way it's supposed to. For others, like me, it does, but some relationships require special note instead of just being added to the long list of people you admire who have been lost. For this, you can hold the anniversary of that person's death like a Sabbat. You can reach out, have a feast or ritual honoring them, or just update your altar by adding some favorite things of theirs.

Because Sabbats are about holding space for yourself and furthering your own intentions, it's important to remember that often the people we love or looked up to in their life can become spiritual allies after their death. The spell below is meant to help you not only honor the spirit of such a person, but also focus on how you can use their energy either literally or as an inspiration to follow your own dreams or work to have your own needs met in the short term.

A Death Day Ritual

Think about the person you are honoring. Do you know them personally? Is it someone you admired from community or other personal connection? Is it someone much more historically notable than you consider yourself? Really think about this person and your connection to them because that changes how the rest of the ritual is performed.

Once you've put the relationship between you and them in explicit words, think about what this person considered their life's work to be. How does that align with your current needs or goals? What traits did they possess that made that life's work possible?

Using the above questions as reference points, design your spell. What are you asking for, and how is this specifically the person who can help? Write out any mantras or incantations you want to use, as well as any specific things you want to tell this soul that you don't want to leave out.

Now think about this person's favorites. If it's someone you don't know personally, you might have to research to figure out if there were favorite colors, flowers, and the like, that you can use in your spell. Once you know, pull some of those things together for your ritual. If this is an ancestor or a known entity (like a celebrity or famous activist) then you might have to either guess, depending on how much you know about this person, or use standard working-with-spirits correspondences like the colors black and brown, decorative skulls, and flowers you associate with funerals.

Pick a time on this person's death day, or a day you've designated as the Sabbat to celebrate them. Bring some bread and juice or wine into the space you'll be working. Pull the correspondences from above. Sit comfortably, ideally with your back against something.

Take a few deep breaths and close your eyes. Imagine a circle of light or smoke surrounding you so that you are safe.

Once the circle is up, arrange your magickal tools the way you want them. Invite any other spiritual entities that you want to work with into the circle.

Specifically ask for the person this ritual is based around to come into the circle, be that through spirit, energy, or inspiration.

Give it a few minutes. Ask again if you need to. Verbally offer the bread and drink, the flowers, and the rest.

Once you feel their presence, talk to them. Ask for help in the intentions you realistically think they can help come true. If you wrote a mantra or incantation, use it. If you created anything specifically for this ritual, call the person's attention to it. Ask them to really see it and look at it.

Once you've said what you need to and asked for what you need to, take a deep breathe again. Invite this spirit to speak to you if it wants to. Sometimes people are clairaudient meaning they hear what spirits or spiritual entities have to say. Sometimes you'll feel what the spirit tries to say. Sometimes random images or words will pop into your head. Sometimes you'll just know something that you didn't know before. Give this several minutes, too. Just like we have to build trust in the spiritual world, it has to build trust in us, too. Your first couple of times, you might not get anything.

You will get a hunch that your ritual is done when it's time. At that time, you can thank this energy for being here and release it. Move the physical things you used for the spell to an altar. Spend some time decompressing or journaling. Talking to the dead can be incredibly emotional. Give yourself space after. Don't make plans to rush right out for happy hour. Let it sit for the evening.

Visit this altar and refill anything that needs refilled, relight candles, and the like frequently over the next few days. Always thank this person and their spirit for hearing you and helping you.

BIRTHDAYS!

I hate when non-witches ask me what my favorite holiday is, because the truth is it's my birthday, tied with the birthdays of my favorite people. Birthdays are so special because we are literally celebrating the simple fact that someone was brought into this world. For most of us, what we're actually celebrating is how this person's birth and the life they've lived has impacted us and brought us joy and sadness and empathy and intimacy. I don't officially hold everyone I love's birthday as a Sabbat, but like a good Pride festival, most of these events have the mark of one anyway. That includes debauchery, offerings (a.k.a. gifts), and often greeting cards filled with simple poems and incantations of well-wishing. When we shift our thinking about loved ones' birthdays, we realize how Pagan they inherently are. This allows us to honor that by intentionally and willfully casting easy spells of luck and success for those we are celebrating.

You can absolutely take this a step further and inform your sister, best friend, or nonbinary datemate that you are in fact throwing them a Sabbat for their birthday. In this case, your goal would be for everyone to gift them either enchanted objects, spells, and stories, or, for nonwitchy folks in attendance, gifts that would advance the birthday person's current dreams and intentions. You could do this every year, but you could also just re-up the spellwork done on the Sabbat year and carry on like a regular birthday (which is still very Sabbatish!) in following years.

Celebrating your own birthday as a Sabbat is a little bit different. When it's someone else that we love and value, we want to celebrate, bang pots and pans, and generally make a big noise. We need and should shout a hearty "thank you" to the Universe for their existence. Our own birthdays as Sabbats should be used more as a time to receive gifts and attention, but also to take stock of where we are in our life. A lot of people set New Year's resolutions that they can't or don't reach. (Congratulations, seriously, if you're in the minority of the population that does set and reach yours every year.) What ends up being more successful is declaring your birthday a Sabbat where you're meant to look at your life plan, your short- and long-term goals, and assess where you are. This is the perfect time to make commitments (not resolutions) for business, spirit, and pleasure over the next year to further your ultimate goals. Once this work is done, go party! (Whatever that means to

you.) Treat yourself to those glittery Doc Martens you've been eyeing or even just a fancy cold press. Let your friends spoil and celebrate you. Remember, especially as queer people who have faced a huge pile of rejections in almost every area of their life, that you deserve this. Your soul, your heart, and your body are worthy of a Sabbat, too. Let yourself shine on your birthday of all days.

OTHER PERSONAL TIME MARKERS

In case you haven't gotten the hang of this section, any day that is special and important to you can be held as special and holy, potentially even reaching Sabbat status. If you are a trans person and you want to celebrate when you announced your true name, gender, or both, the date you started Hormone Replacement Therapy (HRT), a surgery date, or any other date that has been critical, special, and worthy of celebration on your path, do it! Set aside the day for gender magick and revelry. Bring together all of the most supportive people you know and have all of them bring you well wishes and gender-affirming gifts.

Anniversaries of relationships that changed our lives can also be big—for anyone, sure—but especially for queer people whose greatest loves are not limited to romance or sex but certainly can include those things. It's pretty common to celebrate anniversaries, including friendship anniversaries, in this day and age, but you can add magick and imagination to any of them to take it a step further. While my queerplatonic partner and I do celebrate the anniversary of the night we met, we also celebrate a day called "Otter Day," which is the day, about seven years ago, when an incredibly obese otter ran by, stared at us for a minute, and ran off. We don't live in an otter heavy area and the whole thing was strange and hilarious. We use this day to honor the playful spirit of the otter, do something ridiculous, and bring the idea of "strange and hilarious" into our daily lives. Anniversary Sabbats are not at all limited, but do choose them carefully. When you love someone and share a life with them in any capacity, the important anniversaries can pile up. Remember that a prayer or even a wish can be a spell too, and that you do not have to celebrate every magickal occurrence every year if you do find that your special days with your college roommate are starting to outnumber the not-special ones.

When I was twenty-one and had already been an undergrad for way too long, I decided to move halfway across the country to finish school. It prolonged my education but got me out of several toxic and unsafe situations all at once. As a stepping stone, I moved in with my queerplatonic partner and their grandma in a state I hadn't lived in yet. I celebrate two days as Sabbats every year: "Escaped Mars Hill Day" where I left the oppressive school and small town that was choking me, and "Moved to Iowa Day" where I got to start my life over again as a genuinely out, queer, and proud person with resources to start moving on from my trauma. While my degree means a lot to me, I actually don't even remember what day I finally graduated college, what day I started reading tarot professionally, or when I got on the arthritis meds that made my current life possible. For LGBTQQIA2SP+ people, the time markers we note and the instances that change our lives don't look like what we'd expect. On the surface, moving from North Carolina to Tennessee for one summer doesn't seem that important. It was the first step into taking my life back, though, and for that it deserves a Sabbat.

I say all of this just to say that you know your life better than anyone. You know what days stand out as life changing and which ones do not. You know, in your soul, which ones are worth marking as Sabbats and which ones are not.

Journal Prompt

Think back through your life over the past couple of years. What dates and instances seem noteable and, in your mind, Sabbat worthy? Journal about those dates and how they changed your life. Go further back if you feel comfortable doing so and do the same thing. Once you've written about how these times changed your life, think about your understanding of Sabbats. How could each of these days be signified and celebrated as a Sabbat? What might your rituals look like? What idea would you be celebrating and how? Take some time after this journaling to do mini-rituals on these things now, and then stick them in your calendar for next year.

MADE-UP HOLIDAYS

Did you know that January 2nd is Science Fiction Day? I don't celebrate this most years, but one year I'd recently reread some Octavia Butler work that fired up my activism to the point of no return, so I bought some flowers and orange candles and thanked her for everything she's done for me. Many of us know March 14th as Pie Day, a day where we literally just . . . eat pie. For kitchen witches this could be a great pie-baking day, and for the rest of us it's an excuse to laugh with our friends at our favorite diner. There's literally no end to days like this. There was a notable day in the past year that I saw referred to as a day of visibility for a queer identity, a day of doughnuts, and several other seemingly notable things all at once. They are literally piling up on top of each other. As people trying to navigate through this wild Internet time, it can seem overwhelming or like it's too much. It can also be . . . fun? You definitely don't have to celebrate all or any of these, and certainly not as Sabbats. But you can.

If I were a Virgo or a Capricorn I would tell you to use Google Search to find a list of such wacky holidays and note the ones you want to use as a Sabbat. As a double Pisces I'm just gonna tell you to do what feels right. Follow online pages for your favorite silly days, or just put them in your calendar for next year when they come up this year. If they come up unexpectedly, you could even move your afternoon meeting and go get some pie. It's up to you how you navigate this, but one thing I absolutely love about some of these days is that they give us more reasons to do something fun, eat good food, or spend some unexpected time in spellcraft that we desperately needed.

There are obviously exceptions to my flippant-but-accepting attitude towards these days. For queer people especially, days of Visibility and National Coming Out Day can be and often are *huge* deals. The pressure to come out on those days can be intense, and they don't need to be used for that. I came out slowly, one person or group of people at a time until suddenly there was no one left and I was just . . . out. National Coming Out Day then is a celebration of that coming out to me, not a day to pressure others to do so. On those days of visibility I sometimes try to help someone else on their journey just by being outspoken about who I am. They can also be times when I quietly give thanks to my gods for making me this way and allowing me to live in a time and space

where it's possible. Not everyone is or will ever be that far on their journey. If you are one of the lucky ones, do try to give thanks or give back on these days. If you're still struggling, celebrate yourself by looking for those allies and resources that might help you practically or emotionally on these days.

There are some made-up holidays that predate marriage equality and this dada age of the Internet, like Earth Day and Arbor Day. As witches, we are responsible for guarding and giving back to the Earth. In the early stages of your witchery, I would set these days aside as Sabbats so you can at least learn more about the dangers facing the Earth and our trees, and how they may affect you personally in even a short amount of time. Additionally, we have a responsibility to take care of and help each other. Martin Luther King Jr. Day or Juneteenth, for example, are days when non-Black allies should do some reading and develop a plan to help racial justice movements (that aren't rooted in white saviorism or other tools of white supremacy). Black witches should take this time however they need to, holding it as a Sabbat for planning direct action, or celebrating who they are or what that they've been through, or anything else they feel they need to do. Similarly, Indigenous People's Day is starting to sweep the United States as a replacement for Columbus Day, finally. Allies should really do the homework *and* the work of allyship on this day, and Indigenous People can celebrate themselves (or not) however they wish.

ASTROLOGY

Astrology is basically defined as "the study of the movements and relative positions of celestial bodies interpreted as having an influence on human affairs and the natural world." We'll talk about personal astrology in the next chapter, but for now when I talk about astrology I mean following those celestial bodies as they move through time and space currently. The reason I have such a long chapter on magickal timing is because it's incredibly influential in our magickal practice. For a long time, one missing piece of that was noting what the stars and planets were doing above us and how it shaped our life and magick here on Earth from day to day. For example, if it's Virgo Season, meaning the Sun is in Virgo, any working for career, home, or close friendships (people forget how fiercely loyal Virgos are) is immediately well aspected. If you're looking to make big, chaotic changes in your life, this Sun may not

be the time to do it, as Virgo is incredibly steadfast and Earth prefers to move slowly over time.

Astrology can get incredibly complicated, and that's why a lot of witches get overwhelmed and don't use it in their spellcraft. We're finally starting to see some resources that demystify it though, and even just learning what the Sun and Moon are doing can alter your spells for the better. It's usually easy to know where the Sun is. The Zodiac Calendar moves as follows:

Aries ♈	March 21st–April 19th
Taurus ♉	April 20th–May 20th
Gemini ♊	May 21st–June 20th
Cancer ♋	June 21st–July 22nd
Leo ♌	July 23rd–August 22nd
Virgo ♍	August 23rd–September 22nd
Libra ♎	September 23rd–October 22nd
Scorpio ♏	October 23rd–November 21st
Sagittarius ♐	November 22nd–December 21st
Capricorn ♑	December 22nd–January 19th
Aquarius ♒	January 20th–February 18th
Pisces ♓	February 19th–March 20th

During the time of the Zodiac sign, that's where the sun is. It really is that simple. The moon is different. It changes signs roughly every three days, and usually you need a Moon Tracking app, an astrological planner for the year, or to bookmark a website that tracks the Moon's astrological actions to know. You could also use my super official method of using Google Search to find "What sign is the moon in?" every time you need to know. Once you start digging into the witchcraft junction of the Internet, it gets a lot easier. I can't remember the last day that went by where I didn't see a tweet about what the moon was doing in some capacity. It might take you a while to build up those resources, but know that this isn't knowledge anyone should just expect you to

have. Schedule in some research time to use Google Search for relevant astrology before you do a spell, and after a while you'll get the hang of astrological timing fairly innately.

Pop astrology has really taken off over the past few years, and there might be a few other planetary and zodiac motions you're aware of. Mercury Retrograde is probably the most pervasive. The fear around Mercury Retrograde has been really overblown, but it can have very real effects on our lives. Mercury is a planet that deals with communication, travel, and technology. Retrograde means that a planet appears to be moving backwards because of how Earth is aligned with the rest of the planets. Astrologically, that means that anything that the planet is supposed to help with can suddenly become disastrous. Mercury Retrograde can see major communication mishaps, technological malfunctions, and travel plans getting blown apart. Yet the planets really don't mean to break our lives apart. Usually a retrograde serves to bring existing problems to light, and that's a useful thing to know for your magickal practice. Mercury Retrograde wants us to learn to make backup plans and get our cars serviced regularly, to continue working on our communication skills, and to learn how to be flexible when ultimately those things still fail us. Spells to allow for fluidity and flexibility during Mercury Retrograde can be incredibly effective, as can spells meant to open our minds so we can see how other people are thinking and experience empathy instead of annoyance if words fail one or both parties.

Any planet can be retrograde, so you may want to do precautionary searches before diving into spellwork. If I'm setting up a love spell but I find out Venus is retrograde, I will either wait to do the spell *or* ask Venus to help me find love in unexpected and maybe even silly ways. Retrograde is not the only thing that affects how the planets influence your spellwork though, and if this part of the book is exciting to you I strongly encourage you to continue learning and doing astrological work to help with your spellcraft. Other astrological occurrences to research might include figuring out when planets that you think affect you a lot are conjunct (meaning they're in the same sign), or trine, when multiple planets are in angles to support each other.

Seasonal Shifts and Changes

Of all of the magickal timing we'll discuss in this chapter, none affects my magick more personally than the simple climate, weather, and seasons happening outside of my window. Your magick should support what's happening in the natural world and vice versa. As witches, we are meant to ebb and flow with nature. As queer witches, we should be actively working to pull away from societal constructs and constraints and learn to flow with our own bodies and desires. These are very often affected by the seasons more than anything else. The Sabbats in each season are set to support the season itself, and again, vice versa. Still, if you can't imagine after reading this chapter that you can keep track of *any* of this, following simple seasonal cues will help.

SPRING

Spring is a time for new growth and new life. When the snow melts and the weather starts warming up, it's time to think about where your life needs something new or some growth and to set your magickal intentions for it during this time. Spring is also when people living in really frigid places start leaving their homes again and see their Seasonal Affective Disorder melt away, meaning any community or group workings are starting to come together for potentially the first time of the year. Healing work is good in Spring, especially if it's healing parts of you that are holding you back from the joy and ecstasy that you might see the rest of your queer friends engaging in.

SUMMER

Summer is about new connections, summer fun, and showing off. Any glamours, gender magick, or confidence boosting spells are well received here. Working with Sun deities is, too. Sex, love, and big wish magick are met beautifully in Summer months. For queer people, this might be a time where we take our goals and intentions for queer community or activism that we set during Spring and do the magick of putting them into tangible actions. It's also the time to focus your sex magick on anything kinky or quirky that you're looking for, and to widen your circle of queer collaborators, co-workers, or chosen family.

AUTUMN

Autumn is when things start dying, school starts back up, and we start planning for the mainstream holidays and embracing that chill in the air. Magick in Autumn can be about harvesting, about learning new skills (magickally or otherwise), or learning to work with the weather itself in your witchcraft as it shifts and changes. Just like each passing school year denotes a year we have grown and learned, taking time each Autumn to see where we are as students of life (as corny as I know that sounds) is a great idea and can help us figure out what intentions to set in our next several rounds of spellwork.

WINTER

Winter is about resting, resetting, and hibernating. This is our best season for solo magick, for magick meant for ourselves and not the collective, and for honoring darkness by doing shadow work or working with gods considered to be dark. For queer people or anyone who's been marginalized, this is a beautiful time for scheming how to best hex the patriarchy or to look at how much we've overcome and map out how we're going to keep healing next. This is a good time for healing work too, for yourself and others.

Subverting what seasons mean to you is also completely acceptable. I do not do well when the world is at its hottest, so I do a lot of my sexier witchcraft in Spring when I'm trying to heal the things that hold me back sexually, or in Autumn when I'm looking to get cozy with someone new. Autumn itself has always bought fresh, new energy into my life whereas Spring, for whatever reason, usually allows me to continue working intentions I've already set. Shadow work is work I do consistently, regardless of season. When I described the seasons and how we can use them magically, I meant only to give you a basic framework to start from. Like any framework or structure that anyone throws at us, queer or otherwise, we have the power and the self-knowledge to take the parts we like and rewrite the parts we don't. Witchcraft is a queer, marginalized person's way of writing their own life in their own way, and you don't have to subscribe to any certain magickal element in any certain way to do that.

Journal Prompt:

Seasonal Witchcraft

Journal about the season you are currently living in, and how it both inspires and disappoints you. Where in your body do you feel your positive feelings right now? Where do you feel your negative ones? What do you think of this season? What are positive things that have happened to you so far in this season? What are negative things that have happened to you? What does that tell you about the kind of magick you might best utilize right now? Do some additional journaling on ways you think you can perform magick that fits into the season.

5

TOWARDS A
DIY WITCHCRAFT

You don't have to be an expert on queer community to see that LGBTQQIA2SP+ people, especially trans people, live in disporportionate amounts of poverty. That means that a lot of books about witchcraft (even those aimed at beginners) aren't a good fit. Those books strongly suggest buying certain things or starting a loop of unending reading and research that is both overwhelming and expensive. Even later in this book, my correspondence lists do include stones, herbs, and the like that you might want to buy. This isn't necessary for a holistic witchcraft practice though, and it's not even the most common or visible way witches are doing magick anymore.

The aesthetic of the DIY movement and the aesthetic of queer culture are almost interchangeabe. DIY stands for Do-It-Yourself and brings to mind things like zine making, handmade pronoun pins, and t-shirts that say "Hex the Patriarchy" that your friend ran off in her garage. There's a punk rock look to the whole thing that's appealing even when you're an introvert who would rather listen to pop music. That appeal comes from the look and fuck-the-man attitude itself, but it also comes from the connection of having handmade, community-focused things by your side. That's a type of spell too, keeping mementos from your community close by and it's a starter point into DIY witchcraft.

DIY witchcraft is essentially my same basic principle that everything is magick, but more formalized and reigned in for specific spells. It can pull from the DIY movement and punk rock feeling that we've been talking about, but it can also be something that incorporates a shell you found on the beach or a potholder that your great-grandmother knitted. It's not an anything goes movement, per se, because there's still an art and a learning curve to it. Anyone who says witchcraft has to be a certain way or a

certain thing is full of it, and you shouldn't listen to them, but there does need to be a consistency with your practice. In the above examples, shells are still associated with water. That potholder is still best used for kitchen and ancestral magick. Yet DIY witchcraft does rely much more on personalized understandings of symbols, connections, and interpretations, which makes it a ready-made witchcraft style for queer people.

A lot of times the tried and true symbols that bring straight and cisgender people a lot of success in our society mean little, or worse, mean something triggering or harmful to queer people. In the tarot (which can also be used for spellwork), the Hierophant is traditionally a Papal figure that represents a teacher, leader, or healer. For a queer person coming out of a strict Christian upbring, which so many of us were, this figure is harmful no matter how many positive vibes we are told to associate with it. While it makes sense to read that card to be about leaders in the queer community, there are tons of other cards that those leaders can be ascribed to too. Trying to force someone to see this symbol of Christian supremacy as something positive won't work. A lot of symbolism and tools used in witchcraft work the same way. Symbols meant to protect the home could remind you of an abusive upbringing. While I love and thrive in money attraction magick, a lot of queer people who are hurt and disadvantaged in our monetary system might see dollar signs carved into their abundance candles as hypocritical or even harmful to their goals. Instead, they might create a sigil that represents having stable housing and enough food to share, or find charms that represent those things to them. That's DIY witchcraft, which you were probably doing all along.

The most obvious case for creating DIY symbols and therefore spells comes from the prevalence of what I call *womb worship* magick. Womb worship comes from the idea that the womb or vagina is somehow a magickal powerhouse that connects you to goddess energy and the Earth itself because it can create life. This type of magick is used in everything from the aforementioned money magick to sex magick and love spells to, inexplicably, workings meant to create a more just and equitable world. This is a really damaging point of view.

For starters, we all hold our magick in different places. Some of the most feminist and cisgender women I know frown loudly at the idea that their strongest magick is held in their reproductive system. In some ways

this is anti-feminist, because it says that their greatest value resides in the baby-making parts. Cis women's hearts, brains, arms, stomachs, and so on, are just as strong and magickal and hold just as much value as their uterus and for some cis women, more so. None of this even touches on the idea that this is a dangerously transphobic idea and one that excludes nonbinary people and queer, effiminate men at best and seeks to elim-inate them at worst. Some of the most magickal women I know do not have vaginas. Some of the most Goddess-inspired practitioners I know have penises.

Womb worship also doesn't factor in that some people also deal with trauma and angst around their genitals. For people with vaginas who are survivors of sexual assault, who have body dysmorphia that disconnects them from their body entirely, who are struggling with gender dyspho-ria, who struggle with medical trauma or have lost children, or who have shame and fear around their reproductive system, this kind of magick is never going to serve them. In trying to root them in their vagina or uterus, this kind of witchcraft can push them further away from spirituality that they could easily have full access to. Gender lives in the heart, mind, and soul and so does our witchcraft. There is no need to root it in sexual organs and doing so damages the idea of witchcraft for countless already trau-matized and oppressed people.

I could rant about womb worship forever but why it's so relevant in DIY witchcraft is that our mythos and philosophy are so shaped by how prevalent this practice is, that to move away from it and come into our power differently we almost *have to* move to a DIY inspired practice. Sym-bols, charms, and tools that represent our gender to us, that represent where in our body we feel like our magick is stored, and that represent the goals of the workings we are doing, is the way out from under prescribed, transphobic writings. Unfortunately, because there aren't a lot of gender rebels writing witchcraft books, we have to create it for ourselves. You can do that, though, and in rewriting your own connection and history to your body you are rooting yourself in your spiritual practice.

While there are very few gender and sexuality rebels writing about writing your own witchcraft books, we *do* know there are common symbols and representations that we can incorporate into our spellcraft. Here's a list of common queer culture symbols, ideas, or subversions you can include in your witchcraft and how I see some magickal correspondences.

If my correspondences don't work for you, don't stress. Make your own. If you have an open distaste for anything I list, that's fine, too. Ignore it, and work to include things that represent your own gender or sexuality into your work. Use this as a jumping off point.

- Performing spells in drag, especially if you're doing work to ease transition or change how people see you. You could either play the gender you are to a heightened drag performance, or play with a gender you perceive as the total opposite of yours to bring a specific element into your craft.

- Masturbation, especially to orgasm. We've talked about this some and we'll talk about it again, but it's worth mentioning here.

- Using cold press instead of hot coffee in any spell that calls for coffee. You could also do new spells with cold press, like instead of connecting it to Earth like you would coffee, connecting cold press to the "get up and go" qualities of air.

- Rainbows in any art spells or in any spells that require charms to indicate your gender and sexuality. These are especially useful in spells that require or emphasize strength, healing, and, alternatively, legislative change turning in our favor.

- Glitter is fun in any glamour, which is a type of spell where we reflect a certain vision of ourselves to the outside world. This comes up in glamours about gender and sexuality, especially. Glitter can also be used for any spell about creating *fun* and escaping from a cruel world in our space-making work.

- Condoms or dental dams for shielding and banishing especially in the cases of queer exes.

- During the holocaust, LGBTQQIA2SP+ prisoners were made to wear an upside down triangle and treated especially terribly as a result. Now that triangle has become a symbol of overcoming oppression and refusing to separate our identities from ourselves even in dangerous times, and that can absolutely be used in related spellwork.

- Lube can be used as a candle dressing or water element in any spell where we're trying to make something easier for ourselves or others.

- Poppers, (a *mostly* legal drug that can be inhaled and is thought to have physically relaxing qualities, especially regarding the sphincter) can be used in place of alcohol as gifts to our gods, especially gods who we know are queer. They can also be used in spells to attract sexual partners, if poppers are something we like to use during sex.

- In kitchen magick, brunch is a great stand-in to feed your fellow witches and do some herb witchery since brunch is such a staple of queer community.

- Bricks and chunks of cement can represent defiance, revolution, and the like especially when we connect them to the Stonewall riots and the found objects those queer ancestors used to create immediate rebellion and change.

- Art, music, and writing by queer artists. I try to match the piece to whatever my spell is for, but anything by someone who inspires you or speaks to your spell is wonderful to use.

- I have a specific hanky code charm in the grimoire for this book, but know that the bandanas or hankies used for flagging can also work great in spells! The hanky code (for those who don't know) is the act of wearing different colored bandanas on different sides of your body to signify which sexual acts you're interested in. It is also referred to as *flagging*.

- The color purple normally represents creativity, but it can absolutely represent queer identity and be used for any spellwork that your identity is critical for.

- Beyond rainbows, *any* flag (or the colors of it) that you identify with can be used in your spellwork, especially if the work relates to your gender or sexuality that the flag represents.

Journaling Exercise

Before you continue with this chapter and book, take a few moments and take out whatever tools you're using for your exercises in this book. Take a deep breath if you're physically able to, and close your eyes. Where in your body do you feel like magick is stored? Take a few notes about what your body is telling you, and then do your deep breathing with closed eyes again.

This time, ask what symbols represent those parts of the body to you? What images does feeling your magick in that part of your body bring up to you?

Now, think about your next couple of sets of magickal intentions. How do you see those represented? What symbols, images, or spiritual allies pop into your mind for them?

Take all of these notes and remember that things change. Gender, sexuality, and how our bodies speak to us may all be fluid, so check in with yourself every so often about this, especially if you feel like something has changed or feels blocked in some way.

DIY Witchcraft is also perfect for those looking to connect with their ancestors or those they love who have passed on. While things like tombstones and flowers are relatively universal, nothing relies on a personal touch quite the way working with dead people does. Doing spirit work or death work means acknowledging each soul as an individual, so your tokens, pictures, and offerings will probably look wildly different than your best witch friend's. That's how it's supposed to be. Whether you are doing a spell to call on those spirits or are setting up an altar to honor those you love, go through your belongings. What heirlooms or personal gifts from those people to you can you include? Did your college mentor or close grandparent have a favorite cookie? Make a batch of those. Eat some, and leave some out as an offering.

As a white person, I am very aware that not all of my ancestors were good people. For me to be here, in the United States, they had to be colonizers and therefore relatively unscrupulous. Part of my work with my ancestors is recognizing this unscrupulous behavior and using it as motivation in my anti-racist and pro-Earth workings. It's my job to reconcile and

to try to make right the things that my ancestors did that weren't great. I'm also an optimist when it comes to the afterlife and how souls come to terms with their behavior here on Earth, and I think my ancestors know now that moving here and taking this land and doing who even knows what else was not okay. I think they're trying to use me as a tool to right their wrongs, and that's a responsibility I think white people in general need to take seriously if they're going to work with their familial ancestors. As you're building a relationship with those ancestors, should you choose to, you'll need to find symbols, images, or tools that speak of reconciliation and anti-racism to include in your work. Like our sexuality and gender magick, that often has to come down to DIY practices because there's not a lot in our witchcraft canon that speaks to those things.

Most people have people in their family tree they aren't proud of, even if your ancestors weren't colonizers. Statistically speaking, we probably *all* have a murderer, a sexual assaulter, and a handful of abusers if we go down our family lines far enough. There's a couple of ways to work your ancestral magick here. You can actively choose not to work with those spirits, especially if you're concerned with letting that energy into your home. You can work instead with those ancestors that you feel called and closest to. You can work with those ancestors to try to understand and make up for what they've done by figuring out some DIY things to place on their altar. You can also work with those ancestors, using that anger and rage but funneling it into productive things like taking care of our Earth or protecting your trans siblings. All of that will require you to find your own way in terms of calling in and representing those energies.

Ancestor work does not always mean our literal, immediate ancestry though, and assuming it does leaves out those who have been adopted or the countless queer people who are estranged from their families of origin and wouldn't be able to get the information about literal ancestors that they would need for this kind of work. *For those people and anyone else who wants to look at ancestry through a DIY lens*, there are the chosen ancestors. These can be queer radicals and fighters like Harvey Milk and Marsha P. Johnson. They can be specific people from your hometown who fought conservative city councils to open up gay bars or spaces for BIPOC. They can be the ancestors of people in your chosen family that you have a really solid connection with. I have a high school

friend who's also a lesbian now who had an aunt that I really believe saw and loved us both for who we are. I consider her my ancestor too, and her ancestors are ones I'm willing to work with. There are friends who were like family to me that have passed on that I revere as ancestors even though I knew them personally and intimately. That personal connection is not a hindrance to your craft at all, and in fact, sits right in the center of ancestor work.

Using ancestor work and therefore DIY spellcraft also means deciding what kind of workings you're doing with those energies, because that changes the DIY elements of your craft, too. Are you directly calling those spirits into your home or circle? That means you most likely want a picture or personal belonging that the spirit or ancestor touched or has direct connection to. Do you only want to call on a queer or radical ancestor's energy to inspire your own fight? For that you don't need a personal element, but you do need things that represent the fire and the fight that you're hoping to take on.

I've primarily talked about specific, common forms of DIY witchcraft, because they are the kinds of magick that almost always require us to use DIY principles. This type of witchcraft is also accessible and useful for *any* spellwork that you want to do, and I cannot emphasize that enough. Almost all of the witchcraft I do is centered around personal items and DIY designs, and the bulk of my work is successful. Think about your next few rounds of magickal intentions, and use the worksheet below when you feel the time is right. That will be used to help you build your own spells, available in the next section.

DIY Witchcraft Worksheet

1. How involved of a spell do you feel ready to pull together? Full circle, multiple elements, and some gods? Or something simple and easy?

2. What *is* your next or most recent magickal intention? Are you sowing seeds? Making big wishes? Improving confidence? Healing?

3. To you, what images, tools, or symbols represent that intention? It should be totally personal, not something researched and regurgitated.

4. What personal belongings do you have that you could either charm with your spell's intention or use to amplify or build your spell?

5. Is there anything else you own that you want to add? Look over where we've been in this book thus far. What else will help aid your magickal intention?

6. Pull all of those things together in a space where you can safely and comfortably work some magick. Now that you're seeing them all together, is there anything that you want to add or take away? Do that.

7. I want you to have a concrete list of personal correspondences you can rely on. Think about the main kinds of magick that you plan on working with. Examples include money magick, sex magick, attraction magick, protection magick, healing magick, and so much more. Take a few minutes to jot some quick notes about things you already own that you associate with those spells or ideas. Take your time. Come back to this.

Designing Your Own Spells

The worksheet prior to this section should have given you the time and space for brainstorming to help you build your own spells, but I know for a lot of starter witches or even those like myself who are experienced but just like having formulas to work with, it's not quite enough. Below is a formula you can use exactly as is to create your own DIY spells with some ideas from chapter 1 thrown back in. You can also tweak this formula to do what works for you, since that's the whole purpose of this chapter. Don't get caught up in the specifics I outline, but do know what your own specifics will look like. Intuitive practice is intuitive and personal, but that doesn't mean it's not also a practice that requires learning, patience, and sometimes, repetition.

1. Decide what energies you're working with in this spell. Are you working with gods? Faeries? The Moon? The guardians of the watchtowers of the elements? Your great-great-great-great grandfather's spirit? You can use as many of the spiritual entities that you're familiar with that you want too, but for beginners

I do recommend keeping it to three or fewer to start (with the understanding that the watchtowers, your ancestors, the faeries, and a number of other energies may be used as a single element or energy—or not).

2. What represents those entities to you? What do you already own that would call on those energies and spirits?

3. Decide based on the above two steps what kind of spell this will be. Is this a kitchen spell that will require some baking and attention? Is this a circle spell that requires mantras or chants? Is it a simple mantra and a charm stuck in your wallet? What do you feel ready for and called to for this spell? Build the rest of your spell accordingly. Look over the types of spells in chapter 1, or read ahead to get some new ideas.

4. Is there anything else that you feel like you really need to acquire for your spell to work? If you don't have any money, is there a way to acquire it? Perhaps you can borrow from a friend or find one naturally outside. If you can't acquire it otherwise, get creative. Why do you feel like you need this, and is there an easier substitute? If you do have the money, please do buy whatever you need to, but there's usually a cheaper way if you're willing to research.

5. When you feel like you have everything you need, start writing your spell. Put everything in a logical order and list out the steps you'll need to take. If you're doing a circle and a poppet while you're in the circle, put that in a logical order. If you're doing an outdoor spell, make sure to note when and where so you'll be undisturbed by passersby or law enforcement. If your ideas change as you write out the spell, that's okay. Flexibility is key for witchcraft and sometimes we have to let our subconscious mind call the shots.

6. Sit on the spell for a few days. There's no wrong way to do a spell, especially a DIY spell, but you do want to give it space to evolve.

7. Come back to it in a few days. Make any tweaks that you feel are necessary. In that moment, plan a time and space for that spell.

8. Perform the spell!

9. I do strongly recommend tracking your spellwork somehow, be it in a journal or official grimoire or Book of Shadows. If you're not a writer, a quick sketch of the spell will suffice, or even just scribbling out some basic words that will jog your memory. You'll love looking back at your work later, but writing it out is also a form of strengthening the spell and giving it a permanent space to keep working long after you blow your (literal or metaphorical) candles out.

6

TO PRAY OR
NOT TO PRAY

Working with my gods is a foundational and fulfilling cornerstone of my spiritual practice, but it's not something I came to easily. I identified as a Christian Witch for a long time, and then kind of shunned all deities for a while. I didn't want anything that felt like "God," because that energy (or at least, his people) had broken my spirit, victim-blamed me for an assault, and made me feel like that type of spirituality was not for me. I felt like I didn't deserve it, and I forced myself to stop believing in it. My witchcraft worked just fine on its own, taking from my energy and the energy of my environment. I fell back into working with gods really naturally and I'm not even sure what the instigating factor was. Over time I've found the gods to be an important and vital part of my healing, growth, and ability to thrive, and I have altars to several that I maintain in my home. My journal is full of prayers and I speak even more of them. I feel loved, supported, and fulfilled by the gods I work with, and it's an amazing place to be after years of struggle.

While I know firsthand how meaningful working with gods is, it's nothing I would ever force on anyone else. I think all of us have a connection to the Divine and to Spirit, but if you don't feel yours right now, that's okay. It might grow or you might never feel it. There's not a wrong way to approach witchcraft except with bad intent. If you feel like working with gods and goddesses isn't for you, that is one hundred percent okay. You do you. Skip this chapter, or use it purely for informational purposes. I love reading about gods I don't work with, and maybe you will too. If not, I won't be offended.

For the rest of us, I want to emphasize that when you're looking for gods and other spiritual entities to work with, please start with the pantheons that your own ancestors would have worked with. Cultural

appropriation is a huge problem in the Pagan community, and it's not okay to take something from a culture you have no ties to and claim it as your own. In my experience of working with clients for over a decade, I've found that these callings are mostly false. They are gods that the person likes or thought were interesting, but there was no real connection or wake-up call that led them to that deity. Obviously, there are exceptions. I work very closely with Hecate, a Greek Goddess, and I'm not Greek. Greek mythology was foundational to my learning curve as a Pagan, and I meditated for months before starting my work with her. I say this to emphasize that there are exceptions, but it takes a lot of contemplation and time in prayer to be sure that you're getting a genuine calling.

Of course, everything is myth. Our entire wealth of knowledge about gods and goddesses is all rooted in stories and epic poems. Which means that you might feel like you're getting a calling to a deity of a culture that isn't appropriated, but it's really a calling to a god closer to your lineage that we just haven't heard as much about. Do your research—you might be surprised to see where you're being led.

Some people who are in no way ancestrally connected to a place *might* otherwise really, truly get a calling to work with that place's gods for a number of reasons. Maybe you lived there, giving back to that community and worshipping with other practitioners. It's certainly okay to continue this practice after the fact. You might really be getting a unique or special calling to work with gods because you started that faith in a past life, or just because that god really does want you. Always make sure you're honoring such gods, not just asking them for things. Make sure your practice is about a private relationship, not a public display. Make sure you learn about the cultures that those gods come from and try to give back to and serve those communities. Work with deities does move your magick away from being all about you. For collective spellwork that's really important, and for using your privileges and blessings to help others it can be critical. You've got to be ready for that step though, and in the meantime, there should still be non-appropriative gods for you to work with.

Below is a list of gods with ties to the LGBTQQIA2SP+ community that you can look into or research. I've also listed a couple that are not queer-aligned per se, but are deeply concerned with justice, including and especially social justice. I think these are really powerful gods for queer people to work with because the foundations of our practice are that we're

seeking justice for ourselves and our communities. Gods don't care about human law—they care about what is right, and they are more than happy to align with queer witches doing social justice and empowerment work.

As a final note, this is a short list of gods I'm already familiar with or that someone I know well works intimately (and appropriately) with. Use Google Search to find "queer gods" and you're sure to come up with even more. I also want to point out that gods are above human mores and laws. Any god you'll want to work with will range from "ambivalent" to "enthusiastic" about your sexual and gender identity. Any god willing to offer you aid and comfort will affirm you in meditations and workings—but it's still nice to use those who are queer or known to be allied as a jumping off point.

LGBTQQIA2SP+ or LGBTQQIA2SP+ Aligned Gods

- **Athena**—Greek Goddess of Wisdom and Justice (potentially asexual)

- **Baron Semedi**—Voodoo parent of Ghede Nibo, often portrayed as trans, bi, or both

- **Brigid**—Celtic Goddess of Healing, Poetry, and those who have been othered

- **Dionysus**—Greek God of Wine, Theatre, and Gender and Sexual Fluidity

- **Ghede Nibo**—Voodoo Iwa often seen as a drag queen, inspires sexuality in others, especially lesbian acts

- **Loki**—Norse Trickster God, prone to genderbending

- **Lucifer**—Satanic Deity associated with lust and owning one's sexuality

- **Ma'at**—Egyptian Goddess of Truth and Justice

- **Pan**—Greek and Celtic God of Music; forest-dwelling Satyr and known bisexual

- **Papa Legba**—Haitian Vodou Loa (with other faces seen in other cultures) who served as an intermediary between loa and humans— seen as male and female, often at the same time

- **Samodivi**—Eastern European bisexual spirits; nymph, siren, harpy combos

- **Santa Muerte**—Mexican Saint/Deity who looks out for LGBTQQIA2SP+ seekers

- **Set and Horus**—Egyptian Gods of War and Sky, respectively; both have myths about having sex with male figures—including each other

- **Shikhandi**—Hindu war hero who's also transgender

- **The Morrighan**—Celtic Goddess of War, Fate, and Sovereignty

- **Tu Er Shen**—Chinese Rabbit Diety who oversees homosexual love and sex

Once you've decided that you want to work with deities, take some time to do some deep meditations and journaling on what gods may be calling out to you. Pay attention to external cues. A lot of the gods have animals associated to them, so if you're constantly running into certain animals or animal symbols, it may be that animal's god trying to get in touch with you. The gods may show up in dreams, or show up as a form they've shapeshifted into in a meditation. As queer witches, it's okay to set the intention for a queer god to call you and to start your journey with deities there.

Once you know who you are working with, set up an altar to them—at least a small one. Do some research to find this god or spiritual entity's favorite herbs, flowers, or symbols and set them somewhere visible in your home. From there your witchcraft, grimoire writing, meditations, and prayers can become more targeted. The joy of being a Pagan or witch is that we don't have to stick to one god, one group of gods, or one pantheon. I have been practicing for well over half of my life, and I received a new calling this year. I will most likely receive several more throughout my life. It's important not to overwhelm yourself by trying to get to know several at once, but as many as you feel you can handle and you feel genuinely called to is just fine.

I want to emphasize again as strongly as I can that gods are not solely there to grant our wishes. If you want to work with them, you need to be willing to have a deep ongoing relationship with them and enter into an agreement where sometimes, you will do *their* will instead of the other

way around. *Most* gods will not ruin your life if you behave selfishly or as if they exist only to make your dreams come true. Some will, but many will simply stop working with you. Your magick will become much less powerful, and you may even start to feel the absence of that spiritual presence. Your prayers, grimoire writing, and the like should be focused on relationship building first. Give yourself and the god and or goddess time to figure each other out. Start tributing them, and then, when the time is right (and you'll know) or you just really need them, you can start working *with* them to enact your will in your craft.

7

QUEER DIVINATION

Learning divination starts with understanding how it works. Divination is the art of combining your intuition with a learnable tool or skill set, like tarot, palm reading, or I Ching. Not every witch becomes a diviner of any kind, but for a lot of us the crafts of spellwork and at least one form of divination go hand in hand.

What Is Intuition?

Intuition is an important building block for your craft overall. I do think that every witch is psychic/intuitive. There's honestly not a lot of difference between psychic and intuitive gifts. Some might say the difference is in the practice and how you exercise those muscles, but it also might just be language or comfort using a big word like psychic versus a safer one like intuitive.

Nonetheless, one of the first things you'll want to do as you come in to your witch's power is hone your intuition or psychic skills. You can start with simply paying attention to your body's internal cues and the world around you. Most of your intuition lives right inside of your body, and if it doesn't, it lives just outside of it. In your body it could live in a number of different places. Your gut wants to keep you safe and happy in the here and now. Your higher intuition, around your eyes, wants you to stay on track so you end up where you should in ten, fifteen, or twenty years. Your body itself sometimes has an ache or a zing that tells you something big is happening or changing. Your logical mind just wants to process and piece together the intuition from the rest of your body, providing logical answers to once-overwhelming situations. This, too, is a form of intuition (and an underrated one at that). Your heart wants what your heart wants, and believe it or not, that's also a form of intuition—though it looks different

than we think, and we need to think about our heart's desire for our next fifteen years, and not just today.

As your intuition zings around your body and right outside of it, it wants to help you grow into your magickal self, but it needs some fine tuning to help you develop your gifts (and figure out what they are). Use the journal prompts below to see where you feel like your intuition sits now and how it talks to you. *These prompts and the exercises after them are especially pertinent to queer witches*, because as children when we realize our gender is wrong or our budding sexuality isn't the same as our friends, we often cut off our intuition and try to force it to see or be a different way. Even as we come into our own, come out of the closet, and step into our peace or our power we still often struggle with listening to baseline intuition because for as long as we can remember, we were trying to quiet it about something as important as who we are! That takes more than rekindling a relationship with your intuition. It takes rebuilding it. First though, you'll need to see where you are now.

Intuition Journal Prompts

Sit somewhere comfortable but not so comfortable that you can't write or journal. Close your eyes and take a few deep breaths. Perform what's called a body scan, where you start at either your head or feet, and slowly relax each part of your body as you move down or up.

Once you're relaxed, breathe comfortably but deeply. Somewhere in your body, there is probably a knot of stress, nervousness, or actual anxiety if you, like me, struggle with anxiety. Note where that is. What does it feel like? What has this feeling meant in the past? Is there anything you can do to nurture it so it gets calmer? Is there anywhere in your life where maybe things are going awry that you need to listen to this part of you about? If you can't think of anything, when have you felt like this before? This gets into some deeper journaling, so take your time.

Somewhere else in your body, you feel lighter and more hopeful. Where is that and how does it feel? What is this part of you excited about? What inklings for positive change are you getting from it? When have you felt like this before? If you don't

think positive or good things are coming from you, sit with this happier intuition for longer. What do you see, feel, or hear?

After you take those notes, tune in to your body, mind, and spirit as a whole. What other messages are you getting?

Journal about all of these things so you can look back at it later. Know that your original reads of your intuition might not be crystal clear. You might get colors, images, or words floating around. You might hear your inner voice, and you might not. You might get memories that seem totally irrelevant or a snapshot of a future you're not planning on. Take notes on all of it and (more importantly) what it means to you and leave it sit for a few days. Returning to it, you'll likely find that it makes a whole lot more sense than you gave it credit for.

Once you can see how your intuition is working currently, you can begin to rebuild your relationship with it. Here are some exercises I really like that can help you learn to love and use this witchy skill.

- Revisit the above journal prompt several times a week, and look back over your progress after a couple of weeks.

- Talk to people close to you about their intuition. How do they feel it? How do they work with it? Do they have any examples of how their intuition played out?

- Take note of your dreams and any symbols that jump out at you.

- Take note when you have random thoughts, when you see an animal or other symbol that is out of place or when something reminds you of someone you knew once. I once saw a fox in a parking lot on a crowded college campus. That absolutely went in my notes on my own intuition. Often it's more subtle; a graffitied phrase, or someone who shares your late aunt's unique name on the same day you smell her old perfume.

- Do a body scan and quick meditation daily, even if you don't have time to journal on it. Ask yourself "What do we need to know today?" as you slip into your intuitive state and let your body and soul do the rest.

In this book we've talked a lot about DIY witchcraft. For you to have a good handle on what works for you for DIY witchcraft, you also need to have a solid handle on your intuition. Symbols, colors, images—those things all have ascribed correspondences that you can learn and you can operate that way successfully for your whole life. Figuring out what those things mean to you and using your personal ascriptions, though, that takes your craft to a whole new level. Often, that starts with intuitive practice, and for queer people and those who have been traumatized, it starts with rebuilding your relationship with your intuition to start.

What Is Divination?

Once you have a handle on your psychic skill set, you might be ready for something more. While intuition is powerful and has brought me my entire beautiful, blessed life, it doesn't always show up in the clear and present way we want it too. Sometimes we need specific answers or to see how our options play out in real time. For that, there's divination.

Divination is a system of using a combination of tools and intuition to find answers to plaguing questions, to check in with where you are now and if you're doing everything you need to, or, perhaps, just to see what's coming up around the corner. For me, as a traumatized and empathetic person, learning tarot cards helped me channel my intuition into the cards so that I wasn't constantly overloaded and overwhelmed by other people's thoughts and feelings. Learning the fine art of boundaries was the real breakthrough, but learning the cards helped me learn how to turn a certain amount of that intuition on and off.

Divination has existed, in some form or fashion, since people have existed. There's evidence that Ancient Egyptians used scrying with water and ink, presumably watching the ink form into shapes or images they would then interpret. We've already talked about Ancient Celts using weather divination, and they certainly were not alone in that. Pre-American, Indigenous diviners living on this half of the world would throw a handful of corn onto a white surface and read based on what shapes or images arose. Bonecasting in Africa follows a similar method and doesn't have a clear origin point, because as far as we know, it always existed.

Most of these methods have fallen by the wayside (save for bonecasting, which is all too rare and unfortunately, usually appropriated) in favor of tools that we can put more rigorous structures and rules on. While I do think a portion of that is human nature, I also think that it complicates things for people who have learned to live without those structures supporting us. Like anything else, we need to queer these systems to divine as queer witches. We need to acknowledge that prosperity looks wildly different for people who have never had it, that people who have been traumatized will have unique trust issues that cannot be overcome by deciding to overcome them, and that even a positive future might sound terrifying to people who weren't sure they'd get a future at all and therefore didn't plan for one.

Modern diviners are a lot better at adapting to their clients, for the most part, but there are glaring things that get missed when we don't do the work to queer our systems of divination. There are ways we underserve those we're reading for, even if we're just reading for ourselves. We are the authority on our own lives, and we should be, but the way a lot of these skills are taught can shortchange us and fail to provide us with the information we actually desire. This can make us feel like we don't connect with the tools we've selected. You can learn these tools too, though, by deconstructing and rebuilding them using your current knowledge. That's a better way to learn anyway. We should question everything, especially on a spiritual path. Our divination is no exception.

Divination is wildly misunderstood by the world at large. I love campy, witchy movies and TV shows, but they certainly don't do professional diviners any favors with their wacky and confusing fortune-teller tropes. Some diviners claim to see the future, though if a reader ever insists that certain things are set in stone you should run. Divining the future is never a perfect art, because you have free will. The people in your life have free will. The people running our country, our places of employment, the systems we rely on for health care have free will. At any point, any number of people—including you—can make decisions that were not what they were supposed to be. That can severely alter the course of your life as well as theirs. Instead, if you're interested in the future, the best question to ask when divining is "What is the most likely outcome of this situation?" with an understanding that things can shift or turn at any point.

To queer your divination, do your research and learn about the system you're interested in first. Having some base knowledge will help you queer and personalize it, even if that knowledge is problematic. From there, you can see what resonates with you and what doesn't. I strongly recommend journaling every step of the way, so you can see how your intuitive gifts grow and thrive. Sit with the basic ideas you learn at first and journal about them. After a few days, weeks, or months (depending on how much time you have to devote to your learning) work with your tool again. This time, tear away what you think you know. As the symbols, images, and ideas become clear, what stands out as true to you? What doesn't? How has your experience as a queer person altered your perception of this symbol or message? What do you need or want to subvert? What do you need or want to reclaim in this message? How can you rebuild this message in your own image? This might sound confusing now, but when you pick a divinatory skill from below and start working with it, it should all click into place. Divination is not raw intuition, and you should set your interpretations at some point. That doesn't mean there's no room for growth, and it absolutely does not mean that those set interpretations cannot be rooted in the deeply personal, and in our cases, the deeply queer. Setting your interpretations but allowing them to evolve and develop nuance gives you a personalized and important framework that makes learning and using the skills easier and more reliable. It also legitimizes it.

I am a witch who believes in animism, especially when it comes to divination. Animism is the belief that there's a soul or life force in inanimate objects. I believe that our divinatory tools either come enchanted with a spirit of their own, or that we can enchant them to bring that spirit, which may be dormant, out. Animism is something I believe in, in all of my witchcraft, but for some reason it comes up the most when I'm talking about divination. That's likely because some people will ask me if I think the answers come from myself, the person I'm reading for, a spiritual entity working with me, or the cards. My answer is that I think it comes from all of those things. Most people know where you and I get our magick from or where gods and animal allies might get theirs. I do believe that our divinatory tools, in my case my tarot cards, have spiritual "stuff" in them that makes them magickal and allows them to work, too.

I should mention that you don't have to learn a divinatory skill to be a useful witch. You don't have to do anything you're not comfortable with, don't feel aligned with, or are overwhelmed by. If you choose to learn, learn for yourself first. While I've had a long career in tarot and plan on continuing, you need to learn without expectation of this skill ever leaving your sacred circle. Divination for witchcraft can also look very different from basic divination. Divination for witchcraft means using those tools to help you design and implement your spellwork, as opposed to getting general life guidance. It can mean using those tools to help you settle a bad feeling and get some clarity on how to resolve the situation, but that's still different than using it for general purposes. Learning for witchcraft doesn't mean you'll never learn a different purpose. The opposite is actually true. Learning to divine for a specific spell and for clarity in an intuitive emergency will make a later, more public, learning curve all the simpler.

COMMON FORMS OF DIVINATION

There are endless forms of divination, but some stand out to me as being either useful specifically for our purposes as a witch, or because they're popular and therefore more accessible and easy to learn. I also know a queer reader or several who do each of the below methods, and most of them are quite good. That means these methods can be queered with simple intuition and imagination, so they are our best places to start. When you are first learning to divine, I'd stick with one or two methods. Get to a level of comfort with each one, and then you can pick up more.

Tarot Cards

Today, the most popular form of divination is tarot cards. Tarot cards are a system of seventy-eight cards with four suits (Wands, Swords, Pentacles, and Cups) and twenty-two cards called the Major Arcana. The Major Arcana start with The Fool as card 0 and end with The World as card 21. Everything that happens between 0 and 21 is often called The Fool's Journey, a narrative about The Fool undertaking a journey towards enlightenment in The World. The other cards in the Major Arcana represent someone The Fool meets along the way, an event or action that happens, and the inner work required to reach enlightenment. This can be read literally, if you're reading for witch purposes or

dealing with a client on an intense spiritual quest. It can also be a metaphor for the countless inner journeys we go on as humans. For those practicing traditional or ceremonial magick, the Major Arcana are often considered initiate rites required before becoming a full-fledged practitioner of that path.

A lot of times the Minor Arcana (those four suits I mentioned above) aren't written about with the fervor that the Majors are, but I love the Minors. Focus on the Majors is something those with privilege and clout can do in our society. When they're not fighting to have their basic needs covered, they can do things like focus on enlightenment. The rest of us are still just trying to find love, make enough money to eat, and heal from our trauma. For all of those things, there's the Minor Arcana. I've always seen a huge overlap in the Major Arcana energy and Minor Arcana energy, and it's very true that what is happening to us spiritually or emotionally can and does have big real world implications. For queer (or any marginalized) seekers, the reverse is also true. When our very rights are being stepped on daily, it can make us cynical spiritually. When finding love as a gay person in a small town leaves you with very questionable options, it can throw you into an existential crisis. The Majors and Minors are not separate then, and they are both equally important.

To learn tarot yourself, head to your nearest metaphysical store or bookstore and hold some decks in your hands. While demo stations are not common, they're also not unheard of. If you luck into one, play with several different decks before making a selection. If not, hold the boxes in your hand. Use Google Search to find images of ones that feel good to make sure you truly like them. Find something that appeals to you. Nowadays, my favorite decks come from online, independent publishers. Do your research in these cases on both card images and the author's connection to tarot. The great thing about our modern age of tarot is that anyone can make a tarot deck and sell it. The bad thing about our modern age of tarot is that anyone can make a tarot deck and sell it. Once you think you like a deck, see if you can figure out which system it's based on. It will likely either be the *Rider-Waite-Smith Tarot* (considered the original tarot deck), the *Golden Dawn Tarot* deck, or Aleister Crowley's *Thoth Tarot*. Knowing what it's based on will help you research interpretations and find guidebooks beyond the one that

comes with your deck. It will most likely be *Rider-Waite-Smith*, but it helps to make sure.

Other Types of Cartomancy—Oracles Cards, Playing Cards, and Lenormand

Tarot is not the only accessible form of cartomancy, though it is the most accessible. For those who want something a little bit different or aren't sure they can sign up for learning a seventy-eight-card system, there are plenty of other card related options to choose from. This is honestly not my area of expertise, but I do like getting readings from readers who use cards other than tarot. They get me out of my own head and are just as insightful.

If you like the idea of suits but are wigged out about learning the Majors, a regular deck of playing cards might be the right style of divination for you. In this case, Hearts correlate to the element of Water. Spades correlate to the element of Air. Diamonds correlate to the element of Earth. Clubs correspond to the element of Fire. With your own understanding of the elements, it would be easy to find information about the face cards (which tarot also has its equivalent of) and the numerology of a deck of cards. You could even use a standard tarot guidebook, and just ignore the cards your deck doesn't have. Plenty of resources exist for plain old cartomancy though, so don't be scared or feel like this is an outdated, out of touch system. While it is a lot less common now, it is still used, and in witchy circles sometimes the more old-fashioned is the most attractive. This includes queer witches who, while we may not love the politics of the 14th Century, do find something appealing in the aesthetic of it all.

Lenormand cards are another card-based divination system. The Lenormand deck has only thirty-six cards with no suits. No suits doesn't mean no structure though, and as you're learning you'll notice that these cards do have an easy-to-follow ebb and flow to them. Lenormand cards do include correspondences to playing cards, but those are usually included to indicate timing. I know really gifted Lenormand readers who take from cartomancy to inform their Lenormand practice, but it's not a necessity. Instead, each Lenormand deck includes the same thirty-six cards with the artwork allowing for new or creative interpretation within that basic system. This deck is relatively easy to learn because each card

is thought to have just a few keywords instead of the plethora that tarot can often have. There are books about Lenormand reading, and you can certainly follow the deck's guidebook, too.

If you're not into systems or structure at all (like so many other queers!) but love the idea of holding a deck of bewitched cards in your hand, then you're in luck! Oracle card decks abound as prevalently as tarot and playing cards do and most of them have either created their own system, or don't follow one at all. Because of this, there's not really one way to learn oracle cards. Instead, you'll want to learn one oracle deck at a time. They all have wildly different purposes, artwork, keywords, and the like. I do use oracle cards but the lack of structure actually throws me and it takes me a million years to learn a new deck. Like any other image-based divination though, you can analyze the artwork, personalize what the keyword on the card means to you, and proceed in your learning from there. This practice varies so dramatically from deck to deck, so find a deck whose thesis and artwork appeal to your queer soul and give yourself space and time to form a relationship with those cards.

Runes

Runes are alphabets of yore, reworked as divination systems. Norse runes are the most common, and hail back to the myth of Odin sacrificing his eye to discover and develop the Norse alphabet that also served as a powerful system of and tool for magick. Before we had the alphabets we have today, the letters also stood for ideas and words. In ancient cultures the runes connected people to magick and spirituality, thus deepening the reason and meaning of each rune. From there, we're able to divine with them.

Runes as a divination set are usually carved or painted on rocks, wood, or bone. They're kept in a bag so you can shake them, then dump them out on the table. Any runes face up get read. Any runes face down get pulled out. They're read based not only on the intuition and relationship the reader has built with them (which is based on those ancient keywords and magickal ideas) but also in how they interact with each other—which ones are close together, which ones form almost a grid, and so on. They're incredibly relational, even more so than the card systems we talked about. While each rune does have a deep, nuanced message for us, the number of runes is usually limited. The amount being read is even smaller. There's

no art to interpret, just our spins on these letters and words. This means they are . . . succinct, on a good day, but very abrupt and blunt if you're being foolish and need to know it.

As I mentioned earlier, Norse runes are the most common and are often used as part of Heathenism. Heathenism is a form of Paganism that works with Norse gods, myths, and ideas. Heathenism gets a bad rap because there have been a lot of reconstructionists who are also white supremacists. Like any other subculture they find, they manage to take up a lot of space and often dominate those conversations. They're not the majority of practicing Heathens though. While this is not my lineage or anything I've ever felt drawn to, I know quite a few Heathens actively battling white supremacy in their faith and outside of it. I know quite a few queer Heathens, and quite a few who actively spurn the white supremacy that has poisoned the name Heathenry. Norse runes are powerful and beautiful, but you do need to protect your heart when you're learning them. Books about runes written by women are much less likely to be terrible, and books about Heathenry by Pagan authors you trust (especially queer writers) usually include working with runes. In this day and age though, the Internet may be your best bet to find something honest and inclusive.

My favorite thing about using runes for divination and what makes them incredibly accessible is that you can make a set yourself! I've made them for friends with a woodburner and pieces of bark that I had on hand. I know friends who have painted their own stones or hardened clay. You don't need any specific material you just need one small piece for each rune that is roughly the same size, and something that makes the rune itself visible. (This means you could make small, flat circles out of rainbow-colored clay and glittery runes on them and have yourself an incredibly queer set!)

Astrology

We touched on astrology in our chapter on magickal timing and I do primarily use astrology as a way to work with what the planets are doing above me, instead of accidentally fighting against it. It is primarily known as a system of divination, though. Earlier I mentioned tarot cards as the most common form of divination, but astrology is likely tied with it. To divine with astrology requires a lot of research and practice, so it's not for the faint of heart.

Basically, what astrology as divination boils down to is being able to do your own birth chart, track what the planets are doing over the next few years, and overlay those things to get your personal astrology reading for that time. You can also look over any previous years if you're trying to figure out why something happened or if it truly is resolved now. Astrology is a lot of math, science, memorization, and critical thinking. The best astrologers spend years honing their skills before going public. It's so much more than knowing your Sun and Moon sign. There are dozens of signs based on cosmic action, and each of those is in one of the twelve houses in astrology. The houses each represent something different too. The first house, for example, represents the House of Self, that is the first impression you give off and basic things you project. The second house represents The House of Value, which is where your potential for prosperity lies, but it also shows your self-worth and how substantive of a person you are.

To confuse things further, not everyone has a sign in every house. Not every day has a sign in every house. Some days there may be nothing in the first house and a pileup in the third. Some birth charts might have all the signs on one side of the chart. This all can be learned, though, and unlike some of our other systems of divination there is less room for creative interpretation. That doesn't mean each astrologer doesn't have their own ideas of what a Sagittarius is or what it means to say House of Self. They do, and that's why each astrological reading will be a little bit different, but it also means that those interpretations do generally circle around the same ideas.

Learning astrology starts close to home—with your birth chart. This will help you learn several signs and houses at once, as well as what happens when those are retrograde, conjunct, trine, and so forth. For queer people, I strongly implore you to consider the unique stepping stones and hurdles you have faced because of your gender, sexual identity, or both and how those are reflected (or not) in your chart. As a warning, almost every facet of astrology has a binary male-or-female aspect assigned to it based on tradition. As queer astrologists, you are well within your rights to embrace this and find nonbinary or inclusive interpretation within it, to completely throw out the gendered language, or to decide that some planets, houses, and the like are genderqueer, non-binary, or other genders based on your understanding of them.

Once you know your own chart and the houses, you can start looking at astrological happenings for each day and try to give yourself clarity and advice based on that. Keep researching and learning if this is something you're really drawn too. Take some classes, online and in person, and get several readings from professionals. Gobble up horoscopes from astrologers who know what they're talking about. It's worth learning. Astrology is complicated, but it's also incredibly effective for aiding your spiritual journey. You'll be working with the planets, stars, and Sun to bring your dreams and those for your community into full view, and you'll be incredibly satisfied in that.

Scrying

If astrology is all charts and systems, scrying is the exact opposite of that. Scrying is using a reflective or visual surface to divine. The most common form of scrying is staring into a crystal ball or, in modern day, obsidian mirror, until shapes and images start making sense to you, and then interpreting those shapes and images. Water scrying is also common, where you put water in a clear bowl and either read it as is or drop a (very small) stone or pebble in to read the ripples in the water. My personal favorite form of scrying is surprisingly not water, but smoke. Smoke scrying is burning anything safe to burn—cleansing cedar or lavender sticks, incense, etc.—and focusing on the smoke. Because smoke shifts and moves but does so almost fluidly, it's easy to see not only single images or ideas but also entire scenes.

I was unbelievably skeptical about scrying when I started my journey as a witch, but I feel differently now. Scrying works as well as anything else if you believe it does, but it does require that you are someone who's willing to go all in on trusting your intuition and interpretations. Astrology isn't for the faint of heart, because it's a lot of studying and learning. Scrying isn't for the faint of heart because you need to have a really well developed intuition and a deep, abiding faith in that intuition that so many of us are lacking. For queer witches, I think scrying makes sense not only as a system of divination but also as a tool to develop that self-awareness that we are so often so divorced from.

Pendulums

If you want a quick answer with a tool that takes little memorization, a pendulum is the thing to grab. Pendulums are a stone or shaped metal, usually with a point at the end, attached to a rod, chain, or string. To use a pendulum to divine, you'd hold the pendulum straight out, and try really hard to not move your hand while using it. Because there are a limited number of ways a pendulum can answer questions, it's best to bring simple questions with a clear yes/no or either/or answer.

To start your session, ask the pendulum "show me yes" and "show me no." One way should move vertically, the other horizontally. If you want to get fancy, you can also ask "show me maybe" and "show me 'I don't know'" and the pendulum will likely move on opposite diagonals for each question. If it's an either/or question that you're asking, you would say "show me X choice" and "show me Y choice" to power it up before using it. I have asked the pendulum for help with problems that had three or four options, using those diagonals as the other option placements but I do think those diagonals are best used for sort-of answers like "maybe" or "I don't know." Otherwise the choices start blending together, and even simple work with a pendulum gets muddy.

An energy healer using a pendulum will hold it over various parts of your body, whether they work with chakras, muscle groups, or meridians. Where the pendulum is either creepily still or eerily vibratory is the place the energy healer will start their work. This is a form of divination, too. Various aspects of metaphysical, occult, or Pagan life are not separate from each other and often an energy worker will rely on intuition as much as healing ability. Likewise, I've been called a healer as a tarot reader because I'm able to provide answers that offer peace of mind and closure to those who have been grappling for them for a long time. This lifts that burden off their shoulders and helps them feel better. All of this stuff is connected, but we can untangle it by starting with basic principles like the yes/no of the pendulum.

I like pendulums a lot because sometimes, as humans, we want things to be more complicated than they are. Queer community is particularly bad about infighting and backstabbing for reasons I completely understand. When you've been hurt and pushed aside, and are under resourced for mental health care, it's hard to keep your compassion front and center

the way you'd ideally like too. That goes hand in hand with overcomplicating problems and thinking in extremes. A pendulum can cut to the heart of the matter and provide the answer you most need since it cannot get more complicated than yes/no or either/or.

Palmistry

Palmistry is a pretty simple concept (but is an art and a skill that takes time to learn) where a palm reader looks at your palm or palms and divines advice, guidance, and maybe future outcomes based on the lines, bumps, coloring, and other aspects of your hands. Most people think of palmistry as just the lines, but palm readers take the mounds, indentations, and sizes of various parts of your hand as well as hand and finger health and shape into account. Another thing you probably don't know from watching palm readers on TV is that your hands change over time, as you make choices and learn lessons that you're supposed to learn. Getting a palm reading, just like getting a tarot or astrology reading, is not a one-time experience but it is one that should be reserved for when you feel like there's been a lot of significant changes and shifts since your last reading. Palm readings can be incredibly insightful to figure out where you are and where you could ideally be, and it is one of the more prophetic divination styles.

I will never forget the worst, least inclusive palm reading I ever got. It was when I was still fairly new to witchcraft and divination. I let a random person at a fair read my palm, someone who, in retrospect, had red flags written all over them. They looked at my heart line, which can deal with interpersonal relationships and saw that it was forked at the end. They said this meant I would struggle between two great men (Ha! Error number one) and end up leaving one for the other. There was no idea that balancing multiple relationships was possible or even preferable, and a decent queer-inclusive palm reader will take polyamory into account for that fork. I'm not polyamorous, but I do have a queerplatonic partner with whom I take my partnership very seriously. I also date successfully, because, surprise, chosen family within queer community is not actually received badly—or as if I'll have to make some big, dramatic choice at some point. I know myself and my people well enough *now* to know that that's likely what was seen

in the fork—two great loves, likely coexisting but different. I knew that about myself even then but I was young, insecure, and hanging out with mostly straight and cis people who were *always* telling me that my relationship with my queerplatonic partner would end one day. It messed with my head in a significant way, and I choked down insecurities in part because of this reading for years.

Another bad palm reading that I remember clearly was actually a very good palm reading. The reader read my palm and gave me a fantastic, accurate reading that has since seen everything she foretold happen with one glaring problem: she kept talking about the man I was seeing. I was seeing a transmasculine genderqueer person at the time, but they were not a man and even they were much more masculine of center than my normal dating preference. When I left, because she was so wrong and inconsiderate about my partner's gender, I ignored everything she told me. It wasn't until the things she saw started blowing up that I remembered the reading and reconsidered.

I bring up these stories as we navigate through queering divination so we understand what we're really doing by not queering our readings. It's not just about being inclusive or considerate, but you're literally giving bad readings that clients won't take seriously if you don't take polyamory, significant friendships, and other queer staples into account.

FINAL THOUGHTS ON DIVINATION

The methods of divinations I've listed are accessible in terms of how easily you can find books or online resources and dive in yourself, and how few resources they take to get going. There are countless other forms of divination, like bonecasting (which is largely for people following African traditions like Zulu or Ifa), charm casting (the use of charms or tokens to represent different messages), I Ching (a Chinese divination system using coins with letters and symbols), and mediumship or straight up intuitive reading (using spirits that have passed on or nothing but your psychic mind to divine). If you find something that stands out to you as something you want to learn, study, and perform for your witchcraft, your friends, or to take into the world at large, do it! I ask only that, regardless of your own identity, you remember that there is no one way to have a relationship with your body. There is no

one way to fall in love. There is no one way to have a healthy relationship. Friendships can be just as significant as romantic relationships. Some people are kinky and some people are asexual and some people are both. There are infinite genders and even more infinite gender expressions. Keep an open mind, and learn from that place. It will serve your witchcraft and your divination much better.

8

A QUEER GRIMOIRE

When I was asking my local queer and Pagan communities what they wanted out of a queer witchcraft book, the resounding, almost unanimous first answer was spells. In the DIY Witchcraft chapter we talked at length about how to write your own spells, but it can be hard to get a handle on it until you see and work with several existing spells. My main argument for DIY witchcraft is largely about accessibility in grasp and price, so the spells in this grimoire vary wildly but should be doable at most income levels and with any handle at all on witchcraft or magick. Some of them still require you to trust yourself as a witch, as an intuitive person, as a writer or artist, even if you don't identify as any of those things. Additionally, the burnout queer people feel on a daily basis is very real. While I can usually rally the strength to do a spell, I cannot if I also have to write, design, and gather things for it as well. Because I want this to be an easy, accessible group of spells for you to perform, there are plenty of cheap-to-free options or substitutes you can make (à la DIY witchcraft) for each intention.

It's important to remember that easy to perform and accessible does not mean these are weak and fluffy spells. Queer witches are not weak and fluffy by the very nature of how hard we work to maintain full, rich lives while also having our voices heard, while also sheltering and loving each other, while also working to create very real change in the world. We are powerful beyond comprehension, to the point that it terrifies entire political administrations enough to try and write us out via legislation and whatever other ample tools they have. Yet we exist, and we persist as a community. We create change and screw things up for those in charge every day. We do not and will not back down.

So no, these are not fluffy spells, they are tried and true, powerful and magickal workings. These spells tap into queer ancestors' magick, the magick of this Earth itself, the power of the queer collective coming out to

breathe fire and strength on us as we bring them into being. These spells tap into our deepest selves with our most hidden and archaic knowledge. This grimoire digs deep into your heart and your soul to help you create things you have only dreamed of.

Spellcraft is not a perfect art, and you are not a perfect person. Yet together, you can move mountains.

For ease of finding a spell you need, this section is organized into the type of spell it is. Protection spells in one clump, attraction spells in another, and so on. There is some overlap because sometimes causing a huge shift creates a new need for protection, but I tried to put them in the most logical, organic place they made sense.

Protection Spells

I am starting with protection spells for obvious reasons. We live in a world that is physically, emotionally, and financially unsafe for so many of us. Basic needs like shelter and food often elude queer people, especially trans people of color, especially trans women of color, and that leaves them exposed to the elements, on top of a terribly, transphobic world.

I've also recently learned the hard way what happens if you don't protect yourself spiritually. I thought I didn't need protection magick beyond my home, my shared car, and my health and then someone that I loved platonically and deeply turned out to be someone very different than I thought. This person was arrested, and while I have a deep disdain for our justice system and mass incarceration, this person was guilty of something objectively awful. I made it very clear that our friendship was over because of the unconscionable things this person had done. So they hexed me. Nothing bad happened, I just became acutely and bizarrely aware that there was a hex on me, and an actual friend helped me take it down and return to sender.

When you live in the margins, mostly people are really good. Queer family feeds each other, literally and metaphorically. People are still people though. There are still some who are willing and even desire to cause harm. It feels extra difficult and extra personal when it comes from within our own community or close group of friends. The outside world is so hard to deal with, that things should be softer and easier here. When they're not, it's extra painful and can throw us off track the way a different heartache might not. While we can never guarantee that there aren't abusers

and creeps in our midst, we can use protection magick to make our hearts strong and resilient in the face of this and to keep ourselves physically safe.

Protection magick is also absolutely mandatory for those doing activism. The cops are not our friends, especially at protests, and the system would happily see us sit in jail for exercising our right to assembly and free speech. It can also be physically daunting work, depending on what type of activism we're doing. If we protest or go door-to-door canvassing for a progressive politician, we are taking chances with our feet and our bodies not only because people might lash out, but also, because statistics are not on our side when we're consistently doing physically demanding work. Physical protection magick is key, and again, we should protect our hearts, too. We can't and don't win them all, and it's impossible not to take it personally sometimes. We are people whose rights and lives are being impacted so when we don't gain a right or move towards liberation, our spirits can get dashed and create that burnout that I have seen too many times in exceptional activists.

We are all trying to survive capitalism. We are all trying to survive patriarchy. We are all trying to survive white supremacy. Yes, we're trying to overturn and overthrow those things too, but before we get there we have to protect ourselves. We deserve to feel and be safe, but where a lot of therapy and medical intervention fails is that queer people often are not safe. Spellcraft, then, is a natural place to turn, to ensure as much safety as possible.

From a strictly Pagan perspective, protection spellwork is an important building block of a deeper witchcraft practice. In addition to the cornucopia of ways we want to be protected that I listed examples of above, we also need to be safe when we're working with the spirit realm. We all deserve basic feelings of safety in our day-to-day lives, and as your witchcraft grows, the day to day will include the spiritual, too. This kind of magick feels more aggressive than we sometimes think it will. It's not about merely putting an ethereal shield around ourselves. It's also about trusting that shield to fight out anything or anyone that might try to slide in and cause problems. That means that the energy that comes from you and in to you may feel more connected, more vibratory, and more aggressive than you think it will. Remember that this is a type of aggression that is on your side and that it is necessary now. *You are safe in the face of this deeper spiritual work.* Those who might try to cross you? Not so much.

A Protection Spell for Trans People (Especially in Small Towns)

Trans people face unique barriers to health care, employment, and housing and have the highest likelihood to be victims of hate crimes, unjust policing, and judgment even from their own community. This is incredibly true in big cities where trans people still need protecting, but in big cities there are resources and community members they can reach out to, too. In small towns, there is often no one willing or able to take that call, which is why working to protect trans community members in small towns is especially important. This is a general spell that can be worked to protect any trans person from everything from microaggressions to violence.

You will need:

- A candle that is either a color that is gender-affirming to you or magenta

- A tool to carve the candle with

- A charm that represents protection, like a bear or a horseshoe

- A list of the trans people who have been murdered or committed suicide in your country the year you are performing the spell

- A protective sigil, word, or image of your own design

To perform the spell:

Sit quietly and either call in or honor the spirits of Marsha P. Johnson, Sylvia Rivera, Christine Jorgensen, and other trans trailblazers who have passed on. Breathe deeply and feel the spirit of their humanity and humor as well as their strength.

When you feel the inspiration of those spirits, pick up your candle. Carve the sigil, image, or word of your choice into the candle.

As you carve, say, "May the spirits of the trans lives we have lost be at peace. May the spirits of the trans lives still here stay safe."

Charge the candle with your energy. Light it.

Meditate on what safety looks like for the trans people you know.

When it feels appropriate, blow the candle out and wave the charm in the smoke. Say, "As this flame dies down, may my local trans community remain safe."

If you are trans, keep the charm in your wallet or pocket to help you ward off physical danger. If you are not, place it with the candle.

If you still have candle left, light it nightly and repeat the mantras until it is cashed.

Place your list of trans people who have been murdered or committed suicide in your country in the year you're doing this spell on an appropriate altar—most likely an altar for spirit or ancestral work. Honor those spirits, just for a moment, every time you see that list.

A Protection Spell for QTBIPOC

If trans people in general are under resourced and struggling with basic tenets of safety a lot of the time, then it's even more true for Queer and Trans Black and Indigenous People of Color. This spell is meant for heavier magick against the carceral state and the multiple systems of oppression that QTBIPOC are operating within. Like the Protection Spell for Trans People, this one can be geared to specific people you know or to the QTBIPOC community as a whole (or in a specific city, like the one you live in).

You need:

- Bricks or big rocks
- A decent length of rope and the ability to tie knots
- Scissors
- Something to write with and on

To perform this spell:

Do whatever you do to set up a ritual. Cast a circle, call in the elements, or simply close the door and do some deep breathing.

Think about the dangers that are facing the QTBIPOC population where you live—whatever that means to you. Think about what protecting that population means, and how you can help.

The bricks or big rocks represent the stand against police brutality taken by those at Stonewall. In your spell, they can be charged at any point with the spiritual protection energy you are summoning. After this spell, they can be placed on your altar as a visual reminder to keep working your protection magick.

Take the rope, and think again about the dangers facing this community, in particular. Tie a knot for each worry or concern that you can think of. Alternatively, tie a knot for each danger facing a QTBIPOC that you know (including yourself).

Let the knotted rope sit beside you.

If you *are* a QTBIPOC, take some notes on what safety means to you and what you are asking the Divine for now. You can either keep this list and place it on your altar, or tear it up and toss it (or burn it!).

If you are an ally, make a list of resources you could potentially give to a QTBIPOC in need, including food you could make easily for someone who is hungry or financial resources you have access to that might be useful. A list of trans-inclusive shelters and people you know willing to shelter people is also good. This might take some research. Fold this up and keep it in your pocket or wallet.

Take the scissors and cut above and below each knot on the rope, so you are essentially cutting the knots out. As you do so, say a mantra or incantation to the effect of "May (the QTBIPOC you're performing the spell for) find safety and freedom from harm. May I always ensure that I am doing my part."

Destroy or throw away the knots. Leave the bits of rope on your altar to represent those in need, or conversely, the resources that there are.

A Spell of Protection Against the Patriarchy

Patriarchy is the root of so much queerphobia it's not even funny. Some-times its patriarchy dressed up like religious conservatism, but even that is still designed to keep cisgender, usually white, mostly able-bodied men in power and keep everybody else down. Patriarchy hurts every-body, though here we're mostly concerned with how it affects queer people. Because patriarchy does affect all of us, this is a spell you can use for yourself or other people who are facing rape culture and misog-yny in a tangible and dangerous way.

Also of note in our current time: the United States, and the world, experienced an uprising against white supremacy and police brutality beginning in Minneapolis, MN in late May 2020. Please note that this spell can be changed to address white supremacy rather than patriachy, when needed. It will function basically the same.

You need:

- Something with a feminist or queer feminist statement on it like "Hex the Patriarchy" or "Fuck patriarchy" or "Keep Your Laws Off My Body"—a patch or a button is ideal

- A black candle

- A safety pin—only if you have no history of self-harm and are not afraid of blood

- A mantra or incantation like "Keep the patriarchy and its followers away from me/my friend/someone else in need"

- A second mantra or incantation like "I am as safe as I can be from the patriarchy"

To perform this spell:

Sit comfortably.

Call in a god of your choice or the elements or both.

Recite your first mantra incantation as you light the candle.

Close your eyes, take a couple of deep breaths. Ground yourself. Feel yourself securely against the chair or floor or wall, or whatever you're sitting on and leaning against.

Visualize the last unsafe interaction you or the person you're performing the spell for had, especially if it instigated this spell. Visualize the offending parties backing away from you slowly, and then disappearing. You can make this spell more aggressive if you wish by visualizing the offending parties getting hurt or pulled away by a pack of fierce femmes.

If it is safe and not triggering for you to do so, poke your fingertip with the safety pin with the intention of getting a few drops of blood. Drip them into the candle as it burns.

Once you're cleaned up and not bleeding, watch the flame and repeat your second mantra three times (or until you feel safe).

Release any entities that you called into the space. Move the candle to a more candle-safe space if need be. Let it burn until you have to leave or go to bed or until it goes out, whichever is sooner. As it burns out or you blow it out, wave your patch, button, or whichever object you chose into the smoke. It is now enchanted with patriarchy protection. Carry it with you, put it on your clothing or in your car, or carry it with you in your wallet.

Keep Your Laws Off My Body: A Poppet Spell

This is a spell meant to keep us safe from harmful legislation. It can be used to keep sex workers safe or to keep anyone who lives where there is harmful legislation against LGBTQQIA2SP+ people or sex safe.

You need:

- Fabric, corn husks, or other poppet materials

- A small piece of paper with "Keep Your Laws Off My Body" written on it and rolled up or folded even smaller—anoint with a protective oil if you feel so inclined

- Any protective herbs or charms that you want to add—see correspondence lists in the appendix for ideas

- Some strands or a chunk of your hair

- Poppet stuffing

To perform the spell:

Poppets are a form of sympathetic magick, which means the goals is to put your spirit or energy into the poppet to act as you, almost like a horcrux. That means before performing this spell, you should get into a good head space where you are actively feeling your spiritual energy moving through your body and floating through your fingertips however you need to do that. For some, this requires deep breathing and grounded rituals. Some are able to turn that on just by remembering it and deciding to turn it on.

Once you're centered and your energy is flowing appropriately, start putting together your poppet, intentionally putting your energy into it every step of the way. Fill the poppet with the other ingredients on the list.

As you sew up or tie off your last closure of the poppet, say something to the effect of "my body is safe from legislative harm." Keep the poppet by your nightstand or on your altar so it's constantly taking in new energy.

Anoint with protective oil every few days, saying, "My body is safe from legislative harm" as you do so.

An Anti-Gatekeeper Spell

Gatekeepers are the popular kids in the queer community (because every community does have them) who cast judgment on who is and is not queer enough or cool enough to be at this event or that event. *In a lot of communities, there aren't real gatekeepers.* Sure, there are popular kids in every queer community, but in a lot of places they're open and encouraging to younger queers finding their way. We perceive them to be gatekeepery because of the insecurities we develop as the queer kid in our junior high, high school, or job when we really are different and really do stand out. In those cases we need to address the actual root of our insecurity and work through some healing magick before deciding

if gatekeepers are a real issue for you. If you find they are, after you do that soul searching, then this spell will help you combat that energy and claim space in the face of those gatekeepers.

You need:

- This mantra: "I am enough as a queer/And I deserve to be seen here."

To perform this spell:

Before an event that's giving you some social anxiety or that you think there might be hip, gatekeeping queers, take a few moments before you leave the house to take a few deep breaths, close your eyes, and repeat the mantra three times.

A Spell to Protect Activists

I've defined activism for the next two spells to include those doing paid or unpaid activist, lobbying, or direct service provider work that puts them in harm's way physically and emotionally. For this spell you want a lot of fire energy, because we're working to protect the activist's physical self from police, angry clients, or more unpredictable bouts of harm.

You need:

- A black or red candle

- The name of the activist or group you want to protect (it can be yourself)

- A safety pin or sewing needle

- A protective stone, piece of concrete or brick, or similar object

- A small piece of writing or speech to perform in the spell that addresses the reasons for this protection spell and the specific work or action being done by the activist or activists in question— the following is just an example but you can adapt it

    Please protect me as I march for prison reform tomorrow.

    The laws are not just and the punishment is not fair and it is important that I make my voice known.

But I am afraid of ending up in jail myself, or being hurt by police or outside agitators during this march.

Please keep me physically safe as I march for justice and liberation.

Please keep all of those marching for reform safe as we make our voices and demands heard.

To perform the spell:

Sit down and get into as meditative a headspace as you're able to. Think about the project, work, or event coming out that you're seeking protection for. Imagine everything going off without those fighting for what's right being hurt. Imagine having the work's intentions met without activist casualties. Envision powerful activist work that is still safe for those involved. Visualize police or agitators backing away and letting you work.

Using your safety pin or sewing needle, carve the name of who you're looking to protect on to the candle's side.

Light the candle and repeat your speech or writing several times. Go slow and really feel the words you're saying. You can change or improv in the moment if it feels right. You'll feel when you are done or you can set a number of repetitions that feels magickal to you. (Three, five, or seven are the most common.) Hold your stone or piece of brick or concrete while you do this.

Blow out the candle and say, "My will *will* be done and I will remain safe."

Set the candle and stone in a safe place (like your altar) if you haven't already. Light the candle during regular or daily ritual until it's cashed.

After the spell, develop a list of resources in your area for activists who have been arrested, like Legal Aid, or attacked, like injury lawyers, who are accessible in price and reach to use when you hear of someone who needs them.

A Spell to Protect the Hearts of Activists

Physical harm isn't the only danger that can befall activists. The work we do is often very real and very visceral, and it can lead to burnout and can overwhelm. The risk of having a trauma response triggered is incredibly high. The risk of being newly emotionally traumatized is incredibly high. This spell is meant to protect our hearts and souls as we do our ongoing work as activists.

You need:

- Art supplies—paint or markers (or both!), paper or canvas, glue of choice, old magazines or newspapers, scissors, glitter, and the like

- An idea or image you want to create, recreate, or put a witchy spin on

To perform the spell:

Color the paper with paint or marker a base color that represents protecting the heart to you. I like lavender for this, or a calming version of a color I associate with the work being done.

Start creating the rest of your image. This might mean some extra drawing or painting.

Add some collage elements—anything that makes you think of keeping your heart safe, being strong, or the mission of your activist work.

Once you feel like you're pretty close to done, throw some glitter on it! This is for queer activists, after all.

If desired, say a quick incantation like, "My heart stays safe even when I'm in deep" as you complete your work.

Place this work on your wall, altar, or bathroom mirror. It should be somewhere where you'll see it every day and remember how strong your heart is and can continue to be.

A Protection Spell for Sex Workers

I shouldn't need to explain why this spell is necessary, but I know that I probably do. Sex workers have been a backbone and cornerstone of queer community since before Marsha P. Johnson and Sylvia Rivera, although those are the two incredibly influential sex workers that you've probably heard of who also created hordes of resources for sex workers. To this day, sex workers are people doing hardcore activist and direct service work in the queer community, and yet they remain the most unprotected and thrown-under-the-bus queers that there are. Also, a lot, lot, lot of queer people are or have been sex workers. We see it on *Pose* but things are not so advanced that we're beyond those days in the '80s. My Twitter feed is filled with cam service website links. I know people who were personally affected by the Stop Enabling Sex Traffickers and Fight Online Sex Trafficking Acts (SESTA/FOSTA) and the events leading up to them (*Backpage* shutting down suddenly, for example). Sex work is risky though. Obvious perils of legality aside, there aren't resources and sex workers can't assume safety should they be assaulted and need to report it. Sex workers are often sex workers out of necessity, and so this protection spell also covers things like having their basic needs (food, clothing, shelter) met as well as deeper protection work like keeping dangerous clients away from them.

You need:

- An image of a famous sex worker you look up to—even a bad computer printout is fine!

- A white candle

- Some tinsel, twinkly lights, or other sparkly things

- A protective oil or extract

To perform this spell:

Place the image of the sex worker on your altar, especially in a protection spell section or by a protective god's energy.

Light the white candle and say, "May this spirit of (name of person in image) protect the sex workers (feel free to get specific here) in

my community. May this spell protect them from legislative and personal harm. May this spell keep them prosperous and warm."

Decorate the image with the tinsel, twinkly lights, or other sparkly things. Dab the oil or extract on the corners of it.

Keep the candle going until you have to leave or go to bed. Relight as able. Replenish if able once it's gone.

For allies—while the candle is burning, research lawyers and emergency caregivers who will help sex workers for cheap or free. Put your local Sex Workers Organization Project (SWOP) branch, and any other non-profit you know will help, on it. Use as necessary or have on hand in case you see someone in need of such resources.

A Queer Collective Protection Spell

This spell can be used to protect your local queer community, the national or worldwide community, or any other group of queers who could use some extra protection. It is a more vague, easy spell.

You need:

- Something to represent each element that also represents protection—examples: tourmaline (stone), any evergreen incense, florida water or protection oil, and a black candle

- Something that represents the queer community you're trying to protect (for example, I have a rainbow bumper sticker that says Minneapolis that I use for this spell)

To perform the spell:

Invoke each of the elemental tools you're using with the mantra "I invite Earth to help protect my queer community. I invoke Air to help protect my queer community. I welcome Water to aid in protecting my queer community. I invite Fire to help protect my queer community."

Tap on anything like a stone or a sigil that you're using to wake it up, and say the appropriate mantra then. Light anything lightable, and say that part of the mantra as you're lighting.

Take a few minutes to sit and glow in the awoken elementals. Take a few deep breaths and see if they have any messages for you. Let this take as much or as little time as it needs.

When you feel ready, pick up the piece that represents your queer community. Hold it in your hands and repeat "I protect this community with the aid of the elements." as many times as it feels right. You can set this at a number of times before you start the spell, or go until you feel like you're done.

When done, place all elements on an altar or in a space where animals won't knock it over and it won't get stepped on. Relight anything that needs to be relit.

A Spell to Get Rid of Unsafe People in Your Work or Social Life

In spite of any community's good intentions, unsafe people sneak into communities that are vulnerable all the time. It's extra hurtful to see spaces you thought of as safer be poisoned this way, and that says nothing of the harm that comes from actually being attacked or affected by this person (or these people) directly. This spell was primarily included for unsafe community members, but it is efficient for unsafe people at work or otherwise floating around in your social life, too. It is a basic jar spell and there are countless variations, so feel free to play with it until you find the one that works for you.

You need:

- A jar with a lid

- The unsafe person's name written on a piece of paper and folded up—or a lock of their hair, or something they've touched

To perform the spell:

Put the piece of paper or alternate in the jar

Take the jar to the bathroom and pee in it. As you pee, say, "Be gone from my life (person's name)."

Wash your hands, and seal the jar. As you do so say, "May the harm you do reflect back at you. May I and my community be free from you."

Bury the jar. If you don't live near green space or somewhere where you can do it, sneak out and do it late at night or early in the morning somewhere meaningful to you but more public. Urban problems require urban solutions. Get creative. As you bury it, think of whomever you consider your ancestors, and ask them for help getting free of this person's influence and harm.

A Spell to Deflect and not Internalize Microaggressions

Microaggressions are small acts of bigotry and aggression like commenting that a femme "doesn't look like a lesbian" or that a BIPOC "speaks really well." They are hurtful, and many of us internalize them all the time. I know as a fat person, I walked around for years feeling like I had to be really vocal about my vegetable consumption and workout routines because I'd internalized the microaggression "you aren't like other fat people" that got used against me. This spell is meant to deflect those microaggressions away from you so you don't internalize them and so you can continue your journey towards self-awareness and empowerment.

You need:

- Two small mirrors that can stand on their own

- The image of someone you look up to—dead or alive

- A very small sponge or piece of sponge

- A protective oil or tincture—homemade or bought

- The mantra: "Microaggressions roll off of me/So I can be the person my loved ones see"

To perform this spell:

Set the two mirrors facing each other with the sponge in the middle.

Set the image of the person you admire behind them, propped up.

Focus your energy into the sponge as you repeat the mantra a set number of times. Halfway through your repetitions, put the oil on yourself or take the tincture. When you have only another repetition or two to go, dab a liberal but not drowning amount onto the sponge.

Focus on the feeling of loving yourself and feeling empowered. Focus on those microaggressive voices sounding more and more like a bug's buzzing and then imagine them quieting.

Grab the sponge and stick it in your bag, wallet, or pocket and carry it with you throughout the day. If someone performs a microaggression on you, find a quiet place to hold your sponge for a second and repeat the above mantra.

Power up the sponge on the Full Moon by setting it between the two mirrors, dabbing it with the oil or tincture, and letting it sit overnight.

Spells for Self-Discovery

I've designed these spells over the years to help myself and other queer people discover their truth. So much of my witchcraft is geared towards allowing those who are marginalized to thrive and flourish even in a society that hates them, but sometimes the big barrier in the way is not quite knowing what our truth is. These spells are designed to aid us on that journey, so that we can sit and become comfortable with who we are, before moving further on our path as queer people or witches.

Where Am I Hurting?

In order to heal, we often need to address the source spots of our pain. This can be something as straightforward as the first time we heard our parents say something transphobic, or it can be the complicated weave

of never seeing yourself fully represented on page, stage, or screen. To figure out why exactly you still stumble when it comes to naming and living as yourself, this spell helps pinpoint that pain as well as where it's living in your body.

You need:

- A body

- Optional: any tools that help with clarity, such as an athame, a clear quartz, or a white candle

To perform this spell:

Set your tools up appropriately and then lay down somewhere, as comfortably as you can. On your back is ideal but I *hate* laying on my back, so I usually choose my side. Do not cross your arms or legs.

Take a few deep breaths and close your eyes. Do what's called a body scan, where you slowly relax each part of you starting with either your head or your feet. You'll notice which parts are harder to relax or won't relax. That's where the source pain is living right now.

Once you have those areas pinpointed, slowly sit up and sit comfortably. Continue doing your breath work.

Ask your gods, ancestors, or any spiritual allies to help you find the source of this discomfort or pain, especially if it is spiritual or emotional. Sit and listen. Be open to new ideas, even (especially) if you're usually good at self-awareness. If you don't get any answers, try again on a Full or Dark Moon. You will get answers after several times of working this spell. You may even get answers the next day when you're hopping around, living your life—so get ready for an epiphany!

Once you know where and why you're hurting, we can start working to physically heal that body part or area that is holding your tensions. You can have some energy work done, use a relaxing oil, or even see a doctor or physical therapist. Hot baths with Epsom salts help. Find yoga exercises that stretch those body parts (even if it hurts at first). While the deeper spiritual

awakening may be needed to heal the *why*, we can start focusing on the *where* and heal from the outside in at first.

Keep checking in with your body, because you don't want to give up tension in one area just to have it stockpile in another.

A Spell for Coming into Your Own

For this spell, which is for learning to walk confidently in the world as your truest self, you'll need to identify some favorite colors and magickal tools. This one is more of a spell formula because it's about *you* coming into *your* own. You may also want some charms, stickers, or similar objects that represent your specific identities.

You need:

- Paper

- Pen

- Twine, yarn, or string

- Those favorite magickal tools, which should also include color correspondences to your identity

- Those charms, stickers, or other objects representing your identity

To perform this spell:

Set up your magickal tools and any charms, stickers, or other objects in a way that gives you some flexibility to move but does make you feel like you're in a magickal space.

Use the paper and pen to make two lists. The first list should be all of the things you love about the community of people who share your identity or identities. The second list should be things you love about yourself. It's okay if there's substantial overlap between the two lists. It's okay if there's not.

Roll these lists up, using twine, yarn, or string to keep them tightly bound. As you wind the tying threads around say, "May I embody the best of me and move forward confidently" until you're done.

Leave these on your altar, especially to any gods who represent love or empowerment. If you don't work with such a god, your patron deity or general altar is fine.

Owning and Connecting with Your Intuition: A Series of Small Spells

Queer people are very often shut off from their intuition for a number of reasons. Maybe you grew up needing to be in the closet and you silenced any inner voice at all. Maybe you grew up relatively affirmed and privileged and now struggle to find a safe place to use your voice in your queer community, afraid of overshadowing those who have worse experiences. Maybe you do okay in some areas of your life but not others because of how you've had to prioritize your life. And maybe, just maybe, you've gone so deep into needing to focus on base level survival that curating and nurturing a strong sense of intuition or psychic power never registered as high enough on your "to do list" for you to work on it.

For some of us, it's the opposite problem. I don't have statistics on this, but a lot of queer community and chosen family relationship building veers towards the intense and borderline codependent. We're all works in process, and that's okay. What happens to our intuition in these times though is that it's no longer the sole voice that cares about us and wants us to thrive. Sometimes we're blessed enough to have people who are affirming, supportive, and really want the best for us. Those voices shouldn't override ours, but when we're overwhelmed with gratitude or even just empathetic, they can. Our challenge is then making sure that the voice we hear most loudly and most clearly, truly is our own.

In any case, you are a deeply intuitive person, I promise. You have the ability and the responsibility to live your life by your own inner compass, because it's not wrong. This next group of small spells is meant to bring your intuition into full bloom and allow it to grow as you grow into listening to it more regularly and letting it guide you.

SPELL 1: ASTROLOGICAL SPELLS

For this spell, you'll need to know what element your Moon sign is sitting in and be comfortable working with that element.

From there you'll also need:

- A small purple or black candle

- **For Water Moon Signs—**A small vial of oil that increases psychic awareness or Moon water that *does not* open easily

- **For Earth Moon Signs—**A small stone or pouch of herbs geared at growing your intuition

- **For Air Moon Signs—**A word or sigil on a small piece of paper that represents your psychic awareness developing more deeply (even just the words *psychic power* or *intuition* will work)

- **For Fire Moon Signs—**Something small and carryable that represents intuition to you and has a flame on it, like a picture or charm; alternatively, wax from the candle once burnt also works

To perform this spell:

Once you have your elemental object, light a small candle and say, "As the flame burns, so my intuition grows." Sit and focus on the flame flickering (without hurting your eyes). Hold your hands up to it if you feel like you need too. Let your body absorb the flame's ideals of gut instinct.

Once you're nice and focused, hold your elemental talisman in your hands. Say, "This object is charged with intuition/So long as I carry it/I'll grow my psychic vision," a set number of times.

Sit and listen to your body, your mind, your spirit. What does it feel like it's trying to tell you now? Put the feeling of hearing that voice into your magickal object.

Blow out the candle. Charge your object in the smoke as it clears. Stick it in your wallet, bag, or pocket when you're done.

SMALL SPELL 2: FREEWRITING

This spell is best used when you feel like your intuition is trying to tell you *something* but you don't know what.

You need:

- Pen and paper

To perform this spell:

Sit down with your pen and paper. Clear your mind. Tune into the spots in your body where you think your intuition lives. Start writing. Write anything and everything that pops into your mind. When you feel done or realize you wrote out what that intuitive feeling is, stop. Look at what you've written. Circle or highlight the parts that you feel came from your intuition. Put this writing in a drawer and look back on it in a few days to see if anything new stands out.

Repeat as necessary.

SMALL SPELL 3: MOON WATER SPELL

I've referenced Moon water quite a bit in this book without really going into specifics about it. Here are the specifics:

Moon water is water that is left out and charged during a Full Moon, a Dark Moon, or any part of the Moon's cycle that *you* feel deeply connected too. You can throw a couple of grains of sea salt in there, but for this spell I wouldn't, because this spell does involve drinking the Moon water.

You need:

- A jar or bottle with lid

- Water—purified if possible but it will purify by sitting out overnight

- Optional: a *clean* quartz crystal, a small white candle, and edible herbs that correlate to intuition

To perform this spell:

Pick the night of the Moon's current cycle that you think will work best for a psychic spell. On that night, fill the jar or bottle partway with water. If you're using a stone or herbs to ground the spell or

because you're an Earth Sun, Moon, or Rising sign, stick those in the jar, too. Put the lid on.

Moon water can be used for a plethora of things, so be specific. Write down and place under the jar or bottle *or* say out loud as you're placing the jar or bottle on a windowsill that you're charging water in this specific Moon to increase your psychic awareness and intuition.

If you're using a small white candle, light it and let it die out naturally.

Let the jar sit overnight, soaking up all those witchy moon vibes.

The next day, pull the jar down. Remove crystal if relevant. Thank the Moon for helping you on your intuitive journey.

Drink the water mindfully. As you sip, think about what increased psychic sensitivity would mean for you and how you can let it guide your life. Think about trusting yourself and letting your guard with yourself down. *Optional:* if you don't like plain water (please drink water, but I get it) you can use this water to make coffee, which is connected to the Earth and includes psychic aid. If you don't like coffee or water, use the water to make herbal tea with herbs connected to psychic vision.

Repeat on as many big Moon nights as you feel like you need to to grow your intuition and ability to apply it practically.

Spells for Healing

I want to tread carefully as we dip into the idea of healing spells or healing magick in queer community because I'm not a doctor, a pharmacist, or a body worker and sometimes what you need is genuine medical or psychiatric care. Nothing found in this grimoire is going to replace that care, though some spells are meant to amplify it. I know firsthand that those of us living in the margins are *wildly* under resourced when it comes to medical care, and I'm not here to lecture you to get to a medical facility. You can't always, and those of us living in these shrubs on the metaphorical or literal outskirts of society have always managed

to find a way to function. While I think a lot of herbalism and bodywork can be just as useful as medicine, and it certainly is for me, that's not what this section is because it's not my area of expertise. If you could put a name on my magick it would be queer, eclectic folk witch though my focus has always been on the emotional and the spiritual.

Those are the things this portion of the grimoire hopes to aid in healing—the places where we have been hurt spiritually, intellectually, and emotionally. You still might need additional support and care, but these spells will help prop you up and get you through the current stage of your life. Because affordable care can quickly become an access issue, remember that one major strength of queer community is being able to bond together to take care of our members in need. When possible, do these spells in groups so that a bigger, louder call goes up into the universe and gets answered.

Out of the Closet: Healing for the Next Steps

This is an art spell, though you might be able to use found objects (like a small trunk that you would put a doll in to represent a closet) in lieu of making your own art. Art can be crude. It's meant for spiritual entities, not consumption by others. It is meant for any identity in the LGBTQQIA2SP+ spectrum, for any closet you might come out of. Once I was out as a lesbian back in the mid 2000s (the oughts), I thought the world would be my oyster, but I quickly realized that in addition to battling Bible Belt homophobia I also had to contend with the homophobia I'd internalized, the fear of rejection from my peers, and the intense self-doubt I felt on a daily basis. At the time, I worked through this on my own in spite of having a regular magickal practice at the time. In retrospect, I absolutely could have used a spell like this one instead. As people I cherish have come out of the closet over the years, this is a working I've personalized and performed a handful of times that acknowledges why that self-doubt and internalized homophobia is rampant but still pushes us through the threshold of not holding space for it within ourselves anymore.

You'll need:

- An artistic rendering of a closet, or a small trunk—you can also make your own mini-wardrobe for this spell if you're a sculptor or woodworker

- Pen and paper
- A small likeness of you—a doll, a lego mini fig, a picture of you, a self-portrait
- A small black or gray candle and a small purple candle
- A cup of herbal tea with herbs that are spiritually healing and cleansing *and* yummy to you, like lavender or eucalyptus—make it before performing the spell
- A fire safe receptacle

To perform this spell:

Drink your tea naturally as you perform this spell.

Light your black candle and say, "The closeted and edited version of myself is no more."

Light your purple candle and say, "May I heal from the wounds I acquired in the closet and not live in fear of them anymore."

Create or set up your artistic renderings of the closet and you. You should be *out* of the closet for the art and it should be two seperate renderings. Again, found objects are fine for either.

Once you're happyish with your closet art, write a list of things you're not happy with or struggling with in regards to being a queer person or your life in the closet. When I came out of the closet as nonbinary, mine included everything from the color pink to expectations of performing gender roles and back again. If I'd made one after coming out as a lesbian it would've said everything from the way Jake kisses to lack of representation, and back again.

Sit with your list. In a way, this is shadow work. When you feel ready, on a new sheet of paper or the back of this one, separate this list into two lists. One list is the things you can comfortably say good-bye too, like the color pink or the way Jake kisses. The other list should be the things you *will* have to continuously grapple with and heal from—like lack of representation.

Take the list of things you can say good-bye to, and burn it in the fire of the candle of your choosing. Once it's lit, you can place it in the fire-safe receptacle. Just check on it to make sure it doesn't stop burning.

Once this list is reduced to ashes, put it in your "closet." If you've done a paper rendering, just kind of smear the ashes on the backside of the paper or canvas to represent those things staying in the closet, where they belong and *you* do not.

Place the list of things you're still working through under the representation of you. Place the candles with these other objects. Finish your tea and let the candles burn.

Unlike the rest of the spells we've seen today, don't keep burning those candles once you feel like the spell is done. Instead, dispose of the wax, the closet, and any candle drippings. Clean out your tea mug. It's done. Keep only the representation of you and the list of things you're still grappling with. Trust that representation to keep grappling for you. They will.

Healing from the Wounds of the World

This is a pretty dark title for a pretty light spell, but it's named that because this spell is supposed to represent a wide array of pains from feeling hurt when new, queerphobic laws are passed to the stress of having to deal with parents who commit microaggressions. Basically, if it comes from the world at large, this is the spell.

This is a healing and somewhat of a protective spell, and it is an oil spell recipe. If you are a Fire sign, you might want to take the extra step and light a candle, and run the potion container through the smoke. Do the same thing but with incense for Air signs. Earth signs may want to throw some shards or small pieces of clear quartz or substitute an herb for one of the herbal oils in this spell.

Please note this spell does have several ingredients that cost money. Feel free to make substitutes as needed and appropriate.

Please note, too, that this is a sex/masturbation magick spell. The point just post-orgasm is when you want to hold and charge the sigil so

this does take some self-control to be able to grab the sigil and focus in that state.

You need:

- An appropriate-sized container, with lid

- Aloe vera oil

- Tea tree oil

- Lavender oil or buds

- Sandalwood oil

- A carrier oil like coconut or almond oil

- Something adhesive that we can write on (masking tape is fine) and something to write on it with

- Blue or purple glitter glue

To perform this spell:

Fill about one sixth of your container with your carrier oil. We want to be able to put this on your skin safely.

Add drops of the other oils until you're satisfied with the smell and the amount of oil. Test it on a *very* small patch of skin to make sure it doesn't burn. Add more carrier or aloe vera if it does until you're happy with that result.

Create a sigil for healing or use this one, on your adhesive piece. As you're designing, tracing, or drawing, focus on where you're hurting and what needs to be healed. What are you moving on from and warding off?

Dab small drops of your oil onto your upper thighs, where your heart lies within your chest, and the back of your neck or on your skull.

Say, "I am healing from the outside world/My empowered self is becoming unfurled" as you dab.

Masturbate or have sex with your sigil nearby. As you do, think about what healing from these outside sources actually feels like or looks like for you. After you climax, grab the sigil. Kiss it. Whisper "Thank you for helping me heal," to your genitals and to the sigil.

Come down from the sex magick. Suck on an ice cube or stand in front of the AC. Take some deep, calming breaths. When you feel not quite as post-coital, attach the sigil to your oil's container.

Decorate the bottle with blue or purple glitter glue. As you decorate, say your mantras again—whichever ones from this spell you liked the best.

Three Spells for Healing from Spiritual Harm

This spell is one that I have to use surprisingly often, as most of the witches I practice with are queer, which means most of us are very used to the very real pain that comes from spiritual harm. Spiritual harm can mean a lot of things, but I've used this spell primarily in three different cases:

1. When I'm working with witches who have Religious Trauma Syndrome. This is a syndrome that has a lot of the same Complex PTSD (C-PTSD) symptoms that any kind of abuse in your upbringing can cause, but with RTS you may specifically have a hard time believing or trusting in any god or your own spiritual self even decades after you've been marked safe from that abuse. This is really common among queer witches, who've been the primary recipient of this spell.

2. When someone has hexed me or a loved one. The hex alone is usually easy enough to end and return to sender. What I struggle with more is the feeling that someone that I was close enough with for them to know I'm sensitive to magick, would turn around and try to hurt me. The emotional pain is usually far greater than the spiritual pain, but it can make one overly cautious for a while in their own practice. Again, this is not an explicitly queer phenomenom, but when it does happen from queer person to queer person, the feeling of betrayal can run deeper than that of a hex that is not queer-to-queer.

3. When someone I love has been careless with their magick. This is the least common reason I've used this spell, but it does happen on occasion, like when I call faeries and forget to or just don't take care of them. It does happen on occasion that someone calls a spirit or an entity in and doesn't know how to release it. In both of those cases, those energies aren't necessarily harmful but they do get restless and this can cause spiritual or emotional pain to whoever did the initial spellwork. This is not an exclusively queer experience either, but it does happen to a lot of new and overeager witches, so I wanted to make sure to include it.

Of course, every cause of spiritual harm requires its own healing spell. These are all pretty simple, but may take some thought, planning, and confrontation with self in the weeks leading up to the spell to be everything that they can be.

A SPELL FOR COMFORT OVER RELIGIOUS TRAUMA SYNDROME

You need:

- A couple of weeks to process and think through how RTS has affected you and what it's affecting; you'll also want to think about what your current spiritual beliefs and strengths are and where you're feeling blocked—use a journal and pen when necessary

- Something that represents any god or entity you're currently in collaboration with

- A friend you trust to perform the spell

- A cleansing stick your ancestors would have used (I use cedar or lavender)

To perform the spell:

Once you've done your thinking and you feel ready, sit down with the friend or friends you trust to do this spell with you. Talk through

your current blocks and concerns. Together, create an incantation, appealing to your current spiritual allies for help.

Put up a circle. RTS creates a strong feeling of lack of safety and security, so you'll want all of the extra protection you can muster.

Envision your aura (or have a friend do this for you) as brown, red, murky, angry. Now envision or have your friend perform the acts of picking out those murky parts and throwing them away until your outer self is filled with the more playful or compassionate hues you're trying to live in.

Recite the incantation you wrote as you do this.

Say a quiet prayer to your current gods letting them know that you *want* to trust them, you just are struggling. Listen for any messages from them.

Have your friend light the cleansing stick or wand and wave it around your front side and back side.

Hug your friend and thank them for being there.

Know you may need to repeat this spell, many times, over the next few years as you sort through the trauma of being abused.

Release the circle.

A SPELL FOR HEALING FROM THE BETRAYAL OF BEING HEXED

You need:

- Something that belonged to the person who hexed you: something they gave you, a picture of them, or their name on a piece of paper

- If the thing of theirs can be burned to ash, grab a lighter or match and a fire-safe bowl or receptacle

- A healing oil

- A charm, sticker, patch, or the like, of a heart—yellow or rainbow, if color is relevant, if you're both a queer identity that is best represented by a specific rainbow, that's the rainbow that the heart should be

- Something that represents your spiritual path, like an idol of an animal ally or a deck of your favorite tarot cards

To perform this spell:

Cry if you need to. Scream if you need to. Let yourself be hurt.

Destroy or burn the representation of them. As you do, yell at them that they can't and won't hurt you anymore. If burning, place in fire-safe bowl. Yell until it's gone or destroyed.

Take some deep breaths. Ground yourself.

Dab the healing oil onto the heart symbol. Say something to the effect of "My heart is healing from this betrayal." Keep this on your person or altar as a reminder that you're working on your healing moving forward.

Dab the healing oil onto the representation of your current spiritual path. Say something like "My path is my own, and will not be waylaid by this." Thank the item you're using.

A SPELL FOR WHEN YOU MESSED UP

First and foremost, forgive yourself. Everyone makes spiritual mistakes, and in the grand scheme of things, yours is probably relatively minor. Remind yourself that no one is perfect.

From there, you need:

- An appropriate cleansing stick or wand (like cedar, lavender, or sage if you're Indigenous)

- A bell or something that makes a bell-like noise—a noise on your phone is fine (it's the 21st Century, work with what you've got)

To perform the spell:

Sit calmly in the affected area of your home. Breathe deeply.

Invite the entities in question to commune with you. Let them have their say, even if their say is really freaking you out. They might not say anything. They might give you the feeling that someone is glaring angrily at you. That's okay.

Apologize for bringing them in and neglecting or hurting them. Recognize clearly that you have hurt them and you want to release them now.

Envision them floating through your ceiling and back into the ether.

Light your cleansing stick or wand and move through your space. Ring the bell or play the noise as you do. Say something that gives the effect of "If you mean harm or need more than I can give, please go" as you do.

Healing from a Broken Heart

A broken heart is a broken heart, regardless of identity but I also know that, as a queer person, every breakup feels like I'm getting further from my romantic goals. Statistically there are fewer of us. That pressure and that pain throbs deep into our soul, and it can make us feel totally alone even when we're surrounded by chosen family. Queer heartbreaks and queer breakups are really something you can't understand until you've been through one. Every heartbreak is unique, of course. They are called heartbreaks for a reason. Yet something about the way queer people approach relationships makes every relationship feel like soul mate potential and makes every break up course through us exponentially. Of course, spellwork alone won't heal this. You need community, laughter, and perhaps mental health care if the wounds really won't heal. Your craft can and does help though, and this spell is one I have used more times than I care to list.

You need:

- Symbols or objects associated with the relationship

- A lighter

- A fire-safe receptacle

- Seashells, quartz, or rose quartz

- A song or playlist about heartbreak

- A song or playlist about having fun and loving life

- A purple candle

- Flowers of your choice

- A patch that indicates that you're tough

To perform this spell:

Blare the heartache song or playlist. Cry.

Destroy or burn their things. Put them in the fire-safe receptacle.

Light the purple candle. Ask your gods to help you heal.

Sit with your seashell or stone. Think about your life after this heartbreak. What hopes and dreams do you have for your romantic future? Don't think about getting back together with this person. They probably aren't right for you. Think about what you need in a future partner. Think about all the cool things you can do on your own now.

When you feel ready, charm the stone or seashells to bring you healing and good luck in your romantic life moving forward. Keep it on or with you, or place it on your nightstand so you see it every morning and every night.

Play your fun song or playlist. Thank your gods and allies for helping you in this time. Put your flowers in a vase or cup somewhere prominent. Giving flowers to yourself represents self-love and fun. Now you'll see that reminder for a few days.

Sit back down and turn off the music.

Put the patch in your hands and remind yourself that you've gone through worse times than this. Charge the patch in the candle's

smoke to help you heal and stay strong. Sew it on to something you own and wear a lot or just stick it in the pocket.

Blow out the candle and thank your gods for helping you through this. Release any tension in your neck, shoulders, and jaw and imagine the person who broke your heart slipping through the floorboards.

Healing from Burnout/Exhaustion

This spell is pretty self-explanatory, but I do want to remind you that a good self-care practice to help you avoid getting to this point is really important in your spellwork. You don't want to see your spells, your work, and everything else have diminishing returns, so *you* need to be at your best and strongest. That being said, life happens. I still totally burn out a couple of times a year, and I have an admirable self-care practice. Sometimes life is just life, and if you're traumatized, sick, living in the margins, or any combination thereof you're still going to burn out. That's especially true when life throws a bunch of new changes or obstacles in our way. For those times, this burnout spell is pretty effective.

Before you do anything else though, this spell requires that you think about and maybe jot down some notes about what makes you feel rested and restored. I like a couple of hours with a good book or a really hot bath or both. My queerplatonic partner likes to sit and draw things no one else will ever see while binging *Bob's Burgers* reruns. Sometimes you'll need to get out of town. As you move into this spell, spend some time coming up with answers to two questions:

What recharges and remotivates me, daily or generally speaking?

What do I need most right now?

From there you're ready to move on to this spell.

You'll need:

- *Candles*—in whatever color says rest and rejuvenation to you (If I'm totally burnt out and just need my fire completely relit, I'll use orange or yellow; if I genuinely need the rest, I'll use a mermaid blue or lavender because those shades are really soothing to me)

- Purified water, Moon or otherwise, or a drink made with purified or Moon water

- A scrap of cloth big enough to make a small pouch out of, and something to tie it up with

- Herbs, oils, and maybe a small stone that correlate with healing and rest for you

- Your planner and a pen—unless your planner is on your phone or computer, in which case just pull it up

- Optional: lavender or other soothing oil

To perform this spell:

Light your candles and welcome any spiritual entities that you're inviting in to help with this spell.

Charge your water to be extra restorative in the candle's smoke. Say, "By the power of (your patron deity's name) may this water provide health and vitality."

Drink the water casually as you do the rest of the spell.

As you think about what led you to this place of burnout, start putting your herbs and anything else you are going to add into the pouch.

Dab a couple of drops of the oils you selected on to that herb pile.

Tie off the pouch, saying, "May I heal from burnout" as you do so.

Sleep with this under your pillow until you feel like you don't need it anymore.

Before going to sleep that first night, and before you blow the candle out, write down some self-care dates in your planner based on your answers to those two questions I asked above:

What recharges and remotivates me, daily or generally speaking?

What do I need most right now?

Stick to those self-care dates, and get some sleep.

If you have trouble sleeping add some lavender or other soothing oil to the corners of your pillow.

Manifestation Spells

Most people are drawn to magick because of the thrill and intrigue of manifestation spells. Manifestation spells are the spells we cast that bring the things we desire to us. Money magick, love spells, and most wishing spells are all versions of manifestation spells. Magick is tricky though because the reality is that if something is not in our best interest (or someone else's) or not possible, those manifesting spells still won't come true. It doesn't mean you've done anything wrong at all, it just means that the spell you cast *can't* happen. If I were to cast a spell tonight to make myself a millionaire by next week there is absolutely no way that spell would come true. If I cast one to make myself a millionaire within ten years, and I decided to do the required work to wrangle my finances and take a more lucrative job, then I'm much more likely to hit that magickal goal.

Yes, that's the other caveat to manifestation spells—you have to do the work to make them work by moving yourself in the direction you want to go. If I cast a spell to make new friends and never leave my apartment, where exactly are those new friends supposed to come from? You've got to meet your gods partway. It's also true that sometimes you can be doing everything right, and yet you're still not finding what you need. That's where the magick comes in. I've definitely hit dry spells in my love life where it's the same crowd everywhere I go, even when I'm going to new places and trying to experiment. When I cast a spell to bring some new faces in, ideally with romantic potential, those dry spells shift into something more fun and flirty.

All of that being said, I have seen people make miracles for themselves and their loved ones with manifestation magick. I've seen money come out of nowhere in desperate times as the result of a spell. I've seen housing open up when it gets absolutely critical for someone to find it. I've seen decades-estranged family members or close friendships come back into each other's lives through manifestation and healing spells worked together.

The thing about manifestation spells that gets tricky for queer witches, is that you have to believe that it can and will work for you. I'm not super into the idea that you create your own reality, but I do think if you cast a spell without meaning it, it's not likely to come true. That fifth element, Spirit, needs to be there before you can really do the work that needs to be done. Spirit needs to be strong and faithful—if not in a god, then in yourself and the idea that you deserve to attract the things you want into your life. For people who have had very real marginalizations and oppressions like poverty, racism, and homophobia in their lives it's easy to feel like you don't deserve good things or, even if you know you do, it feels like it's impossible for them to come to you. That means there's healing spellwork that needs to happen before we can dip our toes into manifestation.

Journal Prompt

Think about the first time you were made to feel like your wants and desires didn't matter or couldn't be met. Journal about this experience and how it affects and influences your decisions and behavior into today. Do some journaling as you are able about other experiences that contributed to this story, and where that has left you now.

Finally, do some journaling on times that story hasn't been reinforced. When have you wanted something, no matter how big or small, and how was your right to that desire met or reinforced? How can you start reframing the stories of your desires to focus more on the times you did get what you need? What work can you do, emotional or practical, to get to that place?

As queer people it's also true that we have to think outside the box to do our share of the work. Someone who is trans and has spent their whole life in poverty is probably not going to be able to walk into a bank, demand a high paying job, and have it come to them. It's possible, and I've seen it happen, but it's not very probable. So our money magick means relying on shared wealth with others and often, the gig economy. In 2020 there are also countless corporations determined to prove to us that they are genuine allies who will give us the work we want or need for a prosperous life. It still takes a lot of research to figure out which corporations those are and

how safe you'll be should the social tide move back towards queerphobia. If it's love magick you're into but you live in a small town with few to no queer people, you might have to get creative about where you might find or run into potential paramours. This might mean going online to ensure the people you're talking to are queer (and therefore safer). It might mean doing some really intense research to figure out where the people in your small town are hiding out, because really, there usually are, *somewhere*. It might mean going a town over to see what their nightlife looks like. It's unfortunate that as witches we have to work so much harder to figure out how to meet our goals as queer people, but that is the world we live in right now. However, using your creativity also means there isn't as much scarcity mindset and greed around the solutions you come up with because they're not as sought after so it's ultimately how I try to push *any* of my witchcraft students or mentees.

With that, we're ready to look at some manifestation spells for all areas of your life. As always, if you can't find a spell ingredient, don't worry about it. Use the appendix to figure out what you have that you could use, and rework the spell to make it fit.

Anticapitalist Money Spells

So often, before we can move on or move forward in any area of our life, we need money, plain and simple. The following spells range from super quick and easy to more complex, but there's no need to think "faster spell" equals "lesser spell." All of these, done with intent, are designed to bring about abundance in your life. I call these Anti-Capitalist Money Spells because I don't think we have to condone capitalism to want to survive or even do well under it. None of these spells are meant to equate your worth with the money that the spell can bring. They are all meant to help affirm you as a person while allowing you the piece of the pie you deserve for living in the system you live in.

Everything has its limits, and that includes money magick. It makes the most sense to know where money, opportunity, or as we move forward, friendship, sex, or relationsips will mostly likely come from before starting our spellwork. So, I want to be crystal clear that you absolutely need to leave yourself open to surprises, and to include that openness in your spell. You will become more focused where Ocam's Razor says your luck is most likely to manifest if you have some ideas of where that is first.

Miracles can happen with magick, and if you need one, do a spell for one. Most of the time magick is just about focusing on what our resources are and creating gold out of those.

MONEY SPELL 1: THE STIRRING SPELL

This is a super easy money spell that you can use whether you are cooking or mixing food ingredients that correlate to money magick, stirring cream and sugar into your coffee or iced coffee, or even just drinking some water and wanting to do some quick magick.

You need:

- Foods you are mixing or stirring that have correspondences to money—coffee that you are mixing cream and sugar into, or anything that you can perform the following actions with

- Something to stir with

- A mantra or goal that you're trying to hit, like "Money is attracted easily to me" or "I will see at least four clients at this event"

To perform this spell:

- Grab your stirring implement and stir clockwise, like you're stirring towards yourself.

- Repeat your goal or mantra as you do so.

- Drink up, or bake your food and enjoy, *or* finish cooking and share what you've made with others. As you drink or eat, occasionally reflect on your goal and mantra.

MONEY SPELL 2: BAKING BREAD

The kitchen witch art of baking bread comes from the idea that you're using very few cheap, easy ingredients and putting love, intention, and time into them to turn them into something yummy and magickal. I love this as a form of anticapitalist money magick because you are reiterating that you *can* make do with very little, but that you're trying to do more than survive at this point. In spite of how simple bread can be to

bake, it feels luxurious and indulgent to chow down on some well-done homemade bread. This too is money magick and pleasure activism all in one—enjoying something for what it is and trusting that this is resistance.

You need:

- Something to bake your bread in, like an oven or bread maker
- ¼ ounce of dry yeast
- 2 ¼ cups warm water
- 2–3 Tablespoons of sugar (to taste)
- 1–2 Tablespoons of salt (to taste)
- 2 Tablespoons cooking oil of choice
- Roughly 6 ½ cups of bread flour of choice
- Money ingredients—rosemary and basil for savory, cinnamon and cloves for sweeter, and so forth to taste
- A large mixing bowl and some cooking spray or grease
- Baking pans

To perform this spell:

Bake the bread. Start by dissolving your yeast in your water with a small amount of your sugar—half a teaspoon is recommended. Bubbles will form on the surface when you're ready to move forward.

Take this downtime to meditate on financial gain, whatever that looks like for you. Brainstorm how you could bring in money fast *or* what you want for long-term financial health and success.

Once the bubbles are formed, stir (whisk) together the sugar, salt, money ingredients, and three cups of flour. As you pour the salt, especially, remember that in our society money equals safety, and you deserve to be safe.

Stir oil into your yeast mixture and then stir this mixture into your flour mixture. You may need to beat it, and not just stir at this point. Slowly add flour a little bit at a time until it forms a soft dough.

Lightly flour a large cutting board or your counter and spread your dough out. Knead this dough until it's elastic and not as soft. This should take 8–10 minutes, but I knead slowly so it usually takes me longer.

Grease your bowl and put your dough into it. Cover until the size of the dough has doubled. This usually takes at least an hour. Go do something else, witchy or otherwise relaxing.

Punch the dough down on your floured surface once it's ready, and cut it in half. Put each half of the dough into an appropriately sized baking pan. Your dough *will* rise a lot so plan accordingly. Cover and let rise again, which takes approximately another hour, hour and a half.

When you think you have about ten minutes to go, preheat your oven to 375°. Stand over your bread and bless it. Feel free to touch the pans (but probably not the dough) and put intentions, specific or otherwise, into them.

When the dough is blessed and ready and the oven is preheated, cook for 30–35 minutes.

Let it cool.

Appropriately store both loaves. One is for you and whomever you live with to enjoy. The other should be given to someone who is food insecure. In sharing what we have, we show that we have enough to share, which attracts more to us.

Cut off a small piece for any altar that is dedicated to gods in your home, if relevant. This can be skipped if you have issues with insects or animals who should not, but will, eat the bread.

MONEY SPELL 3: A SIMPLE ELEMENTAL SPELL FOR DESPERATE TIMES

Calling in the elements when we're in need is always a good call. This spell helps us work with the natural world to bring emergency money when we're suddenly finding ourselves food insecure, struggling with housing stability because of money, or under the pressure of debt that we can't get out of.

You need:

- A small green candle—or whatever color means money to you

- Any herbs that correspond with money

- Any oil that is arguably money-oriented—even just olive oil from your kitchen

- An incense stick that corresponds to money, like Patchouli or anything citrus

- A paper and pen for a thank you note

If you're struggling with money and don't have these things on hand, ask someone if you can borrow these items or make substitutions as needed. This should be a quick candle spell with all of the other elements present, however you're able to swing that.

To perform this spell:

Dress your candle in oil and then herbs.

Light the candle and your incense stick.

Say a quick prayer asking for your specific need to be met.

Bury or dispose of the candle end and incense when done.

Put a quick thank you note on your altar once your need is met.

MONEY SPELL 4: A CHARM SPELL FOR OVERCOMING POVERTY TRAUMA

Poverty trauma is called trauma for a reason. Years after we leave the bounds of poverty, or even when we start being truly comfortable but are still under the poverty line, we struggle to remember that our next meal is taken care of and to believe that the money we're steadily making isn't just going to all be ripped away from us. This is especially true for queer and BIPOC people who really do need to watch their backs because we do not live in a society that wants us to succeed or move forward. Yet we do owe it to ourselves to succeed, and we can't give back to our community or redistribute our own wealth if we don't have any.

I created a charm spell to enchant an object that you are meant to keep on your person. This helps draw money to you in real time, and it gives you a frequent visual reminder that you are growing and moving forward.

You need:

- A charm or image of an animal or symbol of wealth and abundance—I suggest cow, which reminds us of the mantra "I have enough," or goldfish, which symbolize wealth and signs that we are moving forward

To perform this spell:

Speak your intentions for this charm while you slowly rub your hands together. It's okay to experiment with the words or work to figure it out for a while. Something like "this cow reminds me I am stable" or "Chan Chu'u brings money steadily to me" is just fine.

As your words set, rub your hands together more and more quickly until they feel warm, and then speed up until they feel hot.

As soon you feel hot and fervored, grab your object or image and hold it between both hands. Let your hands come down. You'll feel some heat and some throbbing. Think of that as energy being transferred into your charm.

An optional alternative amplification of this spell is to correlate this spell with sex magick. As you're working towards orgasm, rub

your hands together or on your thighs or chest. As you cum, grab your object and allow it to stay in your hands as you come down from the orgasm.

Either way, once it's charged, stick the charm in your bag, wallet, or coat pocket and keep it on your person. Pull it out and gaze at it when you feel insecure.

Listen for messages the charm might send you over the next couple of days, and take those to heart.

MONEY SPELL 5: MAY IT COME BACK TO ME

This is another common folk spell that is perfect for those of us who are anti-capitalist but still have financial needs since that is the system we live in. It involves giving back to those who need it and being generous while also leaving plenty of space for our Divine entities to be generous to us. This spell is based on the relatively Wiccan principle of "3 x 3," meaning anything we put out comes back to us times three. I don't believe in the math and some of the darker, spiritual bypassing parts that get thrown in with this adage, but I do think that when we're generous and kind, we foster generosity in our own lives. Sometimes by our gods, sometimes by our own community, sometimes by developing our ability to attract comfort to ourselves.

You need:

- A handful of $1 or $5 bills

- A marker or pen

- Optional: a money, prosperity, or blessing oil

To perform this spell:

Use your pen to write some blessings (prosperity or otherwise) discreetly on the bills. It shouldn't take up so much of the bill that people will notice or refuse to take it. I usually just write something like "Be Blessed" or "May $ Find You Easily" somewhere discreet.

If using oil, dab it in the corners of the bills.

Over the next couple of days, use these bills to pay tips to servers or baristas who seem like they're having a rough day or to give to homeless people who ask for money.

When they're mostly handed out, keep the final one for yourself and place it on your altar or in your wallet.

Spells for Love and Sex

Love and sex spells are controversial in the witch community, but that's mostly because people don't quite understand them. Love spells are wildly effective, and sex spells can be too, so long as you're not trying to bind someone else's free will or cause danger to yourself. It's easy to say then, that love and sex spells are most effective when there's no known target, but there are exceptions to that, too. Spells to keep your relationship healthy, happy, and lasting are obviously safe and effective, as well. Spells that inspire someone to make a move when everyone *knows* you're both too scared to make a move are great. Spells to help heal a relationship that is struggling are wonderful. The key is knowing yourself and any partners (potential or otherwise) well enough to know what the best option is, and to be honest with yourself about that. Fundamentally, you cannot change who someone is or how they feel about you any more through magick than you can otherwise. Furthermore, if you're seeking to gain back an ex who cheated on you, abused you, stole money from you, or any other number of other horrible things I've seen seekers eager to overlook, I would strongly suggest focusing on healing and self-love magick instead. There's not a god out there who will bring an abuser back to you, because that is *not* for your own good.

A love or sex spell that is right for you is one that brings hot, satisfying sex into your life or a healthy, sustained relationship full of laughter and joy or both. That's it. That's the whole secret of what makes them work or not, what makes them good or bad, or any other questions you might have about them. For queer people, especially those who do not live in a big city or their city's gayborhood, love and sex spells are a great ally because they simply allow us to cross paths with more queer people than we otherwise might. A lot of times finding Mx. Right or Mx. Right Now is a numbers game, and magick can absolutely be used to skew numbers in our favor and bring more people into our world. Queer people need that,

so queer people seeking connection do need love and sex magick. Below are a number of spells designed for everything from a queer one-night stand to bonding a polyamorous family together to finding chosen family that will genuinely support you.

START HERE: SELF-LOVE SPELLS FOR THE MARGINALIZED

Whenever we're preparing to learn the art of love or sex magick, we have to start at the beginning—by healing the relationships that we have with ourselves. I don't believe that we have to love ourselves to be worthy of love. I think the sheer act of existing in a world that hates us makes us worthy of love. That means we are worthy of our own love, too. All too often we don't break down the internal walls that reinforce the world's external walls that prevent us from thriving where we otherwise might, if we had learned how to love and respect ourselves. And to be honest, as someone who fought myself and put myself down for years, learning to love yourself feels good. It feels like coming home to your own body again, which is another feeling that, as queer people, we are often led to believe shouldn't belong to us. Even on days my gender dysphoria is through the roof or I feel completely alone in the world, there is a feeling of being rooted and connected to myself that sustains and even lifts me up, and that feels . . . amazing.

Self-love is an art though, and it's a healing more than it's a love spell, if we're being honest. We have to rid ourselves of the *ick* that has been pounded into our brains by our families, by society, by toxic exes, or ex-friends, and we have to build from the ground up, like we would a house. Because we may not be a house, but we are the home for our magick and our capacity for love and everything else contained within us. For some of us, we are the only home we have for a long time—so we might as well learn how to live in it.

Self-Love Spell 1: A Poppet Spell

This spell requires you to do the work of figuring out what correspondences say "self-love" to you as a queer person. I use a lot of the same ones I would for a general love spell, so things like rose petals and orange oil work great. From there, you're ready to jump into this spell.

You need:

- Poppet materials—cloth or corn husks or whatever you're using for the body, needle and thread or thicker strings to sew or tie it all together, and such

- Self-love goodies to fill the poppet with—spend time with the correspondence lists in the back to see what screams self-love to you or start by gathering some of your favorite materials together. I commonly use dried rose petals; orange zest, peel, or oil; and material from clothes I used to love that have since gotten too worn out to wear

- Outer decor for the poppet if desired—I sometimes use patches or pins, sometimes yarn for hair in my hair color, or other decorations

To perform this spell:

Make the poppet (obviously) as described on page 9.

While you're making it, think about times you've been proud of yourself or felt the idea of self-love as something more tangible. Focus on putting that feeling into the poppet.

As you sew or tie the poppet up, repeat to yourself, "I am capable of loving myself."

Decorate the poppet if desired.

Leave the poppet by your bedside, on your desk—somewhere you'll see or interact with it frequently.

Self-Love Spell 2: My Body Is Mine

For most trauma survivors, a lesson that gets hammered home is that our body isn't ours. If we grew up in a conservative religious setting that hated queerness (or outright denied it existed) we were probably also told how to get our hair cut, what to wear, and definitely what *not* to do in terms of wild hair colors or piercings. If we are survivors of sexual assault or domestic violence, we often feel a very real disconnect from our body or get it in our heads that our body is for other people's pleasure and not

our own. Those of us who struggle with gender dysphoria intentionally separate from our bodies sometimes because the trauma of existing in them is too difficult. Chronic pain (which many queer people also face) and sexual dysfunction can cause a similar trauma and therefore disconnect. All of that specifically reflects back on how we see our body, which can affect how we see ourselves.

This spell then is meant to make us feel gorgeous *and* pull ourselves back into our body, accepting it as our own. This can be paired with some mantras or incantations that serve as glamours too, but let's start at the beginning. This spell, it's worth noting, is not for everybody but is incredibly flexible. You'll notice there's not a "You need" list, but you might have, want, or need to pull some materials together before doing the spell. I don't create one for you because this spell is meant to be hyper-personalized, so it really depends on what *you* want to do.

To perform this spell:

Think about a haircut, hair color, piercing, or tattoo you've always wanted or wanted to experiment with, or even one you've become fascinated with lately.

Some of the above are price prohibitive, but there are always options. Tattoos can often be pared down simple enough to let a friend you trust perform a stick-and-poke tattoo on you. You could trade a haircut from someone you know does a good job for some skills you have or products you can make. You can get the cheapest dye from Spencer's or find a reputable discount piercing place. You can also, obviously, save up to get it done the way you really want to.

If any cost at all is prohibitive, think about how your style or clothing could reflect a more radical, queer version of yourself. Slowly start updating your wardrobe or attend a clothing swap to acquire more gender, age, or politics affirming clothes.

Jump in and make the change! As you're getting your hair dyed, nose pierced, or whatever you decide to do, repeatedly think to yourself "My body is mine and I do what I want."

Voila! You now have an updated style that reflects who you are. Whenever you notice it in the mirror it will be drilled into you that this is *you*, a bolder, sexier version of you that you can build from.

Repeat the above mantra in the mirror or while dressing as often as you need to.

OPTIONAL PART 2: GLAMOUR TIME

To add the optional glamour step to this spell, think about how you want others to see you. I often wish to be read as gay or non-binary in a queer space, or to be read as sexy on a date regardless of how I feel that day, for example.

From there, you need:

- Environmentally friendly glitter in a gender-affirming color
- A small white candle

To perform this portion of the spell:

Roll the candle in the glitter or gently sprinkle it onto the candle. Think about how you want people to see you.

Say "I am (your identity—the piece of you you're trying to show the world) and all who see me see this in me."

Light the candle and let it burn as you otherwise pamper yourself or your appearance that night.

Self-Love Spell 3: Water and Air

Self-love comes from anywhere we feel like it does in our body, but the two most common places are our hearts and emotions, which are water energy, and our minds, which are air energy. This spell requires using these elements to inspire self-love within yourself, no matter what else is going on.

You need:

- A tea or coffee that is delicious and accessible for you to make at home

- An incense that smells luxurious to you—Patchouli, Dragon's Blood, Vanilla, Rose, or any floral, are good examples of incense that would work

- A paper and pen

To perform this spell:

Make your tea or coffee. As you're pouring the water focus on your emotions and the idea of love, especially love of self.

Light your incense.

As you drink your tea or coffee and smell your incense, make a list of things you like or love about yourself.

When your drink, the incense, or both are done, you can call your list finished.

Dab the corners of the list with tiny drops of your drink and very faint dustings of incense dust.

Put the list somewhere safe, like in a desk drawer. Pull it out and look at it when you feel sad.

Repeat this spell as often as you can until your self-esteem notably improves. From there you should only need to do it when you feel it dip or when something happens to knock your mood down.

Sex Magick and Sex Spells

Sometimes we're looking for love and sometimes we just have physical desires that we want met, and neither are wrong. As queer people, those of us who are sexually driven should work really hard to embrace and honor the inherent sexuality that we hold inside of us. I look at life through the lens of sex positivity, which is kink aware, consensuality focused, and very concerned with people of all genders' right to pleasure. This seems simple, but so many of us, queer or not, are walking around with huge barriers to sharing mutal pleasure with sex partners because of sexual trauma, the messages society hammers home about sex (which somehow idolize and objectify sex while also punishing us for

enjoying it), or religious trauma. Those of us with sexual dysfunctions (which I do have and am very open about) and those of us with gender dysphoria (which I also have and am very open about) have even more that we have to work through before we can really get there.

I know I say this over and over again in this book, but it's true: magick alone will not heal your sexual trauma, your gender dysphoria, and certainly not a sexual dysfunction. The spells in these books are for those who are already ready to experiment with and embrace pleasure. If you need to skip this chapter for now, or for good, I totally understand. If you want to play with some spells to attract good sex into your life, that can be a healing action too (as can truly consensual and pleasurable sex on its own), but please do make sure you're ready for it.

As you move forward learning sex magick, it's important to know that there are two different kinds of magick referred to as sex magick. One kind is using sex, masturbation, or climax in general for magickal purpose. We talked about this in the introductory chapter, but the basic idea is that we're at our most receptive during and just after orgasm, which means our magick is at its peak. *Any* magick can add elements of sex magick to it to make it more powerful. Sex magick in this vein can also refer to group workings that include sacred orgies and orgasming together, or it can just be masturbating and visualizing dollar signs while you come, so it really runs the gamut.

In this grimoire, because this is a section on manifestation, we're mostly focusing on the other way the term sex magick is used—magick and spells that bring sex into your life and help you hold your sexual desires sacred.

A Spell for Sexual Swagger and Confidence

Of course, the first step to getting laid is unfortunately to respectfully make a move on a prospective sexual partner, be it your romantic partner or a stranger at a bar that you're eyeing. While I want to emphasize not being creepy and hitting on someone out of nowhere, we do actually need to have conversations where we bring up our attraction to someone or a desire to have sex with them if we want to end up having sex with them. This spell for sexual bravado works for all genders and sexualities, but if you have an extra tool you know boosts your confidence that correlates to your gender or sexuality, add that to this spell.

You need:

- Your favorite scented oil, cologne, perfume, or even just soap or hand wash

- Lyrics from your favorite song where the singer is really confident, especially if that confidence includes sexual confidence—hip hop and rock are the most common forms of music used for this, but any genre works

- An index card or sticky notes and a pen

To perform this spell:

Write your lyrics on your index card, sticky note, or other substitute.

Dab it with your scent of choice.

Stick the note on your bathroom mirror or the door you use to exit the house so you see it when you're getting ready or leaving.

On a night you *know* you'll see a prospective partner, put on an appropriate amount of the above scented aspect while meditating on the lyrics.

Freshen up. Redo deodorant, wash your hands, and if you wear make-up, quickly remove any smudges or reapply.

Go have fun! Flirt, chat, and trust yourself to bring up sex when the time is right.

Hanky Code Enchantments

The hanky code, or flagging, was primarily used by gay and bisexual men when it first sprung up in the '70s, but queers of all genders and sexualities have been using this code or a variation thereof for a while now. The hanky code is the act of using handkerchiefs to signify your sexual desires by the color and which pocket you have the hanky hanging out of. For example, a black handkerchief hanging out of your left pocket means you're into heavy BDSM and are a top. In the right pocket, it would flag that you are a BDSM submissive or bottom. Other popular

colors include red for fisting, pink for dildo play, light blue for oral, navy blue for anal sex, and green for sex work. If you don't have pockets you can tie them around the appropriate wrist or ankle (if your ankles are showing). If you're a switch, you can wear just the color around your neck.

There are *long* lists of every color and pattern under the sun in the hanky code, but anything outside of a common color is actually not very common so you might need to spark a conversation with someone and hope they ask about it (or find a way to work it into conversation). Also, as you set this book aside and research what hankies you want, please know that the extended lists have a lot of options that exoticize and fetishize BIPOC and that is *not* okay. Please don't flag with those hankies, y'all.

Hanky code works pretty well to bring you the specific sex act you want over time, so obviously charming them works even better. If you're not in a big city or hanging out where there are tons of queers, you'll likely need a boost from charms. I will say too that flagging isn't nearly as common in the age of Tinder and Grindr, but it does still happen. People will list their colors on their profile sometimes though, so it shows that as a community we've still retained that knowledge and your hankies will likely still be understood. Just in case, even those of us living in a bigger city might want to enchant ours just to ensure it's met with understanding and attraction.

It should go without saying, but seeing someone wearing compatible hankies to yours is *not* a license to grab, pinch, or otherwise invade their space or comfort level without consent. Flagging should start a conversation that is sexy but respectful, and you can negotiate how to move forward from there.

For this enchantment, you need:

- The hanky or hankies of your choice
- Herbs for sexual attraction like cannabis, clover, and diamana
- A fiery stone like carnelian or ruby
- Something scented like Ylang Ylang oil; sandalwood oil or chips; or your sexiest cologne, perfume, or body spray

- Charms or small images that scream sex or sexual attraction to you—can be erotic or not

- Anything else that is small and you think will bring you luck sexually—glitter is good if you're not worried about never fully shaking it off, especially glitter that correlates to your hanky

- A bowl—feel free to use a sex or attraction correspondence for color or stone here but you don't have to

To perform this enchantment:

On a Dark or Full Moon say a prayer to a sex diety like Lilith, Venus, or Dionysus.

Open your hanky and dump all of your other ingredients into it. Repeat or split them up if you're charming multiple hankies at once.

Tie the hanky closed and put it on a windowsill where light hits it. If you have personal outdoor space and the weather is good, leave it against a tree to soak up all that moonlight and the next morning's sunlight.

Let it sit for a solid twenty-four hours. The Moon is sultry and seductive but the Sun correlates to lust and passion. Both are necessary sexual energy that we can utilize in this case.

Take the hanky back to your magickal space. Open it up. Dump the spell ingredients into your small bowl and place that on your altar.

Kiss your hanky. I sometimes even say something silly like "we are going to get so laid" to mine, so it knows we're in this together.

Flag wherever it's safe to do so the next few times you go out. You should attract some good sex partners for yourself pretty quickly!

Re-up on the next Dark or Full Moon if it feels like the magick is waning.

Working with What You've Got:
A Glamour to Attract Sex Partners

For this potent sex spell, you get to charm your clothes, makeup, or even your wallet to attract sex to you. This one can be done in the sun at the start of the day, to put that Sun's fire and excitement into it. I lay my clothes out at night, and usually talk to the Moon about its powers of seduction. Either energy can work, you just need to know which celestial body you're talking to and which of their energies will work best for you.

You need:

- Your clothes, makeup, wallet—anything you're going to be wearing or have on you for the day

- A rose quartz, ruby, sapphire, or any stone that screams sex or manifestation to you

- Your favorite seductive scent, oil, or fragrance

To perform this spell:

If you're charging your clothes, wallet, or anything else that lies flat, lay them out and place your stone on top of them.

For makeup, shaving supplies, and the like, stick the stone in the bag that holds it together. Give it a soft shake. (Nothing that will break the makeup containers, obviously.)

Gently and softly dab your perfume or scented oil on to the ends of your sleeves, your collar, and the other ends of your clothes. Dab on your wallet or whatever else you're using if you do that.

If you're using your perfume or oil on makeup or shaving materials, add just a drop or two on your makeup brush or shaving tools.

Say, "May I attract the sex I desire today," and kiss your outfit, makeup bag, and the rest.

Let it sit while you either sleep or get ready for the day in the other ways you need to.

As you get dressed, shave, or pack your wallet back up for the day, repeat the above mantra.

This one may take a few times of trying for it to work. For sex magick we have to boost confidence first, and then the right sex for us will come.

A Spell for Longer-Term Sexual Satisfaction

Sometimes we're not looking for new or adventurous sex, we're just looking for a boost with our current partners and to ensure that the sex will be satisfying for both of us and won't just peter out at some point. Sex is not the only way to be intimate with someone, but for a lot of us it is a big piece of that. Sex can also be an adventure in connection and healing, and when we have partners that we connect with on that level, we don't really want to lose that piece of it. Also, sex is fun! We deserve to have that pleasure for as long as we want it, and hopefully this spell will help with that.

You need:

- Rose petals, or petals of any flower that screams sensuality to you—deep red petals are great, but black or pink work, too

- An oil of your choice that corresponds to sexuality—I like to use sandalwood or Dragon's Blood

- A charm, idol, or image of a sex diety, even if you don't work with dieties.

- Some smaller charms, idols, or images of goats, rabbits, or hummingbirds (or all of the above), which are all connected to sexual satisfaction, short and long-term

- An image you find erotically inspiring

- Flame-safe rainbow, black, or red glitter

- Tealight candles, as many as you want to have out at a time

To perform this spell:

This whole spell should be performed intentionally, meaning you are focusing on the idea of long-term sexual satisfaction and what it can do for you as you build this altar and perform this spell.

Clear off a section of your altar or clear a space for this new altar.

Place your diety icon center stage, so to speak.

Drip oil on it and rub it all over the icon.

Place your other charms, images, idols, and the like around the altar.

Oil them up too, if desired.

Spread your flower petals out over the altar.

Put a dab of oil and a couple sprinkles of glitter on your tea lights.

Light the tea lights and replace as necessary. If money is an issue, just light one at a time until they're done.

If at any point, space or housing stability is or becomes an issue, this altar can be edited down to one tea light (with the oil and glitter) and only your most important and smallest charms and very few rose petals. You can keep this in an old Altoids tin in your bag or set it up in a smaller space.

Any time the Moon is Dark during a Fire or Water sign, you can re-up this spell. While generally speaking we shouldn't do magick on eclipses because they bring their own power and we're supposed to listen at that time, this one is safe to re-up right before an eclipse. Re-upping just means refreshing the oil components, cleaning off anything that's dirty, maybe adding a couple new petals as well as taking a couple of old ones off, and saying quick prayers to the diety of sex or the animal allies that sit on our altar.

Love Spells for Queer Witches

We've already talked about the pros and cons of love spells so I won't go off on more diatribes now. What I will say is that when it comes to finding true l-o-v-e, the odds are stacked against *everyone*, but especially queer people who are only a wee percentage of the general population, even in bigger cities. On top of that, not everyone is queer the same way we are queer. It's *very* doubtful that I'll end up with a gay man, for example. I'm monogamish in a very polyamorous city, which often feels like my odds of finding a partner are even smaller. There are so many different ways to be queer and I am obsessed with queerness and queer community but holding space for all of those different ways to exist so beautifully also means that our ability to find love can remain ever hindered by the numbers game that even the general population at large is trying to work in their favor, often to no avail. No wonder we turn to magick!

On top of *all* of that, being a monogamous woman or non-binary person is not enough to make me fall in love with you, obviously. You can't be allergic to cats and I need to see genuine kindness coupled with a fabulous sense of humor for me to even consider partnering with you. I'm sure you have your own list of things you need in a partner too. Plus, not to get too dark, but sometimes people are terrible. *We should all be aiming for partners who are respectful, communicative, sexually compatible, and will adore us as much as we adore them.* That almost always requires extremely good luck or a total act of god, both of which magick can bring about.

It also takes confidence that love is real and does exist. A lot of queer people come from broken homes where the fact that love fades was proven true under our own roof. We may have seen that love *can* be real in heteronormative homes, but we didn't have the role models to look up to or see our own experiences or desires reflected. That means the earlier work about self-love is absolutely mandatory to see a way forward where we are loved and supported by partners we are compatible with. From there, there are a few different options, and I've tried to include a variety of spells to work with, depending on your needs.

Love Spell Basics for Queer People
of All Genders and Sexual Identities

If you want to do love spells, you have to know what you're looking for. I outlined what I *need* in a partner in the previous section, but I have other things I look for in a partner, too. I also know *exactly* what kind of relationship I want, and what I want the end game to be. I want a long-term, cohabitating, monogamous relationship where we also live with my queerplatonic partner and their partner, some pets, and occasionally queer youth who need short-term safe places to stay. I know where I have flexibility, too. I'm ambivalent about marriage, for example. If I end up with a partner who doesn't want to give the government our names, who distrusts marriage as an institution, or who is on SSI (Supplemental Security Income) disability and can't get married without losing some of their benefits, then I won't get married. If I end up with someone who cares deeply about marriage, I will get married. To me that doesn't change how a relationship looks or feels, so I'm open to it either way. I'm telling you this not to avail myself to people sliding into my DMs (Internet speak for the Direct Messaging option in most social media) but so you can see what information you might want to gather about yourself before performing love spells. Queer people often have specific needs and desires in relationships that are unique to our community (though often not that unique within our community), but we need to pinpoint them and speak them to ourselves if we want them to happen.

Before you go any further, let's do some journal work so you can gather notes for your love spells.

Journal Prompt

Take some notes on what the best partner for you is like. Please include "treats me well" as part of that, but otherwise you know what kind of person works best for you and what you don't care about. Any deal breakers? Include some nots on this list. Mine would include not Republican, not a hunter, and not allergic to common pets, for example. Don't sell yourself short, but don't pull a Sally Owens from Practical Magic and design an impossible person. Leave some room for flexibility and mystery but do not settle where it matters to you.

Now that you know what the best partner for yourself is like, think about what your ideal relationship looks like in the beginning. How often do you contact each other? What do dates consist of? Go from there and imagine several months or a year into the relationship. What does it look and feel like then? What do you do together? What core values do you share? Are you monogamous, polyamorous, unsure, flexible, or somewhere in between?

Finally, think about the end game. When you've been with someone for ten or fifteen years, what should it look like then? Should you live together? Marriage? Who else (if anyone) do you live with? How do you spend time together and show each other you value each other as you grow older together?

Once you do this journaling, you're ready to start doing love spells. We'll start with a basic one that is effective over time. For those of us looking for love in the next ten years (but with no strict timeline on it), this is the one to go to.

Speak It into Being: A Love Spell

Mantras, paired with correspondences of your choice, make the best love spells. Love is often associated with whispering sweet nothings, and a healthy love is about long and deep conversations as much as it's about anything else. This spell capitalizes on the Air magick that words and communication use, and inspires us to go deeper in our connection to what we want and the power of our words.

You need:

- Paper and pen

- The mantra "I am ready for and open to love."

To perform this spell:

Draw a line halfway down your paper or fold the paper in half.

Make a list of traits that your best partner would have, and throw in a couple of ideal partner traits, too (for example, I would put

"good with cats," not just "not allergic to cats") but leave room for surprise and mystery.

Make a list on the second half of your sheet about what a good, healthy, loving relationship looks like to you.

Speak your prayers or even just read your lists out loud.

Spend about twenty minutes visualizing being in a relationship with someone who is loving, supportive, communicative, and respectful. Think about the idea of romance. Think about being wooed and wooing someone else. Let your imagination run away with itself as you visualize traveling, making love, moving in, and more with a great partner.

Optional: masturbate if you feel driven to as you visualize.

When you feel done or ready, open your eyes and sigh contentedly. Repeat the mantra listed above.

Use these lists and work to develop a mantra or incantation that you can speak out loud daily to draw love to you. Examples I have used in the past are:

"As I move forward in my day, may my dream relationship find its way to me."

"Someone kind and funny too/Someone who loves my QPP and my cats like I do/Someone who wants something built to last/ Bring them into my life fast."

A Spell for Someone Else to Make the First Move

This is the most common love spell that I use these days. I'm pretty happy being single but if I have a crush or am even just open to connection, I use this spell. This spell should never be used to inspire a spark that isn't there or create attraction to you in someone who clearly has none. It can be used by anyone who is anxious, shy, or both but open to love with the right person or the right people.

As a weird sidenote, occasionally this spell has inspired me to make the first move after all. Our gods kind of know who will and won't break

down if they feel like their feelings are mutual. This spell has *mostly* worked as planned in my life—but there have been a small handful of times where I've been hanging out with someone and heard someone hiss *"Now!"* into my head and I blurted out my own feelings in response. It usually ends up with at least short-term dating, but one of the longest relationships I've had was another result. While it is designed to work as it states it will, if you end up feeling inspired or motivated to fess up first, go ahead. It will likely be well met by the other parties.

You need:

- A tool that corresponds with your astrology—if you know what your Moon or Venus sign are, use those in addition to or in place of your Sun sign

- Recommended: an oil for Water signs, flowers for Earth signs, Sigils or power words for Air signs, and an image or charm of flames (possibly surrounding a heart) for Fire

- A charm, small image, or other representation of a plant, animal, deity, or symbol that you associate with love

- Your lists from the above spell work

- Optional: a penny

To perform this spell:

If you choose to work with deities, fae, or animal allies for this spell, great! Call those in, as well as the elements you're working with based on your astrology.

Think about your own shyness, and think about what respectfully getting hit on or someone making the first move looks and feels like to you.

Hold your elemental tools in your hand (or gently dab on, if using oil) and say, "If anyone I know is right for me/May they make themselves known immediately."

I recommend repeating this three times.

Another option is to lay your tools, charms, and such in front of you and rub your hands together, slowly at first, and then quickly as you repeat your desire for a crush to ask you out if they're interested in you. When your hands feel really hot, grab the tools and let that feeling of throbbing push your energy into to the tools.

Take a second to feel as empowered and confident as the heat in your hands subsides.

Thank the spiritual entities helping you and release them.

If you used the penny, find a safe fountain or pond (that is, man-made with no animals living in it) and toss it in before the next Full or Dark Moon, making that same wish.

Everything else, place on your altar, desk, counter, or other space.

Love Potions

Potions are fun because they date back to the high holy days of alchemical study but have been lost or mystified over time (like alchemy itself). Like most myths about witchcraft or spirituality, potion making is rooted in a very real form of witchcraft. While there's not a magick potion to make someone fall in love with you out of nowhere, ingesting a bunch of magickal ingredients can bring in any outcome you desire. I use potions for love magick because while working with your own elements is usually best, love is *such* a Water element type of magick that I want to highlight it. So much of spellwork is also about layering, and adding an additional watery undercurrent to a love spell is always a good idea for a boost. There are several potions listed here, as we segue into love magick for things beyond new relationships.

A General Love Potion

This potion can be made and imbibed for basically any love purpose whether you want to attract a partner, seem more attractive to potential partners, or strengthen an existing love. These are super basic ingredients for love but they pack a powerful punch.

You need:

- Some milk or thicker milk substitute—soy or oat milk are good calls

- Honey

- Spices and edible flowers that inspire love like coriander, rose, jasmine, and cinnamon to taste—honestly, I sometimes add those things until I get the *look* that I want for this milk potion

- A squeeze or two of orange juice from an orange or some orange zest for the top

To perform this spell:

Heat up the milk slowly on a stove and state your intention out loud.

As the milk heats, slowly add honey and your herbs and edible flowers to taste.

When finished, remove from heat for a couple of minutes.

Place in a mug and add your orange element and any decorative flower components.

Drink when cool enough (or refrigerate until cold if you don't like hot drinks).

As you drink, read a romantic book or listen to some romantic music.

A Shared Potion for Repairing a Relationship

Even the best, healthiest relationships hit snags and bumpy times. Moving in together hits everyone hard. Long latent jealousies or insecurities can screech to the surface when we open up a relationship for the first time or bring in new partners for the first time in a long time. The first year of marriage, even among those who live together first, is notoriously tough. Then there are the unpredictable times where just being two humans existing in the same relationship gets really difficult.

I strongly advise clients to seek relationship counseling when the problems run really deep. However, if you're already doing that, if you and your partner are both being really communicative and still not seeing eye to eye (and if you have their consent to do this relationship repair spell), then this is a wonderful (and delicious) potion that can remind all parties involved of why they're together and how beautiful life together can be. You won't get over your issues overnight because of it, but you will start seeing each other's point of view and prioritizing the relationship again instead of stubbornly trying to prove your own point. This is also a good spell to perform when you really can't see the other parties' point of view or believe that they can't see yours.

Sharing is best for this one so while I stress consent for all love spells, this is best when prepared and sipped together or when one person prepares it and both repeat the mantras as they drink it.

You need:

- Apple juice

- Cinnamon and ginger

- Vanilla or almond extract—imitation will work in a pinch or you can skip it since I know this ingredient is cost prohibitive for some

- A tiny splash of real or imitation cream

- Brown sugar, honey, or maple syrup to taste—this will make the drink *extremely* sweet very quickly, so be careful

To prepare this potion:

This one you can make cold but it may be a little grainy or otherwise troublesome to consume.

Heat up the apple juice if desired.

Sprinkle in the cinnamon and ginger to taste. Add the sweetener to your juice.

As you add the sweetener say, "May our eyes be open and our hearts be full."

If you're not heating your apple juice, stir until ingredients are blended into the drink. Use the same mantra.

As you stir, *toward* your body, state "May our love stay strong."

As you stir *away* from yourself, say, "May our love stay safe."

Add one or two drops of vanilla or almond extract. The extract is strong and you want your potion to be drinkable.

Add a splash of cream.

Knock on your mug or glass three times to wake up the magick in the ingredients.

Check the taste. Stir again, repeating the mantras if desired.

Drink (once cool enough). Before your first big drink, say, "Our relationship can be repaired/We are (insert number of people involved) deeply in love/Who deeply care."

Savor the drink—this one is yummy and it gives the magickal ingredients time to fan out and unfurl throughout your body.

A Potion or Tincture to Strengthen Loving Relationships (Especially Useful for Polyamorous or Non-Monogamous Partners)

Most strong relationships don't *need* magick to survive and thrive, but why not protect your love and yourself by using magick to boost the romantic and fuzzy feelings in your relationship?

This potion or tincture *will* work for anyone looking to strengthen their relationships with others, but the ingredients come in batches or groups and therefore work really strongly for people existing in polyamorous or non-monagamous relationships. All spells that involve others should come with consent, but because this spell involves strengthening but not necessarily changing relationships or how they look and is mostly meant to center you as lover or partner it's up to you what consent looks like or how you approach it. With long-term partners and my queerplatonic partner I sometimes say something off and on throughout the relationship like "Just checking in: sometimes I do magick to strengthen the relationship

and keep the love flowing. Is that still okay?" You'll usually get a yes, which is blanket consent for a potion like this.

Sharing is always fun, so if you have witchy relationship cohorts, feel free to share the love (potion)!

You need:

- Water

- Lots of herbs—specifically, basil, coriander, mint, rosemary, and parsley; this should not be a financial stressor, but if it is, you can use more of one herb and less or none of another

- Lemon juice

- A few bay leaves, if possible

- Two containers for the potion—I like jars but anything works

- A strainer, cheesecloth, or coffee filter

- An eye dropper

To perform this spell:

This is a spell best performed during a Waning Moon, or any time the Moon or Sun are in a Water sign.

Heat up the water and herbs until boiling.

As the water heats, think about all of the wonderful things about the romantic relationship(s) in your life.

Boil on high until the water starts absorbing color from the herbs.

Add lemon juice and say, "As this boils, our love is strengthened."

Reduce to medium or low and let simmer for roughly thirty minutes.

Remove from heat. Let cool.

Pour mixture into one of the jars and say, "As I pour, our relationships are strengthened."

Let the jar sit on a windowsill or outdoors overnight. Shake it up a few times if you can and remember to.

The next day, put your filter over the second container and pour the liquid into it. The filter should catch most of the herbs.

Using your eye dropper, pull out some of the liquid and place under your tongue until it disappears. Repeat the mantra "My love and relationship(s) are strong."

Close the container and give it a kiss. Thank this mixture for strengthening your romantic life.

You and your partner(s) can take this every day, but probably not more than once a day. It can also just be a "when you remember" tincture or an "Every Full Moon" tincture or whatever works best, timing wise, for all of you.

A Special Kind of Love: A Spell for Doms, Subs, and Other Kinky Queers

For some of us, myself included, whips and dominant dirty talk aren't just part of an occasional fun night but a very real part of what we need to function well in a romantic relationship. I didn't include this spell in the sex spells section, because contrary to popular belief, kinky relationships or those with a power exchange are *not* solely sexual in nature. They can be! If that's what both parties want! They can also be long lasting, sustenant, and fulfilling beyond having our sexual desires met.

Any of the sex spells I highlighted in that sex spells section can be tweaked to bring you kinky sex, but for those of us looking for a longer term relationship full of kink and power exchange, we need to get specific and down to the nitty gritty in our spell work.

Some of it starts with the lists I had you make earlier. Make sure you include the kinks that you know you need to be happy in a relationship. I know I need a submissive partner but I'm flexible on how submissive and how that comes out or takes form in the relationship. Dirty talk and role-play are musts for me though, so they make my list every time I redo it. Revisit your lists and if they seem weirdly chaste, add in what it takes for your sexual satisfaction and what kind of partner you think is best for

long-term compatibility. Take the time or do the journal work to really figure out what you need and what you would ideally have, but again, leave
room for adventure and surprise. Then move on to the spell ahead.

You need:

- Erotic images that showcase your kinks

- A charm or picture that you drew that symbolizes your kink and
  your role in that kink

- General love spell correspondences—rose quartz, rose petals, spicy
  or citrus scents, red candle, and the like

- If you have a harness, a furry mask, handcuffs, or other props, use
  them in the spell. It's not necessary if you're working up to owning
  these things. If money is a factor, look for something in your home
  that could be used safely for sexual play, and bring that into to spell.

- Optional lube and a sex toy if desired

- Optional deity related tools

To perform this spell:

If you work with deities or spiritual entities, welcome them into
the spell—especially any of them who work with divine sexual or
ecstatic ritual energy. Use tools, idols, and the like if you have
them, but a welcoming prayer is just fine.

If you're bringing your own art (and that can include poetry, prose,
music) you can wait until you start the spell to create it. Do that
now. Hold or place in your lap anything you're using that you
didn't draw or create.

Light your candle and ask the god or energy to bring the right kink
energy into a current relationship (get consent for this) or to draw a
compatible partner who is easy to trust and talk to into your life.

Meditate or visualize a well-rounded relationship that includes
these aspects in it. Masturbate with the toy and lube if desired, or
with your hand. Use your other sex toys and tools safely, if desired.

When you feel like the visualization has concluded, rub your love spell correspondence pieces on your sex tools and toys, your deity tools, and any other spell pieces.

Repeat, "I deserve a love that fulfills me," as you do so.

Finish with a prayer to either love itself or to a god, that asks for help finding compatible kinky partners for long-term relationships.

Thank and release those spiritual entities. Place whatever feels right on your altar *or* on your nightstand to make a makeshift mini-altar.

Allow yourself to daydream over the next several nights until you fall asleep about living with the right kinky partner for you.

A Final Romantic Love Spell: Specifically for Polyamorous Relationships or Polycules

This love spell is perfect for those whose relationship looks more like a Three or Ten of Cups tarot card than the seemingly monogamous Two of Cups. There are two different versions. The first, which is largely an art spell, is to keep communication open and love flowing for multiple partners. The second variation is for when you feel ready to add a partner.

You need:

- Paper and pen or markers
- Rose oil or even rose petals

To perform this spell:

This spell starts with a self-guided meditation. Read this whole section, and then perform the meditation. You can also record yourself giving the instructions for this meditation and replay it, if you're like me and struggle to remember instructions.

Sit comfortably, and close your eyes. Take a few deep breaths until you feel calm and relaxed. Picture your body sinking through the floor and into the Earth. Take your time with this. As you feel

yourself connecting with the Earth, imagine that you are sitting on a riverbank. Picture dirt, not sand. The meeting of Water and Earth are important for sustaining any kind of long-term relationship. Imagine the water giving off a breeze that feels cool and comfortable. As you look out over the river, you decide to stand up and walk along the river's edge. Even if you suffer from chronic pain or are injured, you do not feel tired or like this walk is tedious or arduous. As you walk, you begin to notice several tributaries branching off of the river. There are multiple paths you can go down. Instead of deciding to walk down one of them, wade into the river. The water is cool and still, and it feels good—almost like a cleansing. As you stand in the water, feel your energy and your love spread out over each of the tributaries. There is not a single right path for you, there is only oneness with all of the ways you can use your heart and all of the connections that you have. Breathe comfortably, knowing that walking all of these paths at once is right for you. As you feel happy, warm, and satisfied, slowly come out of the meditation. Make your way back to the riverbank entrance you came through. Smile to yourself, and sit back down comfortably. Count backwards from ten, and open your eyes at one.

You likely feel really good about all of your relationships or relationship potentials right now. Grab your art supplies, and draw the river and its tributaries as you imagined them. You may notice that certain forks probably start to feel like certain people in your life. Use your oil or petals and lightly trace those specific tributaries with them when that happens.

Feel free to pray to a deity, the world, or love itself as you draw, thanking them for the time and love that you share with these partners.

If you're seeking balance between your relationships or relationship-life balance, draw some scales or other symbols that mean balance to you in the river.

If you're open to new relationship, draw tributaries that you didn't see in your vision. Say out loud "this represents the potential for new partners."

Frame this picture and put it up or just tape it on your wall. As you do so, say, "My relationships are strong and full of love," "I balance all of the loves in my life easily and I am grateful for that love," or any other mantra that feels good to you.

Platonic Love Spells for Friends and (Chosen) Family

Not everyone is driven by a great lust for sexual pleasure or for a divine romantic love that sets their heart free, and even among those of us that are, it's true that it takes all kinds of loving and supporting relationships to create a support system and a community for ourselves. It took me a long time to develop spells for friendship and chosen family. Something really troubling that I see in a lot of witchcraft materials is the tendency to say that friendship spells are "like love spells, but weaker." That's absurd. Some of us find forever loves, but many of us do not. Instead, what gets us through those transition times and forms a stable foundation for the rest of our lives are our platonic friendships.

I don't believe we have only one soul mate. I think we meet lots of people throughout our lives who are meant to be in our lives and that make us feel happier and more ourselves when they're around. A lot of those relationships end up being platonic, familial, or queerplatonic (a word my favorite person and I heartily embrace to imply a relationship that is as strong, loving, and important as a romantic, sexual relationship but is not one). A lot of those relationships will blur the line between what is romance and what is friendship. Boundaries are critical for any kind of relationship, but knowing I can treat my friends like I would a romantic partner and not be deemed weird is honestly one of my favorite parts about being queer. The right chosen family or queerplatonic partner for you will be able to negotiate those boundaries while still providing you the care you need in any kind of relationship, but *take a few minutes to journal* about what that looks or feels like for you so you have an idea of what you're looking for as you go into these next couple of spells.

I personally believe that those people that protect us, affirm us, and love us in a very queerplatonic, familial way have a soul connection or soul mate relationship to us, but it's okay if you don't! What I know for sure is that for as long as there have been queer people (which is always,

for the record) there have been platonic relationships being formed that cannot be broken come hell or high water. There have always been chosen families of queer people living together and making a life together. There have always been groups of friends helping us heal from the rejection of the world at large and affirming our identities and who we are as people beyond sexual and gender identities.

Yet, as you're reading this, you may not have found the person or group of people that you need. Magick can help with this, as with all things, and it is *not* weaker magick than romantic or sexual love spells. It just looks a little bit different.

A Spell to Attract Chosen Family Members

This spell acknowledges that you may already have potential chosen family members in your life but leaves plenty of room for new people to come in and fill that role. You never know which person in your life may step up and become the sibling or parent you never had, and you never know how relationships will shift and grow. This isn't the case every time, and because of that we want to leave ourselves open to newness and possibility.

You need:

- An apple (mostly its seeds)

- A knife, dagger, or athame

- A very small bowl or shot glass

- Olive oil

- A small rainbow candle or a small candle of your favorite color

To perform this spell:

Gather your materials during a Dark, New, or Waxing Moon.

Sit comfortably in a sacred space.

The candle brings in the Fire element and will inspire you to reach out to new friends and take action in your social life, as well as bring people with similar passions into your life.

Ask the candle to do these very things, and light it.

Apples represent things that are simple but fulfilling, like queerplatonic or chosen familial love. They also connect to Earth element.

Acknowledge this about the apple as you hold it in your hands.

The cutting implement represents Air and the quickness that we want to inspire with this spell so you're not feeling down and out or lonely for long.

Recognize this, and then cut the apple in half or into slices.

Cut or pull out the apple seeds and place them in the bowl, shot glass, or other container that size. These seeds represent the idea of community, because there are so many of them.

The olive oil represents the peace that olive branches, leaves, and flowers bring, and the peace that comes when we're propped up and supported by others. It also can represent love. Drop a few drops into the bowl. Nothing should be wet—just use enough to represent the Water element in there.

If there are specific types of people you want to form intense social bonds with, ask for that as you eat the apple and place the candle and container on a table, counter, or altar.

As you continue eating the apple, visualize the seeds growing and forming an orchard.

Envision feeling safe and secure in this orchard.

As you finish the apple, thank the elements for bringing chosen family to you and release them.

To recharge this spell, dab the container of apple seeds with olive oil every few days until you feel satisfied by this spell or decide to start over.

A Spell for Platonic Relationships as They Evolve and Grow into More

This is really part two of the previous spell, and it will help you pinpoint and grow into relationships that could serve the purpose of chosen family for you that are already present in your life.

You need:

- Your bowl of seeds from before.

- A couple of flower buds or petals that represent intense friendship to you.

To perform this spell:

Sit with your bowl and take a couple of deep breaths.

Say, "If I already know the right chosen family for me/Let us bond closer/Make each party see."

Slowly place your petals or buds one at a time into the bowl, each one representing a potential chosen family member that you may know.

It's hard, but try not to think of anyone specific, just like a romantic or sexual love spell.

A Spell to Heal Rifts within Your Chosen Family

Human beings, especially queer ones, are (generally speaking) amazing on the whole. They're still human beings though, and they can still hurt us and betray us intentionally or unintentionally. Marginalized people come in to a lot of situations feeling very guarded or on edge, ready to defend themselves, and even a perceived attack can cause them to lash out. This is a lot of what has led to cancel culture and the lack of nuance in those conversations about harm versus forgiveness. As novelist and activist Sarah Schulman boldly stated, conflict is not abuse and we do need to ground ourselves and sometimes decenter ourselves to come out of these conversations feeling like we're ready to move forward.

Of course, not everything is as serious as the situation I outlined above. Sometimes we're just not seeing eye to eye, or we're hurt because our closest people are suddenly very busy and we're feeling lonely again. In either case, magick can help bring those people back into your orbit and bolster those relationships.

This spell can be done without consent if you're very clear and use language like "If we're meant to stay in each other's lives" in your prayers and incantations. Like most things however, I think it works better when all parties are on board and willing to do the spiritual, emotional, and physical work of coming together again.

For this spell, you need:

- Something that represents a hatchet—a charm, a drawing, a photo, or hell, you can even write the word *hatchet* on a piece of paper
- Ideally, an outdoor space that you can bury something in—a small box filled with dirt will work for those without access to green space
- If using an outdoor space, a shovel

To perform this spell:

If you're bringing in a god, singing in runes, adding any personal chants, or the like, do that now. Anytime we're connecting with the Earth in this way it's big magick, and we want to call in all of our reinforcements.

Pray or write an incantation that sums up what's been going on and why you want everyone to come together and forgive each other, and use that incantation.

Now you're going to literally bury the hatchet, so dig into the Earth or dirt.

Place your hatchet there. Cover it back up.

Recite: "The hatchet is buried/And if it's meant to be/My chosen family will come back to me."

You can substitute names for "my chosen family" if desired.

Thank and release any gods or other energies that you brought in.

A Spell for Those Who Have Shunned You to Open Their Hearts

A recent criticism of the language of queer chosen family is that having new people in your life, however close and however wonderful, does not actually heal the wounds that given family or other caretakers from your upbringing can cause when they shun you. I have mixed feelings about that in my own life, as I've seen the stunning healing work that simply being loved right can cause, but I respect that for some people a much deeper healing is needed.

Anytime someone has been hurt and rejected, especially if they were previously unsupported or worse, I strongly encourage or advise towards healing work first. Yet in some cases, people's hearts can be opened and their minds can be changed, especially when it comes to things like gender and sexual identity. As more television characters (especially in prime-time slots) and movie characters are LGBTQQIA2SP+ and as more and more churches rush to prove themselves to be on the right side of history, our parents and grandparents are getting more exposure to identities and viewpoints they may not have considered before. Sometimes they just needed time to process, and now, they're ready to come back.

You do not have to forgive anyone who hurt and rejected you. Period. If you *want* too though, and if you want them back in your life, this spell has proven effective for me and some other witches I've worked with to grease the wheels on that goal.

You need:

- A pomegranate or any substitute that you can rip open, especially if eating it can get a little messy. (If you have mobility issues or access needs with your hands, you can cheat on this spell by cutting it open first, and then pressing it back together.)

To perform this spell

Hold the food in your hand and think about the hurt that's been done to you.

Say to the food "I am ready to let this pain go/If they want back in/Let them know."

Rip the food open, and eat it if desired. Think about absorbing or taking in all of the nutrients in the fruit and how those can represent long-standing relationships and what you get from them.

Discard inedible parts. As you toss them in the trash say, "I'm done with this fruit's part/Just like I'm done with this pain in my heart."

MISCELLANEOUS ATTRACTION SPELLS

Not everything we want to bring into our life is easily divided into "money, love, sex, family." As humans we are driven to pleasure, and as queer people we have a divine right to reclaim pleasure and make it our own all we want. Not every pleasure can be bought or encapsulated by the image of a heart or an orgasm though, and I've got spells for those, too!

A Spell for Personal Political Gains

The next section of this grimoire is on spells for the collective, and there we'll see what it looks like when we do ongoing work for the collective, and not just ourselves. Sometimes our motives for wanting a law to pass or not pass are more selfish though. Maybe we've been working really long and hard on a campaign, and we just want that work to pay off. Maybe we've personally invested in a candidate and we want to see our investment succeed. Whatever your reasons, remember that you're entitled to a little bit of selfish desire, no matter how much greater good it may or may not do.

For this spell, you need:

- The specific political gain you want to make for purely selfish reasons written down on a piece of paper (or typed and printed)

- Some twine, yarn, or small rope—color coded red for attraction or black for Underworld Goddess energy and ferocity if desired (totally optional though)

- Correspondences for *power* and *attraction* if desired—examples would be Dragon's Blood oil or incense

- A small black candle

To perform this spell:

Take the paper with your spell's intention and focus on the words. Put your power into it by visualization or energy work.

If using additional correspondences, apply those now—especially any that you're rolling up with your paper.

Roll up the paper tightly.

As you tie the paper tight with your twine (or substitute), say, "May the law be bound as this intention is now."

Light the candle and as it melts, drip the wax in the middle of your scroll where the paper meets.

Say, "It is sealed" and blow your candle out.

A Spell for Laughter and Whimsy

This book has covered a lot of really tough things that queer people go through—everything from parental rejection to societal oppression to pain from within your own community. One of the most emotionally healing facets of life though, is being able to shrug all of that off, even just for a few moments, and to delight in shared hilarity with friends. I see so many tarot clients who ask *big* questions and get lighthearted cards full of people laughing. When I tell them that laughter and fun are the best cure for them at this time, I get a surprising amount of pushback. "I don't have time for that," or "I don't have anyone that will take me out for a fun night," or "I don't even know how to bring laughter into my life organically," are common responses. While I have a ton of practical pieces of advice in these circumstances, I also have a spell!

For this spell, you need:

- To know what is funny to you—seriously, make a quick list or have a couple moments that always make you laugh in your back pocket

- A small drawing, photo, or charm of lips smiling or someone laughing

- A small white candle

- A bowl of purified water—Moon water is ideal

To perform this spell:

As you pull your tools together, think about the things that make you smile, laugh, and feel like you're having fun. Chuckle to yourself if need be.

Light your white candle and as it burns, think about feeling lighter and lighter. Think about laughing more and more, until your stomach hurts or you collapse. Think about how you deserve pleasure and fun.

Say out loud, "I deserve laughter and fun, too." Say it over and over and over again.

When you feel done or ready, stick your hands in the water. Water is emotions, including happiness. You are washing off the things that keep you feeling stuck or unable to laugh.

Smile and sigh contentedly.

Stick the charm in your wallet so you always have it with you.

A Bath to Inspire Adventure

I can't believe I made it this far in this grimoire without incorporating a bath spell yet, considering that as a double Pisces with Cancer rising, this is one of my primary forms of magick. Baths are normally relaxing, cleansing, or both, but I like exploring Water's other properties with them. As kids we often feel light and adventurous in the bath, playing with our rubber ducks and using our imaginations to run wild. That's the feeling I wanted to bring with this spell—with a couple of additional witchy ingredients added to the mix. Adventure, in addition to laughter and fun, is another way we embrace pleasure and in doing so, heal. This bath for adventure is meant to draw adventure to you, but if you're willing to make your own adventure add a few ingredients of your choice for inspiration and ideas.

You need:

- A ruby or something water safe but ruby colored
- Rose quartz if you have some—you don't need to buy any just for this spell
- A hot bath
- Bath salts or Epsom salts with citrus scent, oils—or peels if you're designing your own mix
- A candle or candles whose color, scent, or both, screams *adventure* to you

To perform this spell:

Light your candles and draw your bath. As you do so, think about what adventure means to you, and times you've felt explorative and adventurous in the past. Adventure means a lot of things to a lot of people. Specifically focus on the experience that *you* are craving now.

As your water fills and heats up, add your salt mixture.

Sit in the water, and breathe deeply. Take a bath, whatever that means to you. I usually just soak.

After a few minutes of relaxing, say something like "I am craving adventure/Please bring it to me/Let me let loose ASAP."

You can repeat this incantation by a set of magickal-to-you number, like 3, 5, or 7 times, or until your bath water and candles feel charged.

Finish your bath as desired (masturbate, relax for a bit, actually bathe, or go ahead and drain the water).

Blow out your candles.

Spells for the Collective

I spent a good portion of this book talking about the collective power our witchcraft has to really altar the world towards progressive and radical values, so obviously I'm including a chapter on spellwork to help you get your head wrapped around what collective spellwork means to you as an individual and when you're working with other witches. When I refer to collective spellwork, I don't just mean group work, as you can see. These are spells that are for the greater good and are meant to help the most marginalized as a group (instead of the individual work in the rest of the grimoire), or are tapping into the collective unconscious of witches doing similar work at the same time even if they don't know it, or both. I do believe that we are all connected—witches, nonwitches, animals, plants, gods, spiritual energies like fae, and animal allies. Collective work taps into that connection and uses the power of connection to make our craft work.

Collective work *is* also for the greater good. Collective work is meant to protect those who are marginalized by those in power (including the social power that keeps so many of us from coming forward and speaking out), and meant to oust those in power so that something more equitable can spring forward. This is very big magick and it does take a lot of voices speaking their truth at the same time. Because of that, I pick *big* witch dates to do collective work: Full and Dark or New Moons, Sabbats, and the nights before big things are scheduled to happen, for example. This allows us to predict that the largest number of witches doing similar work will be doing so right around the same time.

I want to be clear that doing collective spellwork without doing the work to leave this world and society better than you found it is not enough. As witches, we come offering *one* set of tools and skills we have ,but in a world where Black trans women are murdered with alarming frequency and climate change threatens our very existence, it's not enough. We must do the work within ourselves to break down the effects of living under any of the systems that benefit us, like white supremacy in my case. You have to be willing to make the changes necessary, including being willing to give up the privileges you have if it comes to that, and to speak out against injustice when you see it—especially if it doesn't affect you. There is no stronger magick than a whole lot of allies and marginalized

people fighting back, and that's what these moments in history are calling on us to do.

My specialty, study, and background is not in direct action or law, though, it's in witchcraft, and as I've stated multiple times, this is one magnificent and powerful tool we have to start sparking change where it's needed. As we think about collective magick and what that can do, we feel ourselves shifting towards embracing those in the fight with us. Go towards that. I often say that I am not a love and light witch, but that's not entirely true. Love means fighting for those we care about and against those who would harm us. Light means embracing darkness too and learning how to use that to our advantage instead of running away from it. That's what this collection of spells is meant to help us do.

All of these spells use the same "But First . . ." information where you will ground yourself and tap into the collective queer energy in question (as well as any spiritual allies or entitities that you believe to be on your side).

But First . . . Ground Yourself

Close your eyes and ground deeply. In this time, take deep breaths if you're physically able to do so.

Imagine a string connecting you to the Earth's core, pulling you down to sink more and more comfortably into the Earth.

As you sink more comfortably, think about the other witches that you know (even just from the Internet) and their work towards social justice and against climate change. Tap into that feeling that we are all together in this.

Hum, sing some runes in, or call out to your gods to intensify the vibration of your spell.

Feel your feelings. Cry if you need to. Scream. Come to grips with the situation that you're trying to stop or protect others from. Then proceed with the individual spell.

A Spell to Slow Down the Effects of Climate Change

This is definitely a big magic, big Moon spell and requires you to tap into the collective forces trying to slow down climate change and its effects on us.

You need:

- Very magickal timing—one of the rare Full Moons, the nights leading up to an eclipse, or the like

- An ice cube, and a small receptacle for it

To perform this spell:

Do the grounding work found at the beginning of this section.

Once you are grounded, pull an ice cube out of the freezer and place it in its receptacle.

Pray out loud, in whatever way makes sense for you, for this to end and the effects of climate change to slow down. Really mean your words but don't restrict yourself otherwise.

Hold your ice cube in its receptacle. Say "Slow down this crisis/ Slow down this wave/We can end this/We can change." Put all of your focus and energy into this idea and pour that power into the ice cube itself.

Stick it in the freezer.

Release any gods and entities. Thank them.

A Spell to Protect Our Community from Legislative Harm

This spell differs from similar ones that we went through before because this one is meant to tap into the collective queer spirit and protect that same spirit (and the bodies inhabiting them), and because this spell is meant to protect entire swaths of community who we may or may not know personally.

You need:

- A written copy of the law or legislation in question
- A lighter, match, or red candle
- A small protective implement—like a charm or a tourmaline
- A fire-safe bowl or receptacle

To perform this spell:

Do the grounding work found at the beginning of this section .

Think specifically about how this law might affect people.

When you feel ready, light the law on fire and set it in the receptacle. I even like to say "Let this law burn away," as I do this.

Once that paper is destroyed, focus on your protective implement. Knock on it to wake up the magick inherent within.

After the spell, dispose of the ashes however you need to. Returning ash to Earth is best, but just throwing it away if you live in a city is fine.

Repeat the mantra below a set number of times. Pick a number that feels right to you.

> *Queer people will not be silenced or erased*
>
> *We will remain steadfast and protected in spite of attempted harm to us*
>
> *Our community is all power, all grace*
>
> *And we will not be touched or affected by this law*

A Spell to Strengthen Community Bond and Collective Love and Power

This spell's title is fairly self-explanatory. In terms of uprooting the system and creating change, there is power and strength in numbers. In terms of getting through the day with the world as is, there is safety in knowing we are tapped into and protected by a wider community.

This spell works to strengthen the bond that localized communities of marginalized people share, and strengthens the power inherent in those numbers and that love.

You need:

- Rope, twine, yarn, or something similar cut into medium-length pieces. It should be enough to make a garland when fully tied together and finished

- Charms, images, or other symbols that you can hang from those pieces that represent community bonds, strength in numbers, or all of the above—rainbows, unicorns, glitter are all welcome but it can be less fanciful, too

To perform this spell:

Do the grounding work found at the beginning of this section.

Instead of crying, screaming, and such, focus on the strengths of community. Visualize big feasts where everyone is happy, laughing, and eating. Think about sitting together at book clubs and watching shows in bars or nonalcohol cafes, feeling safe and taken care of.

Think of individual queer people that you know and love, respect and look up to.

Start tying the pieces of rope together, saying each time, "When we come together, we are stronger."

When you're finished, bless this garland by saying "Like this garland, we are tied together in our hearts and in our missions." Bask in that feeling for a second.

Start hanging your other pieces from it to strengthen the specifics of your spell.

When finished, hang it over a doorway in your home, or drape it across your altar.

Add new charms, ideas, or other items to it as you find them so you can revisit and recharge this spell.

Spells to Strengthen Ourselves for the Fight

This spell is a way that all of us can get in on direct action, even if we don't feel like we're first-line fighters. As society continues to collapse into chaos we need to face the reality that at some point we have to face the fight, whether it's at work, in our neighborhoods, or in the countries we live in. This is a fortifying spell, one meant to make you see your own inner strength and feel like you can vibe off of the strength of collective and community.

You need:

- A mirror—ideally hand-held

- An oil for protection, like frankincense or benzoin

To perform this spell:

Do the grounding work listed at the start of this section.

Spend a few minutes meditating on or visualizing the fight you foresee that you and the community are strengthening for.

Create a mantra that genuinely makes you feel strong and more than able to handle whatever gets thrown at you. I didn't write one for you because I know a lot of times speaking someone else's words while we're trying to talk ourselves up feels really silly. Take the time to think about your own strength, what you need it for, and how all of that can come into a succinct couple of phrases.

Set a number that feels magickal to you.

Anoint the mirror with oil, and repeat your mantra that number of times. Believe it more each time.

Anoint yourself with the oil.

Hexes

Usually the best option in a given situation is to empower yourself to overcome. However, sometimes people, administrations, societies, or organizations need to be stopped. Sometimes they even need to be hexed. A hex is a spell cast on someone or something outside of ourselves that causes harm to them. While there are lines I draw, it's important to contextualize magick within the society we exist in, and hexing someone so that they lose their power, income, or ability to cause others harm *is* causing that person harm. We have to consider that and move forward with hexing only when we're positive it's the right thing to do.

Sometimes it really is the right thing to do, though. You can only protect yourself, your loved ones, and your community so much when there are dark forces coming from within society that are actively dead set on holding you down. *Hexing oppressors is community care and we are all charged with the responsibilities of community care.*

If you do deity work, hexes are a great time to call on any underworld deities or the more disruptive faces of the Goddess or God. I've worked with everyone from Baphomet to Hekate to Faerie Queens for these, so that can mean literally anything you want or need it to. This is also a great time to tap into ancestral magick. Queer and radical ancestors will want to come in and aid this work, obviously. If you come from a lineage that has been hurt by the powers that be, they'll want to be invited in to take their swings. Even if you are white and your ancestors were colonizers, invite them in as a way to make amends for the harm they caused in life. They can't undo that harm now, but they can help you try to fix it.

With that, here are some simple hexes so you can see how they work and when it's appropriate to perform them.

A Hex for Cruelty in Power

I have used this spell, and I have seen it work. Like all magick, nothing is perfect, and this one can miss, but I have seen it absolutely upend corrupt gatekeepers and politicians where they are. Remember, the more power they have, the more frequently or with an increased number of witches you'll need to perform this spell.

You need:

- A soft block of wood, or styrofoam if your movement or strength is limited

- Small railroad spikes, *or* old, haggard looking nails if spikes are not available

- A hammer

- Black tape

- A big black candle or several small ones

- Things associated with those gods, ancestors, or both—especially anything that you feel connects you right to their spirit

- Some gods or lines of ancestor work have something called *Dark Rites* associated with them. I know firsthand that Hekate does, for example. These are rites that are meant to bring in the meanest, most disruptive face of those gods or ancestors. Do some research, and see if you find anything that speaks to you. Print out or copy and use if so, but, if not, move forward with the spell anyway.

To perform this spell:

Light your black candle and engage the tools for the gods or ancestors.

As it burns and those other tools engage, welcome the elements and those gods or ancestors into the circle, verbally if possible.

Recite your Dark Rites if you have them. If not, state your intention boldly and repeatedly until you feel ready to move on. An example would be "I want _____ to be removed from office immediately," or " _____ needs their power stripped ASAP."

Hammer your spikes into the block of soft wood, repeating your spells intention with each new spike. Occasionally, this does not go as intended, but give it a go.

If it worked, you can skip this step, but I like to do it either way. If your nails wouldn't go into the wood, you *need* this step. Take your black tape and tape the spikes to the wood (or just tape over the whole thing if your spikes did go in). As you do, feel free to cuss out or let the person you're hexing know how you feel.

- Wave this block over the black candle's smoke and repeat "Soon this power will be stripped."

- Thank your gods, ancestors, or other entities and release them.

- This is *your* magick, so bury it closer to home *if* that's an option, or maybe in a witchy or understanding friend's space if not. If there's not a respectable place to bury it, wrap it up in paper or garbage bag, and toss it in your trash can.

- Keep burning the black candle each night until it's gone.

Hexing the White Supremacist Patriarchy

While so many of our problems come down to the failings of late-stage capitalism, even a lot of that can be tracked back to an outstanding patriarchal and white supremacist force that was always designed to benefit wealthy, able-bodied, able-minded, white, heterosexual cisgender men and no one else. So much of what went wrong was actually this system going very right and serving those it was meant to serve. With that, it's time we knock this system down a few pegs.

What does hexing the white supremacist patriarchy *do* exactly? Ideally and ultimately it knocks it out of power. In the short term, hexing white supremacy or patriarchy limits its ability to affect you and yours—and *yours* can and should include communities or entire cities that you have stakes in.

Hexing the patriarchy is obviously not a one-time thing. It happens over and over and over again, ideally daily. Ideally, every time you think about it. This spell then has an active component and a passive component. This work is powerful and important though—arguably the most important work in this book. Repeat as necessary and place reminders everywhere so that you are constantly sending out the energy to hex the white supremacist patriarchy.

You need:

- A list of everything you hate about white supremacy and patriarchy—it might get *very* long so feel free to set a timer to just write the things you can come up with in five or ten minutes

- A candle in a color that speaks to this spell for you.

- A protective oil

- Tea with nettle and your favorite protective herbs—including any kind of black tea itself

- A patch that says "hex white supremacy," "hex patriarchy," or ideally both—multiple patches are great, or you can just write this on sticky notes

- Optional: a fire-safe bowl and lighter or matches

To perform this spell:

Anoint yourself and the candle with protective oil. Sometimes hexing rituals get intense and you'll want the layer of protection.

Invite your gods and other entities in.

Light your candle and say, "Fuck the white supremacist patriarchy. I hex it, and I take away its power."

Drink your tea, which drives out unwanted forces as well as protects, as you move through this spell.

Read your list to your gods, your ancestors, or just the spirit energy at large and say either "Fuck (list item)" or "I hate (list item)" for each one.

Repeat if you feel like you need to.

When you feel done with that part, rip your list into smaller and smaller pieces. Put them in a fire safe bowl and burn them if you want to, or rip them up so small that it doesn't matter.

Give one final "Fuck the white supremacist patriarchy. I hex it, and I take away its power."

Blow out your candle.

Finish your tea.

Trash your tea bag and your tiny papers or ashes.

Sew a patch on something where you'll see it a lot. Or place patches or sticky notes strategically all over your home.

Every time you see one, say, "I hex the white supremacist patriarchy," and go about your day living your empowered life.

A Hex on Those Who Rail Against Queer Rights and Actively Hurt Queer People

The government alone is not solely responsible for stripping us of rights and taking our dignity away. If there weren't conservative religious lobbyists paying to have our rights stripped, they likely wouldn't be. If we lived in a more fair and queer-focused society there would still be those who fought against it and actively worked to take that power from us. Unfortunately, there will always be a fringe demographic of people who will openly and actively attack us and try to take our lives from us for a whole host of reasons—none of which are because we've done anything wrong.

This hex is for those people, the ones who wish to do us harm be it politically, physically, or anywhere in between. What I love about this hex is that it doesn't become active until the party or parties try to cause harm. When they do though (and they all do) havoc can be wreaked.

This is a poppet spell because poppets are largely and primarily historically used for curses and hexes. I had some kinder variations earlier in the grimoire but I love *all* poppet work and wanted to end in a place that returns a modernized form of witchcraft back to its roots.

You need:

- Poppet materials—scratchy burlap or hard cornhusks are ideal

- Needle and thread—for this one I do recommend sewing your poppet shut and not just tying it off

- A small piece of paper with "And it reflect back at you" written on it

- A very small mirror or piece of mirror (a charm of mirror would work too)

- Poppet stuffing—feel free to include herbs, like cinquefoil and mustard seed (common and used for hexing) and dried blueberries (which can cause strife)

- Anointing oil of choice

To perform this spell:

Create a safe, protective, sacred circle around you while you do this work. Hexing can bring in all kinds of spiritual energies and entities and you want to make sure the ones coming in are ones you *want* to work with.

Partially sew your poppet up, leaving an open space to stuff the stuffing into. Say, "As I sew this poppet, I curse those who cause queer people harm."

Start stuffing your poppet, first with the stuffing, herbs, and blueberry you want to use. Think about the people you're hexing and the harm they're trying to cause. Let yourself get angry.

Lastly, put in the piece of paper and the small mirror and say, "May any harm you cause/Reflect back on you/May you feel our pain/Multiplied by two."

Finishing sewing your poppet. Anoint it with oil to activate it.

Stick the sewing needle where the heart would be on a person. Say something like "May your heart open but if not/This poppet will send *you* the pain you've wrought."

Place the poppet on your altar, especially if you have an altar space for queer and radical ancestors.

AFTERWORD

This book was so much harder for me to write than I ever thought it would be, but it was also so much more necessary than I thought it would be. Witchcraft is something that can be so personal to so many people, and I wanted to be inclusive but not appropriative. I wanted it to feel personal, but also like a broad umbrella you could pile under or take from for safekeeping. This book felt so complicated until I decided to make it simple.

I also wrote this book at a time in my life that was harder than I expected it to be. I was undergoing treatment for severe, primary vaginismus while I was writing this book. Vaginismus basically means that my vagina didn't open for most of my life. The disorder can create health problems especially if you're not getting regular checkups, and it's painful at best most of the time. I was also carrying, as a result of vaginismus, a stunning amount of tension in my butt, hips, and upper thighs. Treatment for this problem is invasive, painful, and deeply emotional. I felt really cut off from my magick for so much of it as I wildly disassociated just to get through most of my days.

As I finish this book, my vaginismus isn't cured but for the first time ever I know it will be. The morning I finished the rough draft of *Queering Your Craft* I pulled two tarot cards for myself: The Empress and The Lovers, reversed. I thought it was a little on the nose, regarding this book and being in vaginismus treatment at all, but as I went through my day I felt my magick coming back slowly and realized that *that* is what the tarot cards were trying to tell me. My writing, my body, my magick. It's all the same and as I care for one of those things, I care for all of them.

Magick has saved me over and over and over again, and writing and exploring this book is no different. It brought me back into myself (at the last possible moment, but it did). It made me remember why I was writing this at all, why I proposed this book, why I insisted on an admittedly stressful timeline, why I kept going even when I wanted to give up. It's because I wanted you to find something that saves you the way magick has saved me. I hope it's spellcraft, because I love it. If it's not, that's okay.

Maybe it's queer community. Maybe it's your own strength of spirit that this book helped you see. Maybe it's love of someone, anyone, that made you want to keep going. All of these things have saved me at one point or another, too, and I hope that you have found reflections of all of them in these pages.

Witchcraft is having a moment. Queerness is having a moment. I hope these moments last and change the world, but I know they may not. But you will—your heart, the work you're already doing in your community, the spells you cast. They (and their effects) will last and snowball into other people's hearts, work, and spells. That's beautiful. That's witchcraft. And you've been doing it all along.

ADDITIONAL CORRESPONDENCES

There are countless correspondences for anything you may want or need to do magickally. I included this appendix just to get the ball rolling for you. Please feel free to use this as a reference, a jumping off point, or something else entirely.

Protection—for Yourself, Your Loved Ones, Community Members, and Communities

Colors

- Black
- Magenta
- Orange

Herbs, Flowers, or Plants

- Basil
- Black pepper
- Cayenne
- Cinnamon
- Cumin
- Nettles
- Pine and pine pollen
- Sarsaparilla
- Thistles
- Vervain
- Wormwood

Stones

- Hematite
- Iron
- Obsidian
- Onyx
- Pearl
- Red Coral

Images or Charms

- Animals that you view as protective, such as dogs or bears
- Any religious symbol that is precious to you (cross, Star of David, Pentacle, to name a few)
- Evil eye charms and images
- Gargoyles
- Horseshoes

- Images of places that are known safe (or safer) spaces to you
- Keys
- Nails
- Pictures of, or things that belonged to, people who were or are protective of you in a healthy, positive way
-

Oils, Incenses, and Scents

- Benzoin
- Frankincense

Food and Drink

- Black salt (food grade)
- Coffee
- Cashews
- Garlic
- Onions
- Radishes

Tools and Miscellaneous

- A thin rope and some simple knot magick
- Black salt
- Bricks or red brick dust—to represent our foreparents at Stonewall protecting their community
- Condoms
- Laughter and carving out space for fun and pleasure even when (especially when) you're struggling

Timing

- Noon or midnight, often on Tuesdays (noon may not be right where you live—it's whenever the Sun is at it s highest point)
- Waning Moon

Prosperity

Colors

- Autumn color palette
- Brown
- Gold
- Green
- Red (for attraction magick)

Herbs, Flowers, or Plants

- Basil
- Bay leaf
- Cinnamon
- Cloves
- Mint

- Vervain

Stones

- Citrine
- Garnet
- Jade
- Lodestone
- Peridot
- Pyrite
- Topaz

Images or Charms

- Buffalo

- Cattle
- Ch'an Chu (the three-legged money frog)
- Charms that correlate to your career
- Fall harvest or imagery
- Feast
- Flush bank account
- Koi or Goldfish
- Money (coins or bills)
- Norse Rune FA
- Salmon
- Sheep

Oils, Incenses, and Scents

- Any from the herbs listed above
- Citrus
- Frankincense
- Lemongrass
- Patchouli

Food and Drink

- Citrus
- Coffee
- Cold press coffee
- Honey
- Pumpkins (or any fall harvest food)
- Rum
- Wine

Tools and Miscellaneous

- List of community resources you want to contribute to or start
- Money Tree plant placed prominently in home
- Personal list of financial and career goals

Timing

- Harvest holidays and Sabbats
- Thursdays
- Waxing, New, and Full Moons

Fostering Community

Colors

- Glitter
- Green
- Pink
- Purple
- Rainbow
- Yellow

Herbs, Flowers, or Plants

- Allspice

- Clove
- Honeysuckle
- Jasmine
- Passionflower
- Roses, white, yellow, and purple

Stones

- Carnelian
- Citrine
- Honey calcite
- Tourmaline

Images or Charms

- Images of community ancestors
- Images of potential shared or community space
- Norse Rune Wunjo
- Pack or herd animals
- Rainbows
- The word *community* in big letters
- Upside down triangle—for queer community specifically

Oils, Incenses, and Scents

- Cinnamon oil
- Clove oil
- Rose oil
- Sandalwood
- Sweetgrass

Food and Drink

- Alcohol and sober equivalents (wine and juice, vodka and seltzer, and the like)
- Apples
- Bread
- Floral teas
- Food meant for a group (family size, or a whole cake, for example)
- Pumpkin

Tools and Miscellaneous

- Chalice
- Music that is popular in your community (or would be community)
- Rainbow flags
- Something that represents something unique that *you* have to offer this community
- Tarot Cards: 10 of Cups, 10 of Pentacles, The Sun, or any combination thereof

Timing

- Full Moon for big intentions
- New Moon if community is starting from scratch
- Waxing Moon to grow and foster community

Love—Romantic, Platonic, Familial

Colors

- Pink
- Purple
- Rainbow
- Red
- White

Herbs, Flowers, or Plants

- Catnip
- Coriander
- Fern
- Green carnation
- Honeysuckle
- Mistletoe
- Raspberry leaf
- Rose
- Violet

Stones

- Diamonds—*if* you have some that are heirlooms, thrifted or responsibly and ethically sourced
- Malachite
- Moonstone
- Red jasper
- Rose quartz
- Sapphire
- Seashells
- Stones shaped like hearts
- Stones shaped like rainbows

Images or Charms

- Animals that embody traits you want a partner or partners to have
- Claddagh
- Couples (or throuples, and so on) you admire
- Hearts
- Rainbows
- Swans
- Tarot Cards: Two of Cups or Three of Cups

Oils, Incenses, and Scents

- Amber
- Florals
- Patchouli
- Your favorite perfume or cologne

Food and Drink

- Champagne
- Chocolate
- Red candy (M&M's , Skittles, and the like)
- Strawberries
- Water flavored with any of these things or the aforementioned herbs

Tools and Miscellaneous

- Affirmations
- Bodily fluids
- Chalice
- Love poems and songs
- Mirrors
- Moon water
- Unity candles

Timing

- Fridays
- Full Moon (especially in Libra or Taurus)
- New Moon

Healing

Colors

- Black
- Blue
- Green
- Indigo
- Silver/grey
- Violet
- White, your favorite color, or one that is calming to you

Herbs, Flowers, or Plants

- Aloe vera
- Anise
- Carnation
- Chamomile
- Lavender
- Sage
- St. John's Wort

Stones

- Amethyst
- Aquamarine
- Aura quartzes
- Hematite
- Moonstone
- Rose quartz
- Quartz
- Spirit or angel

Images or Charms

- Angels
- Caduceus
- Djinn
- Dragons
- Faeries
- Lotus
- Saints
- Turtles

Oils, Incenses, and Scents

- Camphor
- Eucalyptus
- Juniper
- Myrrh
- Neroli
- Rosemary
- Sandalwood
- Tea Tree

Food and Drink

- Artichoke
- Barley
- Flower-infused cakes or cookies
- Garlic
- Lime
- Onions
- Paprika added to food
- Wheat

Tools and Miscellaneous

- Chalice
- Epsom salt
- Mirror
- Moon water
- Pendulums
- Pentacle/Pentagram
- Sea Salt
- Wands
- Yoga exercises in ritual

Timing

- Dark Moon
- Sunday and Monday

Inspiring and Taking Action/Activism

Colors

- Colors associated with the activist movement you're interested in
- Gold
- Orange
- Red
- Yellow

Herbs, Flowers, or Plants

- Cayenne
- Ginger
- Passionflower
- Vervain
- Wormwood
- Yarrow

Stones

- Carnelian
- Citrine
- Fire quartz
- Goldstone
- Red jasper

Images or Charms

- Fire
- Images of activists who inspire you

- Sowilo Norse rune (lightning strike rune)

Oils, Incenses, and Scents

- Cedar
- Citrus
- Cloves
- Mint
- Rosemary

Food and Drink

- Black pepper
- Bone or veggie stock broth
- Cold press coffee or espresso
- Fire cider
- Sea salt

Tools and Miscellaneous

- Athame or knife
- Bricks and chunks of cement
- Cauldron
- Hammer
- Match or lighter
- Runes
- Your own hair

Timing

- Full Moon
- New Moon

Creating and Selling Art

Colors

- Blue
- Gold
- Purple
- White
- Yellow

Herbs, Flowers, or Plants

- Allspice
- Chamomile
- Ground cinnamon
- Irish moss
- Nutmeg
- Passionflower
- Rose hips or petals (especially ones that match the colors listed)

Stones

- Flourite
- Lodestone
- Moonstone
- Pyrite

Images or Charms

- Images correlating to your art (paintbrush, pen, drama mask, and the like)

- Orchids
- Tarot card: The Empress

Oils, Incenses, and Scents

- Clove
- Frankincense
- Honeysuckle
- Lavender
- Sandalwood

Food and Drink

- Anything made from scratch (especially if you decorate it)
- Avocado
- Macadamia nut
- Maple syrup
- Pumpkin pie

Tools and Miscellaneous

- Bells
- Cauldron
- Compass
- Pen and paper
- Rainwater
- Tarot

Timing

- Waxing Moon

Sex Magick

Colors

- Black
- Orange
- Pink
- Rainbow
- Rainbow glitter
- Red
- Red glitter

Herbs, Flowers, or Plants

- Cannabis
- Cinnamon
- Clover
- Damiana
- Jezebel root
- Lillies
- Raspberry leaf
- Rose

Stones

- Rose quartz
- Ruby
- Sapphire

Images or Charms

- Any image that turns you on
- Cats
- Fire
- Goats
- Hummingbirds
- Logos of hookup apps
- Personalized sigils
- Rabbits

- Symbols of Lilith
- Symbols of Venus

Oils, Incenses, and Scents

- Any spicy, musky scent
- Jasmine
- Neroli
- Patchouli
- Sandalwood
- Smoky quartz
- Ylang Ylang
- Your favorite cologne or perfume

Food and Drink

- Champagne (or wine)
- Dark chocolate
- Pomegranates
- Raspberry
- Strawberries

Tools and Miscellaneous

- Chalice and wand
- Condoms
- Fire
- Hanky code hankies
- Lube
- Masturbation
- Sexy music
- Sex toys

Timing

- Beltane
- Full Moon

Gender Magick and Magick for Self-Awareness and Identity

Colors

- Any color that (to you) represents your gender identity or the one you're looking to grow and root in
- Purple
- Rainbow

Herbs, Flowers, or Plants

- Angelica
- Barberry
- Burdock
- Calendula
- Chervil
- Damiana
- High John the Conqueror root

Stones

- Apatite
- Aquamarine
- Blue goldstone
- Chrysocolla
- Moldavite
- Moonstone
- Sandstone
- Shiva lingham

Images or Charms

- Images of people's who gender presentation you aspire to
- Symbols of the gender you are or are transitioning to
- Upside down triangle

Oils, Incenses, and Scents

- Florals
- Lime
- Musk
- Neroli
- Vanilla bean

Food and Drink

- Banana
- Black pepper
- Carob
- Carrot
- Ginger tea
- Raspberry leaf tea

Tools and Miscellaneous

- Athame/knife
- Chalice
- Gender affirming clothing (binders, heels, trucker hats, and the like depending on your gender)
- Hair dye and makeup
- Pentagram
- Songs about gender or transition
- Wands

Timing

- Anniversary dates of important transition related dates
- Whenever it feels urgent or important to do this work
- Your birthday

Chosen Family/Friendship

Colors

- Deep red—to invoke the metaphor of blood pacts
- Pink
- Yellow

Herbs, Flowers, or Plants

- Caraway seeds
- Catnip
- Cinnamon
- Dandelions
- Passionflower
- Roses (especially in the colors listed above)

Stones

- Blue agate
- Honey calcite
- Malachite
- Rose quartz

Images or Charms

- Fish
- Pack or herd animals
- Pictures of fictional chosen families
- Tarot Cards: Three of Cups or The Sun

Oils, Incenses, and Scents

- Cloves
- Honey rose
- Patchouli

Food and Drink

- Beer
- Bread
- Casseroles
- Cookies
- Corn
- Honey
- Sugar
- Weed

Tools and Miscellaneous

- Chalice
- Magnets or lodestone
- Wands

Timing

- Dark or New Moon
- Full Moon
- Sabbats Ostara or Beltane
- Waxing Moon
- Your birthday (or the birthday of a beloved friend who's passed on)

Making Space

Colors

- Anything glittery
- Gray
- Pale yellow (invoking open, sunshiny space)
- Rainbow
- White

Herbs, Flowers, or Plants

- Acacia/Arabic Gum, Anything cleansing or clearing (ideally cedar), lavender, milk thistle, motherwort, wormwood

Stones

- Honey calcite
- Quartz
- Tourmalated quartz
- Tourmaline

Images or Charms

- Images of the community you're making space for or the physical space you're envisioning
- Pentacle
- Sigils of safety and community
- Tarot Card: King of Pentacles

Oils, Incenses, and Scents

- Cedar
- Citronella
- Gardenia
- Pine

Food and Drink

- Anything meant to be consumed by groups
- Bread
- Garlic

Tools and Miscellaneous

- Bricks
- Energy work on the literal or metaphorical space
- Moon water
- Pentagrams
- Sun water

Timing

- Dark or New Moon
- Day before you want to open or create space—for example on a Friday if you want a Saturday opening; it does *not* have to be the same week
- Litha or Lammas
- Waxing Moon

Ancestor and Death Work

Colors

- Any color on a family shield, crest, symbol, or other object for your given family's ancestry
- A lost loved one's favorite colors
- Black
- Rainbow for queer ancestors

Herbs, Flowers, or Plants

- Coriander
- Fresh flowers
- Graveyard dirt
- Juniper berries
- Mistletoe
- Mugwort
- Wormwood

Stones

- Amethyst
- Bricks and brick dust for queer ancestors
- Coral
- Obsidian
- Selenite

Images or Charms

- Bones,
- Buzzards or vultures
- Pennies
- Santa Muerte
- Shells
- Snake skins

- Tarot Card: Death
- Things that belonged to your ancestors or the dead
- Yew trees

Oils, Incenses, and Scents

- Bergamot
- Copal
- Frankincense
- Jasmine
- Myrrh
- Pine
- Sandalwood

Food and Drink

- Brandy
- Bread
- Coffee
- Orange and orange peel
- Sweets
- Tea
- Tobacco
- Wine

Tools and Miscellaneous

- Ashes of those who have passed on
- Athame
- Bell or gong
- Candles
- Incense

- Letters written to the ancestors or the dead

Timing

- Autumn
- Birth or death days of those who have passed on
- New Moons
- Samhain
- Saturdays
- Tuesday evenings

APPENDIX B

BOTANICAL CLASSIFICATION

- Acacia/Gum Arabic (*Acacia Senegal*)

- Allspice (*Pimenta diocia*)

- Almond (*Prunus dulcis*)

- Aloe Vera (*Aloe barbadensis miller*)

- Angelica (*Angelica archangelica*)

- Anise (*Pimpenella anisum*)

- Apple (*Malus domestica*)

- Artichoke (*Cynara scolymus*)

- Banana (*Musa*)

- Barberry (*Berberis*)

- Barley (*Hordeum volgare*)

- Basil (*Ocimum basilicum*)

- Bay Leaf (*Laurus nobilis*)

- Bergamot (*Citrus bergamia*)

- Black pepper (*Piper Nigrum*)

- Blueberries (*Cyanococcus*)

- Burdock (*Arctium*)

- Calendula (*Calendula officinalis*)

- Camphor (*Cinnamomum camphora*)

- Caraway/seeds (*Carum carvi*)

- Carnation (*Dianthus caryophyllus*)

- Carob (*Ceratonia siliqua*)

- Carrot (*Daucus carota subsp. sativus*)

- Cashew (*Anacardium occidentale*)

- Catnip (*Nepeta cataria*)

- Cayenne (*Capsicum annum*)

- Cedar (*Cedrus*)

- Chamomile (*Matricaria chamomilla*)

- Chervil (*Anthriscus cerefolium*)

- Cinnamon (*Cinnamomum verum*)

- Cinquefoil (*Potentilla*)

- Citronella or Lemongrass (*Cymbopogon*)

- Clover (*Trifolium*)

- Cloves (*Sygyzium aromaticum*)

- Comfrey (*Symphytum*)

- Coriander (*Coriandrum sativum*)

- Corn (*Zea mays*)

- Cumin (*Cuminum cyminum*)

- Damiana (*Turnera diffusa*)

- Dandelion (*Taraxacum*)

- Echinacea (*Echinacea purpurea*)

- Eucalyptus (*Eucalyptus globalus*)

- Eyebright (*Euphrasia*)

- Fern (*Pteridophyta*)

- Gardenia (*Gardenia jasminoides*)

- Garlic (*Allium sativum*)

- Ginger (*Zingiber officinale*)

- High John the Conqueror Root (*Ipomoea purge*)

- Honeysuckle (*Lonicera*)

- Horehound (*Marrubium vulgare*)

- Irish Moss (*Chondrus crispus*)

- Jasmine (*Jasminum*)

- Jezebel Root or Orris Root (*Rhizoma iridus*)

- Juniper (*Jumiperus*)

- Lavender (*Lavandula*)

- Lily (*Lilium*)

- Lime (*Citrus aurantifolia*)

- Milk Thistle (*Silybum marianum*)

- Mint (*Mentha*)

- Mistletoe (*Viscum album*)

- Motherwort (*Leonurus cardiaca*)

- Mugwort (*Artemisia vulgaris*)

- Mustard Seed (*Brassica negra*)

- Nettles (*Urtica dioica*)

- Nutmeg (*Myristica fragrans*)

- Olive/oil (*Olea europaea*)

- Onions (*Allium cepa*)

- Orange/peel (*Citrus sinensis*)

- Paprika (*Capsicum annum*)

- Parsley (*Petroselinum crispum*)

- Passionflower (*Passiflora incarnata*)

- Patchouli (*Pogostemon cablin*)

- Pennyroyal (*Mentha pulegium*)

- Pine/pollen (*Pinus*)

- Poppies (*Papaver*)

- Pumpkin (*Cucurbita*)

- Radish (*Raphanus sativus*)

- Raspberry Leaf (*Rubus idaeus*)

- Rosemary (*Salvia Rosmarinus*)

- Rose and Rose Hips (*Rosa*)

- Sage (*Salvia officinalis*)

- Saint John's Wort (*Hypericum perforatum*)

- Sandalwood (*Santalum album*)

- Sarsaparilla (*Smilax ornate*)

- Slippery Elm (*Ulmus rubra*)

- Strawberry (*Fragaria ananassa*)

- Sweetgrass (*Hierochloe odorata*)

- Thistles (*Cirsium*)

- Tobacco (*Nicotiana tabacum*)

- Valerian/root (*Valeriana Officinalis*)

- Vanilla/bean (*Vanilla planifolia*)

- Vervain (*Verbena*)

- Violet (*Viola*)

- Wheat (*Triticum*)

- Wormwood (*Artemisia absinthium*)

- Yarrow (*Achillea millefolium*)

- Ylang-Ylang (*Cananga odorata*)

RESOURCES

Botanical References

Miernowska, Marysia. *The Witch's Herbal Apothecary: Rituals and Recipes for a Year of Earth Magick and Sacred Medicine Making.* Beverly, MA: Fairwinds Press, January 2020.

Mindell, Earl. *Earl Mindell's Herb Bible.* New York: Simon & Schuster, 1992.

Vanderbeck, Paige. *Green Witchcraft: A Practical Guide to Discovering the Magic of Plants, Herbs, Crystals and Beyond.* Emeryville, CA: Rockridge Press, February 2020.

Wood, Matthew. *The Earthwise Herbal Volume 1: A Complete Guide to Old World Medicinal Plants.* North Atlantic Books, June 2008.

———. *The Earthwise Herbal Volume 2: A Complete Guide to Old World Medicinal Plants.* Berkeley, CA: North Atlantic Books, July 2011.

Suggested Reading

Allen, Lasara Firefox. *Jailbreaking the Goddess: A Radical Revisioning of Feminist Spirituality.* Woodbury, MN: Llewellyn Publications, 2016.

Brown, Adrienne Maree. *Pleasure Activism: The Politics of Feeling Good.* Chico, CA: AK Press, Match 2019.

Buckland, Raymond. *Buckland's Complete Book of Witchcraft.* Woodbury, MN: Llewellyn Publications, 1994.

Grey, Peter. *Apocalyptic Witchcraft.* Scarlet Imprint, 2013.

Herstik, Gabriela. *Craft: How to Be A Modern Witch.* London: Ebury Press/ Penguin Random House, 2018.

Prower, Tomas. *Queer Magic: LGBT+ Spirituality and Culture from Around the World.* Woodbury, MN: Llewellyn Publications, 2018.

Reed, Theresa and Shaheen Miro. *Tarot for Troubled Times.* Newburyport, MA: Weiser Books, July 2019

Zakroff, Laura Tempest. *Sigil Witchery: A Witch's Guide to Crafting Magick Symbols.* Woodbury, MN: Llewellyn Publications

ACKNOWLEDGMENTS

Everything I do is made possible by a huge team of people who support me, prop me up, and encourage me to continue, and this book is no different.

I first want to thank Thraicie Hawkner and my entire Eye of Horus family. Without this home base for my tarot reading and classes, I would be nowhere in the metaphysical community. You're all more than that to me now though. The past few years have been wild and unpredictable, even by indie bookstore standards, and you have all worked so hard to create a space that feels safe (and refreshed when it needs to feel refreshed) and I love you so, so much.

Similarly, I owe so much to Lacey Prpic Hedtke and The Future, the funkiest space in Minneapolis that I am honored to be a part of. The work you're all doing for the community is outstanding and I will never forget how this time with you all feels, as long as I live. To Lacey specifically, thank you for letting me experiment with classes, finish writing in between clients, and be my weirdest, queerest, witchiest self at all times.

To BethAnne and Troy for dropping things to bring me snacks, meet me for coffee, or let me come eat your delicious, amazing food and ramble incoherently about herbs and ghosts all the time, thank you, thank you, thank you. BethAnne, you continue to show me year after year what kind of friendship I deserve and I love you an unbelievable amount.

A huge shout out goes to Abbie Plouff (Northern Lights Witch) for regular accountabillibuddy dates and for always believing in me and my work. You're a true ride or die, and you were so critical to this specific book's success. Not to mention all the magick!

Thank you to J. Ryan Kent, for always being willing to proofread my book proposals, letting me borrow money, and looking me in the eyes and telling me I'm powerful and important when I don't want to hear it but need to.

Thank you Andrew for showing up even when it's not your thing, to Kenny for just being so nice to me all the time, to Anais for always having an open heart for anyone who needs one.

Thank you to Theresa Reed for showing me how I want to treat others when I'm as successful as you are. You shine such a light for my generation (and the generations that follow us) and are just so wonderful to so many of us. My first book would not have gotten as far off the ground without your support, and I will never forget that.

Thank you to Moon Palace, Cream and Amber, and Next Chapter Books for your ongoing support.

I really, really won the sibling lottery. Every single night when I count my blessings I thank my gods for Zach, Drew, and Chelsea. I really don't feel like I deserve to be a part of the Snow Sibling squad but I am so over the moon grateful that I am. A similar shout out to Bradley, Hope, and Kevin, I count y'all among the Snow Sibling squad, too, and every time I see or talk to you I'm grinning ear to ear for weeks. Of course I owe a huge thanks to my dad, as always, for the very real support that you've given me in so many ways over the past couple of years. You are one of the gentlest, kindest men I've ever met, and the way you can go with the flow when the rest of us have wild ideas is nothing short of admirable. Thank you to Ola—you are the rock of this family in so many ways, and I don't think I'd be here without your work ethic to look up to or your soft heart to lean on when things are hard in my personal life.

Thank you to Aunt Linda and Uncle Jim, too, for supporting even when you don't understand. Thank you to my mom, who is always trying. I see that now.

For Libbie, Kimby, Anne, Courtney, the Villhauers, and all of my other high school and college friends who never let distance or time get in the way of their support of me, a huge debt of gratitude and mutual admiration, forever.

Thank you to The Minneapolis queer community—we're not perfect, but we've got us and you inspire me endlessly.

This work literally wouldn't exist without my Patreon supporters, my Instagram and Twitter followers, my students, my clients, those who reveiwed my first book favorably, and the people who came to *Queering the Tarot* events and bought the books. Thank you, thank you, thank you.

Endless thank-yous to my contacts at Red Wheel/Weiser. Kathryn Sky-Peck is a dream champion to have on your side. Bonni Hamilton, Eryn Eaton, and the company's distributors have busted their butts endlessly

to make so many of my book dreams come true. I am so in love with you all as publishers and as people.

My dearest board of directors and artists working with Gadfly Theatre, thank you for letting me be a real witch in the rehearsal room (ha!) and for insisting I pay myself real money so I don't run out of steam. Thank you for believing in me no matter what I'm doing. You *are* my personal community, and I love each one of your faces so much.

Of course I am *nothing* without the queer radicals, activists, icons, and dreamers that came before me. Elders, those who have passed on and those still doing the work: I don't even know what to say, but my heart carries you with it always.

I end on Manny, of course. I don't want to make enemies, but sometimes I don't think anyone has ever loved anyone as much as I love Manny. A huge thank you for *everything* you do for me, but also: I bet you think I wrote this entire book and forgot who introduced me to witchcraft in the first place, didn't you? I never forget anything you do for me though—and this book literally wouldn't have happened without your fevered exploration of Paganism at a mere twenty years old. For this and so many other things, I love you and I thank you. Forever.

ABOUT THE AUTHOR

Cassandra Snow is a witch, a radical activist and advocate, and a sensitive soul, dedicated to making the arts of witchcraft and tarot accessible and easy to learn. They are a professional tarot card reader who teaches Queering the Tarot and Tarot for Beginners classes and coaches new and intermediate readers. Cassandra is a writer and theatre maker in Minneapolis, Minnesota, one of two artistic directors of Gadfly Theatre Productions, a queer and feminist theatre company. Their work is focused on healing, empowerment, and liberation individually and collectively. In their free time, Cassandra consumes excessive amounts of coffee, reads voraciously, and hikes when Minnesota weather allows. You can find more about them at *www.cassandra-snow.com*.

TO OUR READERS